ROLLING THUNDER

For Margaret

ROLLING THUNDER

A CENTURY OF TANK WARFARE

PHILIP KAPLAN

Pen & Sword
MILITARY

First published in Great Britain in 2013 by
PEN & SWORD MILITARY
An imprint of
Pen & Sword Books Ltd
47 Church Street
Barnsley, South Yorkshire
S70 2AS

ISBN 978 1 78159 243 4

Printed and bound in England
By CPI Group (UK) Ltd, Croydon, CR0 4YY

Pen & Sword Books Ltd incorporates the Imprints of Aviation, Atlas,
Family History, Fiction, Maritime, Military, Discovery, Politics, History,
Archaeology, Select, Wharncliffe Local History, Wharncliffe True Crime,
Military Classics, Wharncliffe Transport, Leo Cooper, The Praetorian Press,
Remember When, Seaforth Publishing and Frontline Publishing

For a complete list of Pen & Sword titles please contact
PEN & SWORD BOOKS LIMITED
47 Church Street, Barnsley, South Yorkshire, S70 2AS, England
E-mail: enquiries@pen-and-sword.co.uk
Website: www.pen-and-sword.co.uk

CONTENTS

ACKNOWLEDGEMENTS

Efforts have been made to trace the copyright owners of all material used in this book. The author apologizes to any copyright owners we were unable to contact during this clearance process.

The author is grateful to the following people for their kind assistance and contributions in the development of this book: Pauline Allwright, Ernest Audino, Fritz-Rudolf Averdieck, Jeff Babineau, Malcolm Bates, A.G. Bramble, Ludwig Bauer, Rex Cadman, Donald Chidson, Valerie Chidson, Neil Ciatola, Jeff Dacus, Daimler-Chrysler Historical Collection, J. Ellison, Chris Everitt, John Ferrell, David Fletcher, Eugene Flowers, George Forty, Will Fowler, Florence Garetson, Gaston Gee, Hans Halberstadt, Robert Hartwig, Douglas Helmer, Laura Hirst, Eric Holloway, James Jinks, Steve Joseph, Hargita Kaplan, Neal Kaplan, Margaret Kaplan, Sam Katz, Johannes Kugies, Martin Langford, Jacques Littlefield, John Longman, Martin Middlebrook, Steve Nichols, John Nugent, George Parada, Heinz Renk, John Schaeffer, Charles Shenloogian, David Shepard, Richard Watson, George Worth.

INTRODUCTION

"Caterpillar landships are idiotic and useless. Nobody has asked for them and nobody wants them. Those officers and men are wasting their time and are not pulling their proper weight in the war. If I had my way I would disband the whole lot of them. I am going to do my best to see that it is done and stop all this armoured car and caterpillar landship nonsense!"

So said Royal Navy Commodore Cecil Lambert, Fourth Sea Lord, in 1915. Lambert clearly disapproved of the Royal Navy Armoured Car Division, an organization established in October 1914 with the support and enthusiasm of the First Lord of the Admiralty, Winston Churchill, to develop a new line of armoured cars.

On 12 September 1914, the German Army lost the first Battle of the Marne and quite soon after that the Royal Navy dispatched some personnel from the UK to France to protect the air base near Dunkirk. A part of their task there was rescuing pilots who had been shot down in that area, and to accomplish that, the Admiralty chose to send over some armoured cars. The Navy bought 100 vehicles from Rolls-Royce and shipped some of them to France where they were fitted with a boxlike armour covering, shrouding the main unit, the front wheels and the driver's head. The balance of the R-R order was modified in England for action later that autumn in the war. They were fairly effective, but did not wholly protect their crews from overhead sniper fire. By December the British "armoured car" establishment had developed a somewhat refined version with overhead armour and a top-mounted machine-gun. This version was more effective and certainly an improvement on the earlier vehicle, but by the time it entered service the battlefield situation had deteriorated into mere trench warfare stalemate. The new armoured cars had shown promise, but they were incapable of crossing the trenches or the barbed wire.

By the following February, Churchill had set up the Naval Landships Committee whose remit was the design and construction of a new, tracked armoured vehicle based on a design of Lieutenant-Colonel Ernest Swinton of the Royal Engineers. Swinton believed he could make a caterpillar-tracked armoured vehicle that would be capable of destroying machine-gun positions and barbed wire barriers, and more importantly, crossing the trenches and other obstacles on the battlefield with relative ease. The early trials were not encouraging, but the Churchill committee pressed on and the result was the vehicle they called Little Willie.

Little Willie aroused the interest of the British Army which liked what it saw, but wanted something with roughly twice the capability. At that point, two of the committee members, William Tritton and W.G. Wilson, joined forces to come up with an entirely new design with tracks that ran around the perimeter of its rhomboid sides. Its armement included two six-pounder guns and four Hotchkiss machine-guns, and it was powered by a 105 hp Daimler engine. It was nicknamed Mother and it performed well in its initial demonstration for Lloyd George, Field Marshal Lord Kitchener, other army and navy officials and cabinet members in February 1916. Orders for 100 of the machines soon followed. The odd-looking vehicles were being built under a cloak of secrecy and both workers and executives referred to the machine as a "tank" and it was destined to completely alter the future of land warfare.

THE ROAD TO WAR

The origins of mechanised land warfare go back to the earliest chariots, which were predecessors of the early armoured cars, an ancestry that greatly predates that of the tank. One dictionary definition of *tank* is: An enclosed heavily armoured combat vehicle that is mounted with cannon and guns and moves on caterpillar treads.

In common with the tank, that early chariot was operated as a military vehicle by a crew. It was composed of a driver, a bowman who could also throw a javelin when required, and, for armoured protection, a shield bearer. It has been established by Russian archeologists that some Bronze Age warriors in Central Asia used chariots as mobile launching platforms from which they shot arrows and hurled javelins at their enemies.

The Hyskos, (or "Princes of the Lands"), an obscure race of mountain warriors from the area that is now known as Kurdistan, are believed to be the first people to have engaged in combat from war chariots. The Hyskos entered northern Egypt in about 1700 BC to establish a dynasty that lasted four centuries, with the key to their military success being a chariot-based mobile strike force. But they were ultimately overthrown by a more powerful Egyptian army.

In 1479 BC the army of the Pharoah Thutmose III, the Assyrian Army, and, in c. 972-931, the army of King Solomon, were all famous for their mighty war chariot forces. It was not until the sixth century BC, however, that Cyrus, the king of Persia, developed the chariot into a what has been acknowledged to be a truly impressive and highly effective fighting vehicle. He designed a very sturdy, long-axled version operated by a two-man crew. The vehicle's axles with small, extended scythes and the horses that pulled it had armour protection. It was quite light in weight, relatively fast, and the most resistant to overturning of any chariot design to that point. Perhaps in a forethought of the eventual tank concept, he also pioneered an enlarged wagon-shaped model that included a central tower, a battering ram, and room for a twenty-man crew.

But before the tank on the field of battle, a period of warfare dominated by the presence of great beasts, elephants adapted to a land combat role of sorts by the mounting of long lances to their flanks and swords on their trunks. The concept was the brainchild in 327 BC of the rajah Porus whose army faced the invading forces of Alexander the Great. The Indian intended that his elephants were to be employed as "infantry tanks" sent forward to part Alexander's lines to allow the supporting Indian cavalry to reach the enemy troops. It is believed that each elephant carried a fighting cage howdah as a "cockpit" with a crew of up to four men. The appearance of and the threat posed by these enormous live weapons must have been awesome and genuinely frightening to Alexander's men, and he was moved by that initial exposure to amass and create an elephant fighting force of his own.

Next in line to field elephants in combat was Hannibal, the son of Hamilcar Barca. Hannibal was a Punic Carthaginian military commander who, in 202 BC thrust his war beasts into action against the forces of the Roman Scipio in the Battle of Zama, Hannibal's final battle. There the shrewd Roman outfoxed Hannibal, whose eighty elephants were sent in to break Scipio's battle line. As the animals neared the opposition, the shattering blast of many Roman horns and trumpets sounded, terrifying and confusing the elephants which then panicked and ran back through Hannibal's own ranks. In the ensuing chaos, the Romans, like Alexander before them, were inspired to build a fighting force of the beasts into their own armed forces, a force they employed effectively for two hundred years.

In a notable battlefield event of 55 BC, reconnaissance troops of the Roman Julius Caesar were met in what they referred to as Brittania by the determined spear attacks of the enemy forces who appeared aboard light chariots. Caesar later reported that the British charioteers crossed the field at great speed, while "crew members" threw javelins at their foes, confusing and disorganizing them. The chariot crews then dismounted and attacked the Romans on foot. The chariot drivers continued on beyond the point of the action and halted, ready to carry their dismounted fighting men away to safety, if such an escape were to become necessary. So devastating were such attacks to the Romans, so substantial were their casualties in the encounters, that many historians have believed they eventually led to Caesar's withdrawal from Britain.

Eventually the interest in and appeal of making war through the deployment of chariots gave way to the simpler and more efficient approach to killing one's enemy from horseback. Many believe that this conclusion was reached after experimentation using horse riders to gather intelligence information on and around battlefields, a concept that is likely much older than the use of the chariot as a military fighting vehicle. In the intelligence-gathering role, a man mounted on a horse on a battlefield was in the favourable position of having more height than when standing on the ground, an obvious observational advantage, together with the considerable speed of his mount, both for approaching the battlefield situation and for escaping it. The role of the chariot in a military context was further eroded with the gradual development of body armour for use by knights in battle. The combination of that development and more sophisticated breeding of war horses for their combat role put further distance between the war chariot and modern military conflict. The chariot was giving way to the cavalry, well-armed horse-mounted soldiers whose primary mission was the breaching of opposition ranks. Then everything changed again.

The key portent in the development and early evolution of useful, effective firearms in the fourteenth century signalled the coming end of the horse as the source of the soldier's mobility. The load being placed on the animal now—the weight of the soldier's weaponry and ammunition, together with that of the armour for man and horse to protect them from the shot of the enemy—left the animal substantially overburdened and inefficient in combat. The virtues of mobility, agility, and speed soon became of greater importance to the fighting man on the battlefield, who quickly shed his heavy armour. A new emphasis on the strength and killing efficiency of greater firepower was seen as the way forward to enhanced battlefield achievement and survivability. The wide-spread use of traditional horse cavalry continued, though, through the years of the First World War, even as the military planners, designers, engineers, and visionaries moved ahead in their thinking and development of the tank concept.

One such visionary, a medical doctor and inventor in Italy, Guido da Vigevano, created a war cart with an exposed wooden gear train. The vehicle was wind-powered, which, of course, severely limited its utility. Science quickly moved on to the visions of the universal genius, Leonardo da Vinci, who 150 years later produced sketches of what he referred to as an armoured fighting vehicle. The thing was bowl-shaped with four wheels and had guns mounted between the basic body shell and what appeared to be a parasol-shaped roof. The vehicle was intended to be propelled by an eight-man crew, all of whom turned cranks to transfer power through an extremely basic gearing system. Of his device Da Vinci wrote: "I am building secure and covered chariots which are invulnerable, and when they advance with their guns in the midst of the enemy, even the largest enemy masses are bound to retreat, and behind them the infantry can follow in safety and without opposition. These take the place of elephants and one may hold bellows in them to terrify horses or one may put carabiniers in them. This is good to break up the ranks of the enemy." All well and good, but Leonardo seems to have provided little in the way of a steering capability, and the extremely low ground clearance of his vehicle meant that it would have frequently bogged down. The very low power-to-weight ratio would have rapidly exhausted the poor crewmen. Four hundred years would pass before the next level of progress began for the tank.

It was to be "the power of those within, the same more easie and more spedie than so many armed men would be otherwise" that would provide the momentum for the 'assault car' design of mathematician John Napier in his 1596 "round chariot of metal. The use thereof in moving serveth to break the array of the enemies battle . . . by continual discharge of harquebussiers [a portable, long-barreled gun dating from the 15th century] through small holes, the enemy being abashed and uncertain as to what defence or pursuit to use against a moving mouth of metal."

More than two centuries later, in 1838, a Cornish engineer named John George, together with his son, laid claim to having invented what they referred to as a "modern steam war chariot, a vehicle which he described as "coke-burning, with sides armoured against muskett and grape shot, and capable of cutting a twenty-three-foot opening in an enemy rank." George's war chariot was operated by a three-man crew and could, he said, "penetrate the densest lines, the firmest cahorts and the most compact squadrons with as much certainty as a cannon ball would pass through a partition of paste board." When he and his son offered to demonstrate a model of their device to the members of the Commons in London, their proposal drew no interest.

Another Briton, James Cowan, was in the process of developing a design for an armoured fighting vehicle in 1854, when it occurred to him to acquire and enclose one of the engines designed and built by James Boydell (the British inventor of the steam-powered traction engine), in an open-topped iron skin or shell. There were gun ports housing a number of cannon, and the track of the machine was made up of many short, reinforced wooden "feet" mounted around the road wheels. The result vaguely resembled what would one day evolve as linked caterpillar tracks that would ultimately enable the modern tank to roll into battle over many kinds of terrain.

But when members of a Select Committee appointed by the then British Prime Minister, Lord Palmerston, considered the Cowan armoured fighting vehicle design, their evaluation found it lacking in many ways. It failed to adequately provide internally for the functions of the boiler, flywheel, and the breech-loading guns, for other machinery, for coal and ammunition storage, and for the driver and gunners. In Palmerston's own view, the design was "repellent" and he publicly described it as "barbaric and uncivilised". The Committee rejected the Cowan design, and Cowan condemned their decision in the press, calling the members "washed out Old Women and Senile Old Tabbies".

Progress, though, would not be thwarted, and many enlightened and visionary men of the time concurred that the way forward for land warfare would include a self-propelled fighting vehicle with excellent firepower and substantial protection for its crewmen. The Cowan episode would actually lead to the birth of that irresistible killing machine, the modern tank.

One significant change of direction occurred in the 1880s when two German engineers, Gottlieb Daimler and Karl Benz, joined forces to design and develop a relatively small internal combustion engine which soon took the evolution of the armoured fighting vehicle away from steam power. The less-than-visionary War Office personnel of the British government, meanwhile, were steadfastly ignoring or rejecting all armoured fighting vehicle designs submitted to them. Next in line for such War Office treatment was Edward Pennington in 1895. Pennington, an American entrepreneur, approached the

Office with his new design for an open-topped, bathtub-shaped armoured car mounted with two machine-guns. Pennington had developed and patented a pneumatic tyre, examples of which were incorporated into his car design, along with a 1.4 inch-thick armour plate skirting around the hull. The skirt ended eighteen inches above the ground and was hung with a chain mail fringe to protect the tyres. The three-man crew included a driver and two gunners. Predictably, it elicited no interest at the War Office and the project was abandoned.

After the Pennington episode, another British inventor, Frederick Simms, came up with the Military Scout, another self-propelled fighting vehicle. The Simms machine was armed with an air-cooled Maxim machine-gun and was powered by 1.5 hp De Dion engine. It was considered quite promising by many knowledgable observers, but once again, it failed to appeal to the War Office. But by the time of the Second Boer War, Simms had developed a little petrol-engined armoured rail-car that he had based on Pennington's design. The well-armed Simms War Car was utilised in the Boer conflict, making good use of a Vickers-Maxim one-pounder gun and two Maxim water-cooled machine-guns. The War Car made a maximum speed of nine mph and was powered by a 16hp Simms-Daimler engine. It was shown to the press and public at the 1902 Crystal Palace exhibition where it impressed the crowds, though not the War Office. This rejection led to Simms moving on to other projects and away from the design of armoured fighting vehicles.

The next appreciable advance in the development of the tank came in 1905 from the Richard Hornsby & Sons firm. From 1828 until 1918, Richard Hornsby manufactured engines and machinery in Lincolnshire, England. Hornsby's company developed one of the earliest track systems for vehicles and then sold the patented system to the Holt Company, the predecessor to Caterpillar, Inc., in the United States. In 1918, the Hornsby company became a subsidiary of the nearby agricultural engineering firm, Rustons, of Lincoln, to form the firm of Ruston & Hornsby, manufacturing stream engines and traction engines.

Then, in an initial connection with the British military, David Roberts, Hornsby's chief engineer and managing director, designed and developed a paraffin-engined chain-tracked steam tractor which the company patented in 1904. During the next year Roberts first demonstrated his invention, to the Mechanical Transport Committee of the British Army and followed with more formal demonstrations at Grantham and Aldershot in 1906, and again at Aldershot in 1907 with an improved version. By November of that year he had completed and demonstrated a tracked trailer on which a gun could be mounted, a showing that impressed members of the Royal Artillery. An additional demonstration of the device and tracked trailer carrying a dummy gun, was conducted in the presence of King Edward VII in which rough ground and obstacles were easily crossed. In addition to the planned showing, the

"Caterpillar tractor" as it was now known, hauled a stuck team of horses from the mud with ease, greatly impressing members of the Motor Transport Committee gathered at the Aldershot ground to witness the presentation. Commenting on the occasion, one newspaper referred to the system as "the germ of a land fighting unit when men will fight behind iron walls." When Roberts went on to show that his device could readily travel more than forty miles without stopping, he was awarded a £1,000 prize by the British War Office for the achievement.

That achievement was followed in the spring of 1910 with the towing at Aldershot of a 60-pounder gun and its ammunition across rough ground. This led directly to an early breakthrough in the developments leading to the concept of the tank when Army Major W.E. Donohue of the Mechanical Transport Committee proposed that Roberts consider the fitting on a single tractor unit of a gun together with bullet-proof shielding, an idea that might have then resulted in one of the first self-propelled guns, had Roberts elected to follow up on the suggestion. He did not, and later came to regret the decision.

In further testing at a North Wales location, in which the Holt-Roberts devices were pitted against Army horse teams, the artillery officers present were less impressed, noting that the device was decidedly underpowered. Roberts then tried converting it to one powered by a petrol engine which raised its performance to 105 brake horsepower.

In a cautionary response, the Mechanical Transport Committee continued to believe in the possibilities exhibited by the Holt-Roberts tractor, with the proviso that it be used in conjunction with teams of horses. The Royal Artillery, however, took a more negative view of the device.

The outlook for the future of the Holt-Roberts tractor was, by 1911, not very promising. While the Mechanical Transport Committee expressed its interest in having one of the tractors for evaluation, the War Office steadfastly refused permission for the MTC to buy one. The discouraged Roberts had devoted five years to developing the tracked machine, the costs involved being hardly covered by the small fees he had received from the Army in the course of the work. In that time he had received no military or civilian orders and had finally sold the patents to the Holt Manufacturing Company in the U.S. for £4,000. Holt registered the name 'Caterpillar' as a trademark in 1911 and when it later merged with C.L. Best the new firm was called The Caterpillar Tractor Company.

With the outbreak of the First World War, Britain was in the position of having to purchase caterpillar tractors from Holt in America to tow the Army's heavy guns. The British had lost their chance to take the lead in tracked vehicle technology and possibly, to create and manufacture the world's first practical tank weapon, a weapon that would be based on American design. However, while the Roberts chain-track design did not contibute directly to the ultimate design development of the early military tank, that vehicle's design was certainly influenced by the fact that British Lt. Col. R.E. Crompton, who would play a major part in military tank development, had attended some of the early trials of the Roberts machine and had been heavily influenced by the experience.

The start of the Great War was near, but in the run-up to that catastrophic event, developments in the area of armoured fighting vehicles were relatively limited, the results being efforts in Britain, France, Italy, and Germany to deploy vehicles of varying capabilities and success in local conflicts. The principal general staff and war ministry personnel continued to operate with predictably narrow, intransigent and reactionary mindsets, showing hostility to most of the new ideas, learning nothing from their own battlefield experience, and perpetuating the delay and sabotaging of virtually all of the promising new developments in the field. Their muddled views and delusions in the area of future tactics condemned them to being wholly unready for the monstrous conflict about to be unleashed.

St Petersburg, 29 July 1914
From: Czar Nicholas II
To: Kaiser Wilhelm II
I forsee that very soon I shall be overwhelmed by the pressure forced upon me and be forced to take extreme measures which will lead to war.
—Nicky

Berlin, 30 July 1914
From: Kaiser Wilhelm II
To: Czar Nicholas II
The whole weight of the decision lies solely on your shoulders now. You have to bear the responsibility for peace or war.
—Willy

There is no question but that the majority of commanders, when the First World War started, should have realized that charging cavalry and massed ranks of infantry could not and would not withstand the withering fire of breech-loading, rifled weapons and machine-guns. Still, most of these field leaders would not even consider possible alternatives to ordering their troops 'over the top' in a mindless and hopeless attempt to overwhelm the enemy.

In 1914, early in that so-called war-to-end-all-wars, the Belgians first employed a type of armoured fighting vehicle mounted with machine-guns on the Western Front. The first thing they found when putting their wheeled vehicles into action on the seemingly perpetual muddy battleground was that they were entirely unsuited for the sticky conditions.

The mindlessness of the entrenched static warfare on the Western Front by 1915 had brought with it a death toll so enormous that none of the combatants could continue to justify the tactics on which they had come into the war. The incredible massed infantry charges over the ruined no-man's land, resulted in immense losses among all the participants as they were mowed down by the artillery barrages and the withering machine-gun fire. By this point, the commanders at the Allied General Headquarters in France were beginning to see the light and calling for some sort of way out of the hopeless, static trench warfare stalemate.

In February of that year, Winston Churchill, who was then First Lord of the Admiralty, set up the Naval Landships Committee whose purpose was to design and build a new tracked, armoured vehicle based on a proposal by British Army Lt. Col. Ernest Swinton, Royal Engineers. The idea was that such a petrol-powered caterpillar-tracked armoured vehicle with hardened steel plate tracks should be designed to destroy machine-gun positions and barbed wire barriers and, importantly, to easily cross the many trenches and obstacles of the battlefield. The Committee then commissioned Naval Air Service Lieutenant W.E. Wilson and William Tritton of the William Foster Company of Lincoln, to construct the small landship. The work went on under a strict veil of secrecy, the project given the code-name 'Water Tank', a wartime handle that would eventually be shortened by troops to 'tank'.

The British referred to the vehicle as the 'machine-gun destroyer' and both Churchill and the rest of the Landships Committee were undeterred by the disappointing initial test results of the device. The prototype was demonstrated for the Committee on 11 September 1915. It was a start, but it failed to cross the broad trenches prepared for it. The failure prompted Wilson and Tritton to rethink the premise and come up with another approach, that of running the tracks right around a body designed in a rhomboid shape, pointed at the top and front and sloped downward at the rear. The height was kept to a minimum through the use of sponsons on both sides of the vehicle, each of them mounting a six-pounder naval gun, rather than a top-mounted turret. The vehicle had fixed front and rear turrets, with the front turret accommodating the tank commander and the driver who sat side by side. The rear turret housed a machine-gun and there were four Hotchkiss machine-guns in all, with four doors behind the sponsons as well as a manhole hatch in the top of the hull. To the rear of the hull was a towed two-wheel steering tail. The 'tank' was known as Big Willie, but more commonly as *Mother*. It weighed twenty-eight tons, was eight feet in height and twenty-six feet, five inches long. It was powered by a 105 hp Daimler sleeve-valve engine.

Mother was put through her paces on a brisk February day in 1916 at the Hatfield Park, Hertfordshire estate of the Marquess of Salisbury. Those present included the Minister of Munitions David Lloyd George, later to become prime minister, Field Marshal Lord Kitchener, other cabinet members and representatives of the Army and the Admiralty. Mother was driven through a specially prepared obstacle course with craters, ditches, wire entanglements, streams, and wide trenches. It performed well, in the collective view of the Landships Committee. Kitchener was somewhat less than enthusiastic about the demonstration, but the Army representatives were impressed and a production order for 100 of the Mothers resulted. Fifty of the vehicles were ordered with the same armament as that of the Mother prototype, and these would then be referred to as 'males.' The other fifty tanks would be armed with six machine-guns, four of them mounted in smaller side sponsons. These vehicles were referred to as 'females' and their job on the battlefield was to prevent the 'male' tanks from being swamped by the enemy infantry.

At the Foster's workshops where the new vehicles were being constructed in deep secrecy, the workers referred to them as 'tanks' and pondered whether they would indeed totally change the nature of land warfare. The now common reference, tank, was an attempt to conceal the project; the term landship being too close to the mark, and tank would very soon become the generic for the machine.

From the drawing board to actual assembly of the Mark 1 tanks, pressure on the shop workers allowed just twelve months and, as might have been expected, the results left room for considerable improvement. The gravity-fed fuel system was found to starve the engine as the vehicle manoeuvred with its front end in a steep climbing or descending attitude. And the fire risk to the crewmen was greatly increased due to the placement of the fuel tank inside the vehicle. Strangely, sterring the vehicle, even with the help of the wheeled steering tail, required the teamwork of four men. David Fletcher of the Bovington, England, Tank Museum, a leading authority on tanks, and author of *The British Tanks 1915-19*, described the procedure of the early tanks: "Four of the crew served the guns; a gunner and loader on each side. The others were all required to operate the controls. The driver, sitting to the right of the commander, was effectively there to make the tank go. Apart from the steering wheel, that was almost useless, he had no control whatever over turning, or swinging the tank, to use the contemporary term. He controlled the primary gearbox, clutch and footbrake which acted on the transmission shaft, along with the ignition and throttle controls. The commander operated the steering brakes and either man could work the differential lock which was above, between and behind them. The two extra men worked the secondary gearboxes at the back, on instruction from the driver who had to work the clutch at the same time.

"It was, according to the instruction book, possible to steer the tank by selecting a different ratio in each of the secondary gearboxes although the experience soon proved that this would result in twisted gear shafts. Thus, except for slight deviations when the steering brakes were used, the standard procedure for steering was to halt the tank, lock the differential and take one track out of gear. First was then selected in the primary box and the other secondary box, the brake was then applied to the free track and the tank would swing in that direction."

Early in 1917, the Marks II and III had been shipped into combat with only minor improvements over the Mark I. However, by April of that year the Mark IV was ready for service and proved to be a much improved weapon system with much better armour protection. This tank incorporated a vacuum-fed fuel system, a revised cooling and ventilation system, an exhaust silencer, and a rear-mounted external fuel tank. The 'males' carried the same armament as the prototype and the 'females' were armed with five Vickers and one Hotchkiss machine-guns. Prior to the entry of the Mark V in May 1918, 420 male and 595 female tanks had been produced. The Mark V was easily the best and most advanced version of the basic design. It incorporated an entirely new epicyclic steering system designed by the now Major W.E. Wilson, and had an extended hull to increase its trench-crossing capability. Increased power from a 150 hp Ricardo engine gave it a maximum speed of 4.6 mph and Mark V production totalled 400 male and 632 female tanks.

Through considerable trial and error the first rather crude British tanks had been developed, shipped to the Western Front and sent to lead the attack on the Somme of 15 September 1916. Historical records indicate that, of the forty-seven tanks brought to the front for the attack, only eleven actually entered the battle. While shocking and frightening for the Germans, these tanks were, in fact, quite unreliable and underpowered for their weight and role. Certainly, they were too few in number to make the desired impression for the British. And this is where the original thinking, even genius perhaps, of Lancelot E. DeMole comes in.

DeMole was an Australian, a draughtsman and inventor who had worked in mining and surveying projects in his native country. Among his many clever designs was an early automatic telephone system which he developed fully three years before a similar system was introduced in the United States. His interest in the development of a chain rail traction system for heavy haulage arose during his work in the challenging countryside of Western Australia and resulted in his design for a chain-rail armoured vehicle, drawings of which he submitted to the British War Office in 1912. DeMole's 'tank' could be easily steered over rough, difficult ground and trenches, turning to left or right by changing the direction of the chain-rail being laid. The War Office rejected the design in 1913. Friends and associates of DeMole urged him to try to interest the German consul in Western Australia in his tank idea, but he refused on the basis that the Germans might one day be the enemy. And with the British declaration of war against Germany in 1914, Australia, as part of the British Commonwealth, also declared war on the Germans.

Unaware of the existence and work of the Landship Committee and their tank development activity, DeMole re-submitted his drawings and proposal for his tank in the summer of 1915. The British Munitions Inventions Office declined to forward his design to the Landships Committee, possibly because that office may also have been unaware of the Landships Committee and its work.

It was after the worst fighting in the Battle of the Somme that the secret of the Landships Committee tank became common knowledge and DeMole realized that his own tank design was, in fact, superior to that of the Committee vehicle. With the financial assistance of his friend, Lieutenant Harold Boyce, a man who would one day become the Lord Mayor of London, DeMole engaged the firm of Williams and Benwell in Melbourne to construct a 1/8 scale model of the DeMole tank to be demonstrated to the British military authorities. During the sequence of two demonstrations, DeMole was stymied before the second when the German forces launched their spring offensive of 1918. After the war's end in November, a Royal commission reported its findings on rewarding certain inventors for their contributions to the war effort. DeMole and a few others had lodged claims re tank development. The commission found that the credit for designing the British tank should be given to Mssrs Wilson and Tritton, along with a joint award of £15,000. The commission awarded £1,000 to Lt. Col. Ernest Swinton for his part in the early British tank development. They found, in the matter of Lancelot DeMole's claim, that he was certainly owed considerable credit for "having made and reduced to practical shape as far back as 1912, a brilliant invention which anticipated, and in some respects, surpassed that which was actually put into use in the year 1916. It was the claimant's misfortune and not his fault, that his invention was in advance of its time and failed to be appreciated and was put aside because the occasion for its use had not yet arisen." The commission regretted that they could not recommend any award to him, explaining that a claimant must show causal connection between the making of his invention and the use of any similar invention by the government. They did, however, award the sum of £965 to cover DeMole's out-of-pocket expenses.

The DeMole tank would have been, in all probability, far more manoeuvrable than its British tank competition machines, with far better handling, turning, climbing and descending capabilities, and was also able to back itself out of problem situations. But the DeMole machine was never actually built. It existed only on paper and no full scale version of his tank was ever made and tested to prove the accuracy of the inventor's predictions for his creation. There is no way to actually measure the extent of DeMole's contribution to the development of the early tanks, thus most tank authorities and historians have tended to credit Wilson and Tritton with by far the greatest achievements in that development. Shamefully, DeMole's innovative work, his considerable genuine contribution and achievement in the field of early tank development, and the man himself, have been virtually reduced to a mere footnote in history.

In 1916 the British Army was busily establishing its armoured striking force under the overall responsibility of Lt. Colonel Ernest Swinton. The General Headquarters representative for tank development and policy at the time was Lt. Col. Hugh Elles, an officer in the Royal Engineers, who was soon appointed the British field commander in France. Initially named the Tank Detachment, the force was redesignated the Tank Corps in June 1917, and renamed the Royal Tank Corps in 1923 when so awarded by King George V, and was later renamed the Royal Tank Regiment, becoming a part of the Royal Armoured Corps. Lt. Col. Elles had, in 1916, assembled an excellent small cadre of officers for the effort on the war front in France. Among them were Major J.F.C. Fuller and Captain G. Martel, whose foresight brought predictions of the coming battles between opposing tank forces. Their evolving tactical ideas would change land warfare fundamentally. Their vision of the tank weapon in 1917 was encompassed in Fuller's writing: "It is, in fact, an armoured mechanical horse."

Britain's first tanks of the Great War arrived in France covered in canvas wraps and entered the battlefield against the Germans in September 1916. Col. H.C.B. Rogers described the equipment and supplies accompanying those early British tanks into battle: "Rations for the first tank battle consisted of sixteen loaves of bread and about thirty tins of foodstuffs. The various types of stores included four spare Vickers machine-gun barrels, one spare Hotchkiss machine-gun, two boxes of revolver ammunition, thirty-three thousand rounds of ammunition for the machine-guns, a telephone instrument and 100 yards of cable on a drum, a signalling lamp, three signalling flags, two wire cutters, one spare drum of engine oil, one spare drum of gear oil, two small drums of grease, and three water cans. Added to this miscellaneous collection was all the equipment which was stripped off the eight inhabitants of the tank, so that there was not very much room to move about."

An immediate weakness was the crew training of the men sent to war in the new tanks. Their instruction had been sub-standard, with virtually no emphasis placed on the essential co-operation between the tanks and the infantry. The two forces agreed only on the necessity of the tanks reaching their initial objective five minutes before the infantry forces and destroying the enemy strongpoints which were holding back the advance of the infantry.

Only thirty-two of the forty-nine British tanks meant to deploy against the enemy were able to be fielded. Of these, nine were halted through breakdowns, five were halted when they became stuck in trenches or soft ground, and a further nine were unable to maintain the pace of the advance and lagged behind the infantry troops. Still, the nine remaining tanks completed the mission and inflicted heavy losses on the German forces. While not achieving all their objectives, the tanks that were successful in this first effort made a definite impression on the Germans they encountered, sending many of them fleeing well before the menacing machines were even within firing range.

The operating conditions in these early British tanks at the midpoint of the war were powerfully described by historian / author Bryan Perrett in his excellent book *Iron Fist*: "Such intense heat was generated by the engine that the men wore as little as possible. The noise level, a compound of roaring engine, unsilenced exhaust on the early Marks, the thunder of tracks crossing the hull, weapons firing and the enemy's return fire striking the armour, made speech impossible and permanently damaged the hearing of some. The hard ride provided by the unsprung suspension faithfully mirrored every pitch and roll of the ground so that the gunners, unaware of what lay ahead, would suddenly find themselves thrown off their feet and, reaching out for support, sustaining painful burns as they grabbed at machinery that verged on the red hot.

"Worst of all was the foul atmosphere, polluted by the fumes of leaking exhausts, hot oil, petrol, and expended cordite. Brains starved of oxygen refused to function or produced symptoms of madness. One officer is known to have fired into a malfunctioning engine with his revolver, and some crews were reduced to the level of zombies, repeatedly mumbling the orders they had been given but physically unable to carry them out. Small wonder then, that after even a short spell in action, the men would collapse on the ground beside their vehicles gulping in air, incapable of movement for long periods.

"In addition, of course, there were the effects of the enemy's fire. Wherever this struck, small glowing flakes of metal would be flung off the inside of the armour, while bullet splash penetrated visors and joints in the plating; both could blind, although the majority of such wounds were minor though painful. Glass vision blocks became starred and were replaced by open slits, thereby increasing the risk, especially to the commander and driver. In an attempt to minimise this, leather crash helmets, slotted metal goggles and chain mail visors were issued, but these were quickly discarded in the suffocating heat of the vehicle's interior. The tanks of the day were not proof against field artillery so that any penetration was likely to result in a fierce petrol or ammunition fire followed by an explosion that would tear the vehicle apart. In such a situation the chances of being able to evacuate a casualty through the awkward hatches were horribly remote. Despite these sobering facts, the crews willingly accepted both the conditions and the risks in the belief that they had a war-winning weapon."

"They looked like giant toads", according to one British corporal. What an ominous, foreboding image 400 tanks crawling out of the early morning mist and ground fog near Cambrai, northeastern France on 20 November 1917 must have been. Their appearance was the turning point in the war after literally years of trench warfare, attrition and stalemate. That stalemate had agonizingly dominated the trenches of the Western Front throughout 1917, with the Allies totally bogged down and unable to breach the German defences. Finally, in November of that year, the key Allied armoured commanders proposed launching a massive tank offensive against the heavily fortified enemy defences near the town of Cambrai. There the well-drained, gently rolling terrain suited their plans for a surprise attack that would develop suddenly and quietly with none of the conventional softening-up artillery barrage beforehand. The idea of the armoured commanders was that the gigantic tank force would arrive quickly, hit with maximum destructive power inflicting major damage, and depart the area just as rapidly.

The bold plan of the armoured commanders had been presented to Douglas Haig, British Commander-in-Chief, Western Front, during the preceding summer, at a time when Haig was experiencing enormous losses in the Passchendale swamps some fifty miles north of Cambrai. In the circumstances Haig showed little interest in the scheme. By November, however, the shattering events of Passchendale had forced him to reconsider and approve the great tank offensive plan, which now required the massive tank armada to force a breakthrough between the two canals at Cambrai, capture the town itself, along with the high ground of the village of Flesquieres and the Bourlon Wood. Many of the tanks would be carrying enormous bundles of brushwood to be used as fill-in for the trenches they would encounter when reaching the Siegfried Line defences. The plan called for the tanks to approach the area in a line-abreast formation with the accompanying infantry troops following in columns close behind and defending against close-quarter attacks. It also called for the use of deception and diversionary tactics in the days immediately before the attack. Heavy smoke, gas, and dummy tanks would all be employed to fool the Germans. The men and equipment were all brought up by night and carefully hidden in the daytime. A huge force of 381 tanks was set to advance along a six-mile front towards Cambrai.

One of the British commanders, Major-General G.M. Harper of the 51st Highland Division, though, chose to deviate from the plan of action. Harper apparently took the view that the strange new tank vehicles could probably not manage to breach the Siegfried defences as rapidly as the plan required. On the day of the attack, he chose to delay sending his tanks and infantry forward until an hour after the rest of the tank and infantry force had depart-

ed. This odd delay worked in favour of the Germans, allowing them sufficient time to position their field artillery and take out five of the British
tanks. Much of the remaining armour and infantry, however, did manage to
cut efficiently and lethally through the German lines in a dramatic five-mile
advance to Bourlon Wood by midday. It was an impressive accomplishment
for the British tank crews and it continued the next day with a push that
included the capture of Flesquieres and a further 1.5-mile penetration into
the enemy territory. Their achievement was cast aside, however, on 30
November when fresh German forces counter-attacked, forcing the British to
retreat and retaking all of the territory they had lost in the great tank-
infantry offensive. The Germans took some 6,000 British prisoners in the
counter-attack, but the Allies had learned some valuable lessons about the
effective use of tanks in concert with infantry.

German tanks first appeared on the battlefields of the Western Front in
March 1918. The German A7V was considerably larger and heavier than the
main British heavy tank of the period. The German machine weighed thirty-
three tons and was operated by a crew of eighteen men. The armament
included a forward-mounted 57mm gun and six machine-guns positioned
along the sides and rear of the hull. With a maximum armour thickness of
30mm, the A7V was able to resist direct hits from field guns at long range;
the overhead armour, though, was not thick enough to provide adequate protection for the crew. The crew were endangered too by the susceptibility of
the hull to bullet splash due to the way in which the armour plating was fitted. The tank was powered by two Daimler sleeve-valve engines, each producing 150 hp. It could make a speed of eight mph—high for the time—on
its sprung tracks when traveling on smooth, level ground. When crossing
poorer ground conditions, though, its design and low ground clearance made
for far less impressive performance.

The entire production of A7V tanks by the Germans was limited to just
fifteen machines. They were introduced to combat in an action in which four
of the big tanks were employed together with five captured British Mark IVs.
A month later, thirteen A7Vs, nearly the entire force, took part in the assault
and capture of Villers-Brettoneux, in a kind of reciprocity for the shock
effect of that first British mass tank attack. It was soon after the Villers-
Brettoneux success for the Germans that the world's first tank-versus-tank
engagement occurred in the same part of the French countryside. In the
early hours of the morning three British Mark IVs were sent up to stop the
German penetration in the area. Some of the British crewmen were suffering
from the effects of gas shelling, but all of their tanks advanced on one of the
A7Vs. The British machine-guns were all but useless against the German
tank's armour and two of the British tanks were taken out by the enemy fire.
The remaining British tank then manoeuvred to take a flank shot at the

German machine. The British crew scored a direct hit and the crippled German tank ran up a steep embankment and overturned. At this point two more A7Vs arrived to attack the British tank. One of the German pair was destroyed by the British crew and the crew of the remaining German tank abandoned their vehicle and ran off.

These early tank actions served to influence the conduct of later battle action in that final year of the war. In the decisive battle of the war, a huge force of 456 British tanks were engaged in the Battle of Amiens on 8 August. The action was strung along a thirteen-mile stretch and was set to begin with the mass of tanks moving to the start line at 4:20 a.m. There was a heavy mist lying over the field of action which worked to help conceal the British force, achieve largely complete surprise, and aid in overrunning the German forward defences.

In that action, the main Allied attacks were to be delivered by the Canadian Corps on the right flank and the Australian Corps on the left, both units operating south of the River Somme. North of the river, the British Third Corps had the job of covering the left flank while making a limited advance. As the Canadian Fifth Tank Battalion was under way towards its objective, it came under heavy fire and suffered the loss of fifteen tanks, and that of a further eleven tanks in achieving its second objective of the day and having only eight machines still operable. While achieving its initial objectives with relative ease, the Canadian Fourth Tank Battalion then came under very heavy German artillery shelling and lost all but eleven of its tanks in the fighting.

The Australian Corps tanks, meanwhile, achieved all of their objectives, eliminating much of the enemy opposition. They then stormed through the German defences, outpacing the tanks.

In the lull after this devastating engagement, most of the tank crewmen were the worse for their having spent more than three hours buttoned up in their tanks with their guns firing. Most suffered with headaches, some with high temperatures and some with heart disturbances. Amiens had been a major Allied success. 22,000 German prisoners had been taken and it led to capitulation by the German High Command. It was clear to them, and to their political leaders in Berlin, that the Allied tanks had brought about the end of their resistance against the Allies. The Kaiser, it is said, told one of his commanders, "It is very strange that our men cannot get used to tanks."

I met her paddling down the road, / A vast primeval sort of toad, / And while I planned a swift retreat / She snorted, roared, and stamped her feet, / And sprinted up a twelve-foot bank; / Whereat a voice cried, 'Good old Tank!'

She paused and wagged her armoured tail, / There was a 'Jonah' in the 'Whale,'

Since from her ribs a face looked out; / Her skipper hailed me with a shout, 'Come on and watch my beauty eat / A batch of houses down the street!'

It was pure joy to see her crunch / A sugar factory for lunch; / She was a 'peach' at chewing trees— / The Germans shuddered at her sneeze— / And when she leant against a wall / It shortly wasn't there at all.

I stroked the faithful creature's head; / 'What gives her greatest bliss?' I said. Her skipper glibly answered, 'Tanks are crazed about Abdullas . . . Thanks! She waddled off— and on the air / Arose Abdulla's fragrance rare!
—*The Ways of Tanks* from an Abdulla cigarette ad in the 2 November 1918 issue of *The Sphere*

THE GENIUS

He came from the town of Kulm on the Vistula River, south of Gdansk in Poland. His father, Friedrich, was an officer in the 2nd Pomeranian Jäger Battalion of the German Army. Heinz Guderian was born on 17 June 1888 and by the time he was sent off to boarding school at the Karlsruhe Cadet School in Baden, he was serious, articulate, and at times, quite cold in his manner. In 1908, he received his commission as an officer in the Army and on 1 October 1913 he married Margarete Goerne. They had two sons, both of whom served in the *Panzertruppen* in the Second World War.

"His ability as a commander, came not from recklessness and intuition, as with Erwin Rommel, but from knowledge. He knew exactly how far every tank could go and over which landscape." —George Parada on General Heinz Guderian

Twelve-year-old Heinz studied at the Karlsruhe Cadet School for two years and then, in April 1903, at the age of fourteen, transferred to the Main Cadet School (*Haupt-Kadetten-Anstalt*) at Gross Lichterfelde, near Berlin. He recalled his training there as "military austerity and simplicity, but founded on kindness and justice." Training for a life and career as an officer in the German military before the First World War was unlike that in America or Britain at the time. The selection and grooming of the potential officer candidate for the German Army began in childhood. Military school education was strict and serious. The schooling, mentoring, discipline, and guidance came from teachers who were serving officers, non-commissioned officers, and senior classmen, all people who had been through the grinding, demanding, unyielding system themselves, to become skillful, able soldiers, ready for whatever awaited them. It was a no-nonsense environment and it suited the young Guderian, who was both highly intelligent and tough. Being bright, self-disciplined, and determined, he successfully met and passed all of the phases of his training, including a brief detachment to the 10th Hanover Jäger Battalion, which was then under the command of his father, and the formality of being selected for and elected to membership in the regiment, receiving his commission into it as a 2nd Lieutenant in January 1908.

Guderian's connection to the *Jäger* (Light Infantry or Rifle Battalions of the Imperial Army) was quite significant to his future career as his unit was intended for reconnaissance to an infantry corps or support to cavalry troops. The unit was issued with an ample supply of bicycles for the mobility of its role. Heinz and his fellow troopers, many of whom had been mountaineers and foresters, had been cultivated to think and operate with a high degree of independence in the field, a capability he developed far in excess of that expected of the average German soldier.

The clever Guderian was well regarded and, in 1913, won selection to the German Army Staff College—the *Kriegsakademie*—an essential prerequisite to the career of a German officer on the rise. His selection was of particular note as he was among the youngest students ever to be so honoured. With the outbreak of the First World War in 1914, the current training course at the Kriegsakademie was dissolved and the students were moved into appropriate staff appointments. Guderian, with a period of assignment to a wireless station in his background, was a natural choice for an appointment to the 5th Cavalry Division's wireless station. He served there, and as Assistant Signals Officer to the Headquarters of the 4th Army until April 1917, during which time he had been promoted to Captain. The promotion led to a General Staff appointment with the 4th Infantry Division, which was then holding down a captured sector near Champagne. For the balance of the war, with a single brief interruption when he commanded the second battalion, 14th Infantry Regiment, he continuted to serve in various General Staff appointments, and by war's end he had risen to the most prestigious of German Army staff posts, 1a—General Staff Officer, Operations.

Lili Marlene is a song based on a German poem of the First World War. It was a favourite of both German and British troops in the desert war in 1941, and with the arrival of American forces in North Africa in 1943, its popularity was extended when the German-born actress and singer Marlene Dietrich, made it famous. From *Lilly Marlene*: Aus dem stillen Raume, / aus der Erde Grund, / Hebt mich, wie im Traume dien verlieber Mund, / Wenn sich die spaeten Nebel drehn, / Werd ich bei der Laterne stehn, / Wie einst Lilli Marleen, wie einst Lilli Marleen.

From *Lily Marlene*: Resting in a billet, just behind the line, / Even tho' we're parted your lips are close to mine; / You wait where that lantern softly gleams, / Your sweet face seems to haunt my dreams, / My Lily of the lamplight, / My own Lily Marlene.

"It's a beautiful song, and the only redeeming thing is the rumour kicking around that *Lily* is an ancient French song, stolen by the Germans. It may not be true, but we like to believe it. *Lily* got a couple of artillerymen in trouble in France. They were singing it at a bar the day after this particular town had been taken. Some local partisans came over and told them to shut the hell up. The guys understood, apologized, and bought drinks all around."
—Bill Mauldin, WW2 cartoonist

With the end of the war, Heinz Guderian found himself having to deal with many problems and concerns relating to the armistice, organization, withdrawal, and demobilisation, as well as the wholesale reduction and practical elimination of the German Army. By December 1918, the regular German

Army had few soldiers left under its command.

Guderian remained on active service after the war. What had been the remains of the German Army had been reconstituted into what became known as the *Reichswehr*. Under the terms of the Versailles Treaty at the end of the war, the strength of the German Army had been reduced from about 500,000 to about 100,000, of which 4,000 were to be officers. The intention of the Allied powers had also been to close the German cadet schools and thus eliminate the source for the Prussian officer element in the army command structure. This, of course, included the Kriegsakademie, which was dissolved. In practical terms, Germany was no longer allowed to have tanks, heavy artillery, aircraft, or anything beyond the barest necessities of military equipment. Germany had no choice but to accept these conditions. Not to do so would have meant an invasion by France and Britain, which the Germans could not have resisted.

In the circumstances, the German government was faced with the problem of selecting appropriate applicants from among the 32,000 army officers who had returned from the war still fit for duty, to fill the relatively small number of permanent commissions available in the new army. The government was looking for applicants who had shown significant courage in combat, together with suitability for promotion to the next higher grade in the event of war. With little actual combat experience, a non-aristocratic background and average family circumstances, Guderian could not have been considered a hopeful candidate for retention with a permanent commission. What was working in his favour though, was his superb reputation as an experienced staff officer and, by the end of 1919 he was confirmed as an officer of the new Reichswehr.

In 1922, he was surprised to receive an appointment to the General Staff (then disguised for treaty purposes as the *Truppenamt* and its Inspectorate of Transport), an organization with which he would serve for thirteen years, a period in which it became the parent branch for the Panzer Corps. Heinz Guderian had been brought into the unit specifically to study the theoretical uses of motorized infantry in combat, but as so often occurs in military contexts, he was almost immediately reassigned to another job that had no relation to his experience or interests. While disappointed in this unwanted diversion from his career path, he spent his spare time studying the theory of mechanized warfare and paid particular attention to the writings of the British tank pioneer, Major-General J.F.C. Fuller, and those of the military theorist Sir Basil Liddell Hart who had, after his service in the First World War, developed the concept of mechanized warfare to replace the absurd static warfare he had known. Their ideas, together with Guderian's own theories, formed the foundation of what would be his own extraordinary contribution to the evolution of armoured warfare.

In the terms of the Versailles peace treaty at the end of the First World War, Germany was not permitted to develop an effective army. She was forbidden construction and / or possession of tanks, armoured vehicles, or any similar equipment which might be used in war. And while Britain, France and other countries experimented with the development of tanks and other armoured weaponry, without any particular fervour, many in the new German Army were coming under the strong influence of another brilliant theorist and advocate of mechanized warfare, General Hans von Seekt, a man who would contribute greatly to the reformation and reorganization of that army.

In their zeal and enthusiasm about tanks and armour, the Germans made a secret arrangement in 1928 with the Soviet Union, giving Germany access to a test facility near the Volga River, a facility in which the two nations would share ideas, technology, and some small British Vickers-Loyds tanks the Russians had acquired. The new arrangment enabled Germany to pay lip-service to the armaments restrictions of the Versailles Treaty, while she was actually working and experimenting behind the scenes towards the development of a new and fearsome armoured capability. Not one to be tight-lipped about his views, Heinz Guderian moved smoothly through the lecture circuit in the 1920s and into the '30s, delivering his thoughts and theories on the uses and implications of armour, motorized infantry, and aircraft in future conflict. As a keen observer of developments world-wide in his area of expertise, he took a special interest in the progress then being made in Britain in radio communications for tanks and armoured vehicles. All that he said in these addresses enhanced his reputation as the budding 'Father of the Panzer Force.'

Adolf Hitler was Chancellor of Germany by 1933 and, in the following year surreptitious progress was being steadily achieved by the Daimler-Benz Company on its design and construction of a promising new prototype tank, the PzKw *Panzerkampfwagen*. At a secret ordnance test centre in February 1935, Hitler observed trials of the new tank weapon and commented: "That's what I need. That's what I want to have." The new Panzer tank was indeed what he needed; an inexpensive, capable light tank that could be had in large numbers once Germany had overcome the problem of serious shortages in steel, fuel, and rubber supplies. The excited German leader immediately authorized the establishment and creation of three panzer divisions. The post of Chief of Staff of the new German armoured force was given to Colonel Guderian in the autumn of 1935, who had greatly impressed Hitler with his concepts of armoured warfare and his ideas about the required tactics and equipment. Hitler found the funding for the new armoured force mainly at the expense of other army organizations which were made to do without some of their own needs. Even under Hitler's wing, however, Guderian found that he was still unable to acquire the particular tracked armoured vehicles that he believed to be essential to the fulfillment of his armourized warfare philosophy, one that required the ability to move motorized infantry overland in concert with his tanks. He devoted himself wholeheartedly to expanding his knowledge, understanding, and experience of mechanized warfare through the 1940s, and was widely recognized and acknowledged as a genius at the forefront of armoured mechanized warfare for the future. Not merely a theorist, Guderian believed in leading from the front and was highly instrumental in the design, development and manufacture of his tanks. He had a key role in the design and development of the PzKpfw III and IV tanks, the former armed with a short, large-calibre cannon for hitting at soft targets, the latter with a long gun for tank-killing. Meticulous, thorough, and especially detail-oriented, he was keenly interested in all aspects of the tanks his panzers would be riding into combat.

Two events of the mid-1930s impacted on armour-meister Guderian. One was his promotion to the rank of General, and his book, *Achtung—Panzer!* (Attention—Tanks!) was published. Of the book, Liddell Hart wrote: ". . . of great interest as a self-exposition of the specialist mind and how it works. He had far more imagination than most specialists, but it was exercised almost entirely within the bounds of his professional subject, and burning enthusiasm increased the intensity of his concentration." And Paul Harris wrote: "*Achtung—Panzer!* is one of the most significant military books of the twentieth century. Guderian distillled into it about fifteen years' study of the development of mechanized warfare from its origins in the First World War until 1937. [In it] he sought to demonstrate that only by the intelligent use of armoured formations could Germany achieve swift and decisive victories in future wars, and avoid the ruinous attrition experienced in 1914-18. Although a number of conservative senior officers were sceptical of Guderian's message, by the outbreak of the Second World War it had gained a good deal of acceptance. The panzer (armoured) divisions became the cutting edge of the German Army in its spectacular victories of 1939-42."

One key point made by Guderian in his book was: "We believe that by attacking with tanks we can achieve a higher rate of movement than has been hitherto obtainable, and, what is perhaps more important, that we can keep moving once a breakthrough has been made."

So impressed was Adolf Hitler by *Achtung—Panzer!* that, in February 1938 he promoted Guderian to the rank of Lieutenant-General and appointed him to command the world's first armoured corps. The position spotlighted his tank units and their substantial capabilities in 1939 when they became the lead force in Hitler's annexation of Austria. To the rest of the world they exemplified a strange kind of ruthless efficiency in the essentially bloodless takeover of Germany's neighbour, but in fact, Guderian's tanks were insufficiently supplied in the effort, his logistics organization for it ill-conceived. Forward progress for his petrol-engined tanks was achieved only through re-fueling at civilian service stations along the invasion route. Food and ammunition were in critically short supply and the breakdown rate among the tanks was reportedly 30 percent. The experience caused Guderian to rethink and reconstruct his supply system.

The British government of Neville Chamberlain had guaranteed Poland's integrity in the late 1930s and for that reason, Hitler postponed his planned attack on Poland of 26 August 1939, in the belief that something in his favour might yet result from his diplomatic exchanges with Chamberlain. That was not the case, however, and on 31 August the German leader alerted his armoured divisions to be ready to move against Poland immediately. Hitler had loathed redrawn Poland that had been created by the Versailles treaty at the end of WWI. Some of Germany's former territory had gone into the new Poland, and he saw the move as part of a French plot to encircle Germany in order to keep it under surveillance. And, ideologically, he had a political commitment to the acquisition of *lebensraum*, living space to the east of the German nation. He was probably emboldened too, by the weakness of the British and French position on Czechoslovakia the previous year.

By 22 August, Hitler had successfully concluded a non-aggression pact with the Soviet Union in return for agreement to partition Poland between Germany and the Soviet Union. The agreement with the Russians afforded Hitler a new freedom of movement in Europe.

According to author / historian John Keegan: "To Germans of Guderian's background, class and profession . . . the most enduring and important factor in the history of that Baltic coast-line and its hinterland is the Prussian presence, which brought civilisation and Christianity to the region and ensured order, government and trade for 500 years. Hence the untroubled tone of Guderian's description of the Polish blitzkrieg of 1939—viewed by the west as the unjust destruction of a national and sovereign state, but by Prussian military professionals as the breaking of a purely arbitrary re-arrangement of the political geography of the area imposed by the western powers for their own selfish strategic ends."

How did the German and Polish forces compare in late summer of 1939? The German Army was capable of deploying fifty-two divisions, roughly 1.5 million men. The Polish Army could field thirty-nine infantry divisions, as well as seventeen miscellaneous brigades, mainly cavalry. But only two of the brigades were motorized; none were armoured. The Germans were prepared to field ten panzer and light tank divisions. In terms of air power, the German Luftwaffe had 1,500 aircraft ready for the assault, while the Poles had approximately 1,000. The quality and capability of the German aircraft was superior to that of the Poles, and the airfields from which the Polish Air Force was operating were inadequately defended.

The German battle plan for the Polish invasion called for the establishment of a junction across the neck of the Polish Corridor and the assignment was given to the XIX corps under the command of General Guderian. Guderian had nearly missed this opportunity, discovering only by accident that he had previously been nominated by the War Ministry to take command of a reserve infantry corps in the event of war. He, thus, had to argue to get the XIX command. That corps contained the 3rd (original) panzer division as well as the 2nd and 20th Motorized Infantry Divisions, and some of the panzer and reconnaissance battalions of the German Army. It was comprised of just the sort of units and organization that Guderian had been clamoring for for years and this attack would be his first opportunity to show what such a force could achieve. It required him to take his force across the River Brahe just beyond the edge of the Polish Corridor, and on to the Vistula by the frontier of East Prussia, quite near where he had been born, at Kulm.

Guderian: "On the 1st of September at 04.45 hours, the whole corps moved simultaneously over the frontier. There was a thick ground mist at first which prevented the air force from giving us any support. I accompanied the 3rd Panzer Brigade, in the first wave, as far as the area north of Zempelburg where the preliminary fighting took place. Unfortunately, the heavy artillery of the 3rd Panzer Division felt itself compelled to fire into the mist, despite having received precise orders not to do so. The first shell landed fifty yards ahead of my command vehicle, the second fifty yards behind it. I reckoned that the next one was bound to be a direct hit and ordered my driver to turn about and drive off. The unaccustomed noise had made him nervous, however, and he drove straight into a ditch at full speed. The front axle of the half-tracked vehicle was bent so that the steering mechanism was put out of action. This marked the end of my drive. I made my way to my corps command post, procured myself a fresh vehicle and had a word with the over-eager artillerymen. Incidentally, it may be noted that I was the first corps commander ever to use armoured command vehicles in order to accompany tanks onto the battlefield. They were equipped with radio, so that I was able to keep in constant touch with my corps headquarters and with the divisions under my command.

"Messages from the 2nd (Motorized) Infantry Division stated that their attack on the Polish wire entanglements had bogged down. All three infantry regiments had made a frontal attack. The division was now without reserves. I ordered that the regiment on the left be withdrawn during the night and moved to the right wing, from where it was to advance next day behind the 3rd Panzer Division and make an encircling movement in the direction of Tuchel.

"The 20th (Motorized) Division had taken Konitz with some difficulty, but had not advanced any appreciable distance beyond that town. It was ordered to continue its attack on the next day.

"During the night the nervousness of the first day of battle made itself felt more than once and shortly after midnight the 2nd (Motorized) Division informed me that they were being compelled to withdraw by Polish cavalry. I was speechless for a moment; when I regained the use of my voice I asked the divisional commander if he had ever heard of Pomeranian grenadiers being broken by hostile cavalry. He replied that he had not and now assured me that he could hold his positions. I decided all the same that I must visit this division the next morning. At about five o'clock, I found the divisional staff still all at sea. I placed myself at the head of the regiment which had been withdrawn during the night and led it personally as far as the crossing of the Kamionka to the north of Gross-Klonia, where I sent it off in the direction of Tuchel. The 2nd (Motorized) Division's attack now began to make rapid progress. The panic of the first day's fighting was past.

As the visionary creator of the theory of *blitzkrieg* or 'lightning war', Guderian believed passionately that a powerful, well-supported armoured force was best utilized in a high-speed, long-ranging push deep into enemy territory, achieving rapid, sustainable gains while wreaking maximum confusion, chaos and panic as it travels. He believed in versatility and adapability in combat, and cherished the radio capability that enabled these qualities. His watchwords were mobility and velocity. Basil Liddell Hart wrote of Guderian: "Sixty percent of what the German Panzer forces became was due to him. Ambitious, brave, a heart for his soldiers who liked and trusted him, rash as a man, quick in decisions, strict with officers, real personality, therefore many enemies. Blunt, even to Hitler. As a trainer—good; thorough; progressive. If you suggest revolutionary ideas, he will say in 95% of cases, 'Yes', at once."

Guderian: "On the 5th of September our corps had a surprise visit from Adolf Hitler. I met him near Plevno on the Tuchel-Schwetz road, got into his car and drove with him along the line of our previous advance. We passed the destroyed Polish artillery, went through Schwetz, and then, following closely behind our encircling troops, drove to Graudenz where he stopped and gazed for some time at the blown bridges over the Vistula. At the sight of the smashed artillery regiment, Hitler had asked me: 'Our dive bombers did that?' When I replied, 'No, our panzers!' he was plainly astonished. During the drive we discussed at first the course of events in my corps area. Hitler asked about casualties. I gave him the latest figures that I had received, some 150 dead and 700 wounded for all the four divisions under my command during the Battle of the Corridor. He was amazed at the smallness of these figures and contrasted them with the casualties of his own old regiment, the List Regiment, during the First World War: on the first day of battle that one regiment alone had lost more than 2,000 dead and wounded. I was able to show him that the smallness of our casualties in this battle against a tough and courageous enemy was primarily due to the effectiveness of our tanks. Tanks are a life-saving weapon. The men's belief in the superiority of their armoured equipment had been greatly strengthened by their successes in the Corridor. The enemy had suffered the total destruction of between two and three infantry divisions and one cavalry brigade. Thousands of prisoners and hundreds of guns had fallen into our hands."

Guderian chose not to mention the disproportionately high casualty rate among his officers. He was well aware that the initial battles of a war invariably claim high casualties in the officers, who are frequently required to be self-sacrificing in their leadership of troops new to combat.

"Our conversation turned on technical matters. Hitler wanted to know what had proved particularly satisfactory about our tanks and what was still in need of improvement. I told him that the most important thing now was to hasten the delivery of Panzers III and IV to the fighting troops and to increase the production of these tanks. For their further development their present speed was sufficient, but they needed to be more heavily armoured, particularly in front; the range and power of penetration of their guns also needed to be increased, which would mean longer barrels and a shell with a heavier charge. This applied equally to our anti-tank guns.

"With a word of recognition for the troops' achievements Hitler left us as dusk was falling and returned to his headquarters.

"On the 6th of September the corps staff and the advance guards of the divisions crossed the Vistula. Corps headquarters was set up in Finckenstein, in the very beautiful castle that belonged to Count Dohna-Finckenstein and which Frederick the Great had given to his minister, Count von Finckenstein. Napoleon had twice used this castle as his headquarters. The emperor first came there in 1807, when he took the war against Prussia and Russia over the Vistula and into East Prussia. After crossing the poor and monotonous Tuchel Heath, Napoleon exclaimed at the sight of the castle: 'Enfin un château!' His feelings are understandable. It was there that he had planned his advance towards Preussisch-Eylau. A mark of his presence was still to be seen in the scratches left by his spurs on the wooden floor. He was there for the second time before the Russian campaign of 1812; he spent a few weeks in the castle in the company of the beautiful Countess Walewska. I slept in the room that had been Napoleon's."

Following the success of the German Army in the Polish campaign, Guderian and his armoured corps devoted much of the winter months of 1939-40 in preparation for the coming campaign against France, Britain, and the neighbouring countries. In October Hitler told his key military commanders of his decision to go ahead with the attacks. The primary objective for the Germans was the Channel coast of France.

In Guderian's opinion, the "finest operational brain in the German Army" was that of Generalfeldmarschall Erich von Manstein. The initial plan for the German invasion of France, Fall Gelb (Case Yellow) had been prepared in October 1939 by Commander-in-Chief of the Army, Generaloberst Walther von Brauchitsch and General Franz Halder. The plan involved an encirclement attack through the Netherlands and Belgium and neither Hitler nor Manstein were satisfied with it. Manstein believed such an attack, coming from the north, would both lack the surprise element and gravely expose German forces to counterattacks from the south. In addition, he thought the Belgian terrain unsuitable as a base for further attacks on France and believed that campaign would certainly not succeed in wiping out the enemy and would, in all probability, lead to stalemate and WWI-style trench warfare. At the end of October, Manstein had prepared the outline of an alternative plan for a German invasion of France and submitted it to his boss, Generalfeldmarschall Gerd von Rundstedt, Commander of Army Group A. Manstein's plan was developed with the help of Heinz Guderian. It proposed that the panzer divisions would attack through the wooded hills of the Ardennes forest, where no one would expect them. They would then quickly establish bridgeheads on the River Meuse and push rapidly on to the English Channel, and in the process, cut off the Allied and French armies in Belgium and Flanders. The Manstein plan proposed too, a second thrust that would outflank the Maginot Line of fortified defences where it ended in the southern tip of the Ardennes, enabling the Germans to force the positioning of any future defensive line further south.

The Manstein plan was rejected, with Halder particularly opposed to it. But on 11 November, Hitler ordered the mounting of a surprise thrust attack on Sedan, a move that appeared somewhat aligned with the direction of the Manstein proposal. Halder and Brauchitsch opposed the possible implementation of the Manstein plan rather than their own, and Halder had Manstein removed from Rundstedt's headquarters and reassigned to a command at Stettin. Hitler, however, was looking for a more aggressive approach to taking France. He met with Manstein on 17 February and approved a modified version of the Manstein proposal.

Guderian personally led his panzers through the Ardennes and across the Meuse, breaking through the French lines at Sedan. He led his tanks and armour in a series of rapid, blitzkrieg (lightning war) advances in a "race to the sea", splitting the French armies and the British Expeditionary Forces and depriving them of food, fuel, spare parts and ammunition. Approaching the Allied beachhead at Dunkirk, Guderian's advance was finally halted by an order from German High Command.

In 1941, Guderian commanded *Panzergruppe 2* in Operation Barbarossa, the German invasion of the Soviet Union and in early October he led the redesignated Second Panzer Army in a spearhead to quickly capture Smolensk, preparatory to launching a final assault on Moscow. Instead, Hitler ordered him south towards Kiev. He protested Hitler's decision and, on Christmas Day, 1941, was relieved of his command. On his dismissal, Guderian and his wife retired to a country estate in Reichsgau Wartheland.

When the Germans were defeated at Stalingrad in February 1943, Hitler appointed Guderian Inspector-General of the Armoured Troops, to develop strategy and oversee tank design and production, as well as the training of German panzer forces. He was to report directly to Hitler, avoiding involvement in the Nazi bureaucracy. In fact, his role and power there were rather limited.

Was Guderian possessed of the military genius that so many historians and military professionals who knew him, and others have proclaimed of him? Clearly, he shaped, fully developed, and powerfully advocated the blitzkrieg strategy as the one sure way to make the mobile and armoured divisions of an army coordinate with and work in support of each other to successfully achieve the objective. He was absolutely convinced that the need for technological development, in support of the blitzkrieg concept, particularly in radio communications and visual equipment for every tank in the German armoured force was key to enabling the tank commander to successfully execute the blitzkrieg. Guderian: "In 1929 I became convinced that tanks working on their own or in conjunction with infantry could never achieve decisive importance. My historical studies; the exercises carried out in England and our own experience with mock-ups had persuaded me that the tanks would never be able to produce their full effect until weapons on whose support they must inevitably rely were brought up to their standard of speed and cross-country performance. In such formation of all arms, the tanks must play a primary role, the other weapons being subordinated to the requirements of the armour. It would be wrong to include tanks in infantry divisions: what were needed were armoured divisions which would include all the supporting arms needed to fight with full effect."

Historian John Keegan: "For someone whose first extended period of command authority was as commander of a Panzer Corps, Guderian showed an astonishingly sure touch. Perhaps he was not really tested during the Polish campaign, the powers of resistance of the Polish army being as unequal to the Germans as they were. But he showed from the outset that readiness to expose himself to danger, to set a personal example, and to go and see for himself, to judge by his own senses the intensity and pattern of the fighting and the reaction to it of the men under his command, which were to make him such an outstandingly inspiring leader and uncannily accurate forecaster of events and master of timing. He was to display all these qualities to full effect both during the overthrow of the Western Allies in 1940 and during the blitzkrieg in Russia in 1941. Nor, despite his peripatetic style of command, did he ever fall into the trap of losing sight of the whole picture in whatever zone he was responsible for. 'Forward control', of which he was a pioneer, did mean control to him, even if he spent a great deal of time forward even of his advanced headquarters. It was here that his long training as a signal officer stood him in such stead; and indeed, one might argue that if Guderian were not remembered for his experimental strategy with armour, he would be celebrated for his demonstration of the potentialities of wireless as a means of command in war.

"On the other hand, Guderian was not an easy subordinate. Nor was this the familiar matter of the cleverness of a junior upsetting his less quick or able chief. The final answer is probably that he pushed his differences with his seniors to the lengths that he did because he had a sense of being right; that he was, in short, doctrinaire—and all the more stubbornly so for having invented the doctrine which he wished to see translated into action."

With the end of the war in Europe in May 1945 Heinz Guderian became a prisoner of war, surrendering to a unit of the United States Army. The Russians wanted to see him face justice in the Nuremberg War Crimes tribunals, but the Western Allies did not, accepting that his actions and behaviour were consistent with those of a professional soldier. Germany's greatest tank man, perhaps history's greatest tank man, spent two years in West German prisons before his release in 1948. He retired to his home in Schwangau bei Fussen where he wrote his memoirs. He died there on 14 May 1954.

BLITZKRIEG

"You'd think, to hear some people talk, / That lads go west with sobs and curses, / And sullen faces white as chalk. / Hankering for wreaths and tombs and hearses. / But they've been taught the way to do it / Like Christian soldiers; not with haste / And shuddering groans; but passing through it / With due regard for decent taste.
—from *How to Die* by Siegfried Sassoon

Sometimes referred to as "the father of the blitzkrieg", the German Lieutenant-General Heinz Guderian, evolved a theory for fielding a highly mechanized mobile army and then expounded on it in his book *Achtung Panzer!* which impressed the German Chancellor Adolf Hitler who, in 1934, gave Guderian the task of perfecting the fighting technique and capability of Germany's armoured fighting forces, supported by infantry and aircraft. This resulted in the famous *blitzkrieg* (lightning war) method of warfare. The concept and strategy of spearheading fast-moving tanks, followed by motorized infantry and supported by dive-bombers was first proposed by British Army Colonel John Fuller, Chief of Staff of the British Tank Corps. In frustration over the way in which tanks were used in WWI, Fuller devised a plan calling for long-range mass tank attacks supported by strong air, motorized infantry, and artillery. He developed the idea in considerable detail in his books *Reformation of War* (1923) and *Foundation of the Science of War* (1926). Fuller: "Speed, and still more speed, and always speed was the secret . . . and that demanded audacity, more audacity and always audacity." The British Army showed little interest in Fuller's ideas, but they aroused considerable interest in Germany where the military devoted considerable time to the study of Fuller's books and the government eagerly ordered the production of new tanks.

Prior to the First World War, many Germans had perceived their country as being surrounded by threatening enemy nations with greater resources. German strategists of the time, and Count Alfred von Schlieffen in particular, believed that Germany could not win in a long, protracted military struggle against such adversaries. He believed that, for Germany to achieve victory against those enemies, she would have to defeat them quickly and decisively and, as she would always be outnumbered by her enemies, she would have to be fully prepared for such conflicts with better quality training, equipment, planning and execution than her opponents could field. Schlieffen created a doctrine for the German Army whereby it would outfight its opposition using great speed of manoeuvring and attacking the enemy where he was weakest. He wanted to wrong-foot the enemy, forcing reaction for which the enemy was unprepared, and always maintaining the initiative. He proposed achieving this through the use of a flexible command system as proposed earlier by Helmuth von Moltke the Elder. The German Army would in time accept that, as conditions on the battlefield tended to change quickly and orders from higher command were frequently overtaken by events, it was desirable to encourage field commanders to make quick, independent, opportunistic decisions without waiting for orders from their superiors. In so doing, the Army anticipated creating many new aggressive, flexible leaders in command positions.

Schlieffen, and his successor Helmuth von Moltke the Younger, gradually trained the German Army in what they called the "war of manoeuvre", and by the early months of WWI German Army units were mostly outfighting the Allies in their early encounters. But in 1914 when that war began, the German Army was not mechanized and was unable to move long distances rapidly. Thus, it was unable to achieve truly decisive victories and had to reluctantly settle into trench warfare.

The problem of the trench stalemate was finally addressed by the German officer corps in the spring of 1918 when they elected to apply Schlieffen's operating principles to the smaller army units as well as the large ones. They chose to decentrailize command and at the same time increase the firepower of the infantry. They wanted to create a lot of platoon-sized units that could act independently in combat, with freedom to engage as they thought most appropriate in the situation.

"The European war will be an industrial war of aircraft, tanks and movement."—Dwight D. Eisenhower, while he was an aide to General Douglas MacArthur in the Philippines

The term *blitzkrieg* was actually coined by western journalists during the German invasion of Poland in 1939 and its meaning has usually been linked with a series of rapid, decisive brief battles intended to knock out or destroy the enemy force before it can fully mobilize and react. Functionally, it has been generally accepted to be a coordinated military effort by tanks and other armoured vehicles, mobilized infantry, artillery, and aircraft to quickly establish overwhelming combat superiority and break through the enemy lines. An additional element that the Germans brought to the concept was psychological. The employment of terror lending further chaos, confusion and enhancing the fear of the sudden attack was exemplified in the use of the noise-making sirens fitted to the Junkers Ju 87 Stuka dive-bombers the Germans used in support of their armoured and infantry forces.

Early references to the term blitzkrieg are relatively rare and do not occur in handbooks of German Army or Air Force doctrine. German press uses of the term were rare and did not occur before 1939. A few early references exist relating to German efforts to break the stalemate and win a quick victory in the First World War, but were not specifically related to the use of armoured or mechanized forces or aircraft. It was used in the context of Germany needing to develop self-sufficiency in food and other areas in the event of her becoming involved in a wide, protracted war. A 1938 article appeared on the matter of Germany developing the capability to launch a rapid strategic knockout blow, but acknowledges the difficulty of accomplishing such a result in a land attack in modern circumstances, especially relative to the problems posed by fortification systems such as the Maginot Line unless considerable surprise is achieved. There is also a reference in a book by Fritz Sternberg, *Die Deutsche Kriegsstärke* (German War Strength), published in 1939, and an English edition published in 1938 called *Germany and a Lightning War*, in which the author uses the term blitzkrieg arguing that Germany was not economically able to sustain a protracted war, but might be able to win a quick one. He does not elaborate on any tactical or operational considerations, nor does he advance the notion that the German armed forces have developed such a method of warfare. Adolf Hitler supposedly said in a November 1941 speech: "I have never used the word *blitzkrieg*, because it is a very silly word."

In the terrible, stalemated trench warfare of the First World War, kill zones had been established with barbed wire and the brutal crossfire of machine-guns keeping either side from making a breakthrough to the enemy lines. In an inspired effort to end the stalemate, the British introduced the first tanks to the battlefields of France. These early armoured vehicles were essentially invulnerable to machine-gun fire and were able to cross most trenches and breach the barbed wire, breaking a pathway for the Allied infantry troops to follow in their wake. Initially, they achieved some success in penetrating the German lines, and certainly managed to shock and frighten the Germans in the early days of their entry in the war zone. The British, though, were not able to produce enough tanks by the war's end to demonstrate the sort of capability that was to come in later years. But the appearance of those early tanks certainly intrigued the Germans with the battlefield potential of the new weapon.

With German defeat in the First World War came the limitations set by the Versailles peace treaty, among them the limitation of any new German army to a total of 100,000 men with no more than 4,000 officers. The framers of the treaty reasoned that such a limit would effectively prevent Germany from ever again deploying the masses of troops that had been the basis of her battlefield strategy. Technically, the German General Staff had been abolished by the treaty, but in reality it continued to function in the guise of the Truppenamt (troop office), the secret General Staff. Comprised of veteran staff officers, these men drew on their WWI experience to draught reports that resulted in training manuals and doctrine which led to new standardized procedures that would be employed in WWII.

From 1919 through 1935 that new German army was called the *Reichswehr* (Reich Defence). In 1935 it was renamed the *Wehrmacht* (Defence Force). Notable was the criticism levelled at much of the German officer corps its essentially collective failure to grasp many of the technical advances of the First World War, including that of the machine-gun, and for placing tank design and production on such a low priority. Most of these officers studied in military technical schools during the period of rebuilding the army after the war. Much of their focus centred on the infiltration tactics developed by the Germans in WWI, and the use of decentralized groups to strike at weak positions and attack rear-area communications facilities, supported by coordinated artillery and air attacks which were a prelude to bombardment by large infantry forces to destroy the centres of resistance—all of which would become the foundation of German Army tactics in WWII.

Among the first moves towards the direction of a blitzkrieg approach to future warfare came when the Chief of Staff of the new German Army, Generaloberst Hans von Seekt directed a shift in doctrine from what he believed to be excessive emphasis on encirclement to something based on speed and mobility. Von Seekt would develop the doctrine for the operation of the Wehrmacht in WWII. It was published by the army in 1921 under the title *Command and Combat with Combined Arms*.

In 1928, Seekt's book *Thoughts of a Soldier* was published. In it he was critical of the huge conscript armies of the recent past, claiming that technical science and tactical skill would win the wars of the future: "The whole future of warfare appears to me to lie in the employment of mobile armies, relatively small but of high quality, and rendered distinctly more effective by the addition of aircraft, and in the simultaneous mobilization of the whole forces, either to feed the attack or for home defence."

Seekt had the problem of maintaining the morale of the German armed forces in spite of the limitations imposed by the Versailles treaty. He began by reshaping the German Army into a thirty-five-division mobile shock force. His approach was called *Bewegungskrieg* (manoeuvre warfare) which actually introduced a leadership system of mission tactics where local commanders were authorized to take immediate, on-the-spot decisions about how to accomplish the tasks of their missions. Incorporating the ideas of Schlieffen, this system was vital to the success of the blitzkrieg concept, providing a powerful advantage to the Germans over their adversaries. It was key to the operation of the "lightning war" technique, but in early 1942 the OKW (*Oberkommando der Wehrmacht* or High Command of the Third Reich armed forces) called a halt to it in the belief that there was too much risk involved in allowing German Corps and Army Groups to be commanded and run wholly independently by a single field commander. When the German

Army of 1940 went to war in the west, it did so on an offensive doctrine built around swift decision-making, rapid manoeuvring and decentralized fighting. It was influenced in large part by Schlieffen's emphasis on high speed action, encirclement, flanking attack, and the vital importance of achieving decisive combat results. It included his tactical concepts for the operational level as devised during the First World War and incorporated the developing technology of the 1920s and 1930s of tanks, motorized armoured vehicles, aircraft, and radio communications. Most of the military and political leaders of Germany in the 1930s were in agreement that application of the new offensive doctrine was as important at the tactical operating level—speedy manoeuvre and independent fire—as it was at higher levels. In 1940 at least, that application enabled elements of the German Army to prevail, outfighting the Allies (even when outnumbered in equipment and personnel), and frequently leading to collapsing Allied resistance.

They called it the "Phoney War", the period between the German occupation of Poland in the autumn of 1939 and the German invasion of Norway in April 1940. In that strange time the British were persuaded by the French to hold off bombing targets in Germany. The French worried about German reprisals and tried to prepare themselves to resist a German move against France, pinning their hopes and their future on their Maginot Line of fortifications. They, like the British, and the Americans, seemed stuck in an old set-piece battle mindset in which their mechanized forces were mainly meant to keep up momentum on the battlefield, much as it had been in the First World War. They showed little interest in concentration of forces, deep penetration, or the use of combined forces.

The British continued their tank development and to an extent maintained an interest in a mechanized role for their army in reaction to the heavy casualties and lack of progress on the battlefields of WWI. Still, in this period they failed to develop a strategic policy in line with their technical developments. One man among the Allies who did think along the same general progressive line as Seekt and Guderian was then Colonel Charles De Gaulle. In that period De Gaulle wrote a book called *Vers l'Armee de Métier* (Towards the Professional Army) in which he advocated the concentration of armour and aircraft and maintained that France could no longer have the sort of large army with which it had fought WWI. He believed in the concept of using tanks, mechanized forces, and aircraft to enable a smaller number of well-trained and well-equipped personnel to achieve far more on the battlefield. He did not endear himself to the French High Command with his perspectives, but he may well have influenced Guderian.

Meanwhile, in the Soviet Union a prominent Red Army officer, Marshal Mikhail Tukhachevesky, was developing the notion of deep operations in warfare, based on his experiences in the Polish-Soviet conflict. Mindful of the limitations of cavalry and infantry, Tukhachevesky was promoting the use of mechanized formations and large-scale industrialization to support them. Unlike the standard definition of the blitzkrieg tactic, however, the Soviet concept advocated total war rather than limited operations and several large-scale simultaneous offensives instead of a single decisive battle.

Another condition of the 1919 Treaty of Versailles prohibited Germany from operating any form of air force. It also prohibited the production or import of any form of aircraft in Germany. In 1922, that clause was modified to allow the production of civilian aircraft in Germany and, a year later, the control of German airspace was returned to the nation. Production and operation of any aircraft for military use was still prohibited. But the Reichswehr was sensitive to the evolution of aircraft and tactics for aerial warfare and was not willing to lag behind the rest of the world, regardless of the Versailles treaty. It began with the normalization of relations with the Soviet Union in 1922 through another treaty.

Germany had been required to pay reparations after WWI and, when in 1923 she defaulted on those reparations, French and Belgian forces occupied part of the Ruhr Valley. The action shifted the German position on obeying the terms of Versailles, triggering an order by the German Army for 100 new aircraft from the Fokker company in the Netherlands, fifty of the planes being the new Fokker D.XIII. The following year, the crisis in the Ruhr ended and the new Fokker planes were due to be delivered shortly. The Germans approached the Soviets about the possibility of developing new aircraft in the Soviet Union and the Russians were interested.

June 1924. The Germans assigned retired Colonel Hermann von der Lieth-Thomsen as permanent representative of the Truppenamt, in Moscow. Seven German flight instructors were then sent to work with the Red Air Force, and in the following April, Leith-Thomsen signed a contract establishing the German fighter pilot school at Lipetsk, some 230 miles from Moscow. By spring 1926 extensive construction work had been completed and the training of new German fighter pilots and fighter ground personnel began. The pilots and ground personnel would also serve as instructors upon the formation of the new German Air Force in 1935. Training continued at the Lipetsk base until 1933 when the Nazis came to power in Germany and their ideological differences with the Soviets led to the closure of the Lipetsk school and the ending of the Russo-German pilot training arrangement.

With the Spanish Civil War in 1936, the German Panzer Battalion 88—three companies of Panzer I tanks—were provided by the Nazis to the Spanish Nationalists, while the new German Luftwaffe sent squadrons of dive-bombers, fighters and transport aircraft to action in the conflict, aircraft and personnel of the Condor Legion, which was made up of volunteers from the air force and the army. They served in Spain from July 1936 to March 1939, and there developed methods of "terror" bombing, demonstrated infamously in the raid on Guernica. The aircraft units of the Condor Legion were commanded in Spain by Hugo Sperrle and the ground units by Wilhelm Ritter von Thoma. The controversial attack on Guernica is thought by many historians to have been intended as a demonstration of the worth of the Condor Legion's contribution to the Nationalist cause.

The application of Guderian's concept of armoured warfare in Spain was, in his words, "on too small a scale to allow accurate assessments to be made." That would have to wait until the start of the Second World War in 1939. The first testing of the Ju 87 Stuka dive-bomber was conducted impressively by German volunteers in the Spanish Civil War, an effective proving combat environment for the various new German aircraft and tactics.

On April 9, Hitler's forces invaded Norway and Denmark, in part to isolate Sweden whose iron ore resources he coveted.

When German forces had invaded Poland in early September 1939, many newspaper writers in the west referred to the action as a blitzkrieg but, in fact, the action was mainly a conventional envelopment. The three primary panzer units were dispersed rather than concentrated. The use of tanks, dive-bombers and infantry was largely conventional. According to historian Matthew Cooper, ". . . throughout the Polish campaign, the employment of the mechanised units revealed the idea that they were intended solely to ease the advance and to support the activities of the infantry . . . thus, any strategic exploitation of the armoured idea was still-born. The paralysis of command and the breakdown of morale were not made the ultimate aim of the German ground and air forces, and were only incidental by-products of the traditional maneuvers of rapid encirclement and of the supporting activities of the flying artillery of the Luftwaffe, both of which had as their purpose the physical destruction of the enemy troops."

The first major examples of employing the blitzkrieg idea came with the German invasion of France and the subsidiary thrusts into Belgium and the Netherlands. Operation *Fall Gelb* (Case Yellow) began as a swift move against Belgium and the Netherlands by German paratroopers and two armoured corps on 10 May 1940. The German armoured units, against all expectations of the French, drove quickly through the Ardennes, cutting off and surrounding Allied forces that had moved into Belgium. The Allies had fallen into Hitler's trap.

From the personal papers of Generalfeldmarschall Erwin Rommel, commander of the 7th Panzer Division during the German invasion of France in 1940, and who would later be known as 'The Desert Fox' for his leading role in the North African campaign, and his command of the German forces defending against the Allied cross-Channel invasion of June 1944. In an extract from his journal, Rommel wrote of the blitzkrieg drive of his panzers skirting the Maginot Line fortifications and racing to attack French forces near the River Meuse on the Belgian border: "Rothenburg [one of his tank commanders] now drove off through a hollow to the left with the five tanks which were to accompany the infantry, thus giving these tanks a lead of 100 to 150 yards. There was no sound of enemy fire. Some twenty to thirty tanks followed up behind. When the commander of the five tanks reached the rifle company on the southern edge of Onhaye wood, Colonel Rothenburg moved off with his leading tanks along the edge of the wood going west. We had just reached the southwest corner of the wood and were about to cross a low plantation, from which we could see the five tanks escorting the infantry below us to our left front, when suddenly we came under heavy artillery and anti-tank gunfire from the west. Shells landed all around us and my tank received two hits one after the other, the first on the upper edge of the turret and the second in the periscope.

"The driver promptly opened the throttle wide and drove straight into the nearest bushes. He had only gone a few yards, however, when the tank slid down a steep slope on the western edge of the wood and finally stopped, canted over on its side, in such a position that the enemy, whose guns were in position about 500 yards away on the edge of the next wood, could not fail to see it. I had been wounded in the right cheek by a small splinter fron the shell which had landed in the periscope It was not serious, though it bled a great deal.

"I tried to swing the turret round so as to bring our 37mm gun to bear on the enemy in the opposite wood, but with the heavy slant of the tank it was immovable.

"The French battery now opened rapid fire on our wood and at any moment we could expect their fire to be aimed at our tank, which was in full view. I therefore decided to abandon it as fast as I could, taking the crew with me. At that moment the subaltern in command of the tanks escorting the infantry reported himself wounded, with the words: 'Herr General, my left arm has been shot off.' We clamored up through the sandy pit, shells crashing and splintering all round. Close in front of us trundled Rothenburg's tank with flames pouring out of the rear. The adjutant of the panzer regiment had also left his tank. I thought at first that the command tank had been set alight by a hit in [the] petrol tank and was extremely worried for Colonel Rothenburg's safety. However, it turned out to be only the smoke candles that had caught light, the smoke from which now served us very well. In the meantime Lieutenant Most had driven my armoured signals vehicle into the wood, where it had been hit in the engine and now stood immobilized. The crew was unhurt."

From behind the structures of the Maginot Line, Rommel's forces raced north to attack the fortifications from the rear: "The tanks now rolled in a long column through the line of fortifications and on towards the first houses, which had been set alight by our fire. In the moonlight we could see the men of 7th Motorcycle Battalion moving forward on foot beside us. Occasionally an enemy machine-gun or anti-tank gun fired, but none of their shots came anywhere near us. Our artilllery was dropping heavy harassing fire on villages and the road far ahead of the regiment. Gradually the speed increased. Before long we were 500-1,000-2,000-3,000 yards into the fortified zone. Engines roared, tank tracks clanked and clattered. Whether or not the enemy was firing was impossible to tell in the ear-splitting noise. We crossed the railway line a mile or so southwest of Soire le Chateau, and then swung north to the main road which was soon reached. Then off along the road and past the first houses.

"The people in the houses were rudely awoken by the din of our tanks, the clatter and roar of tracks and engines. Troops lay bivouacked beside the road, military vehicles stood parked in farmyards and in some places on the road itself. Civilians and French troops, their faces distorted with terror, lay huddled in the ditches, alongside hedges and in every hollow beside the road. We passed refugee columns, the carts abandoned by their owners, who had fled in panic into the fields. On we went, at a steady speed, towards our objective. Every so often a quick glance at the map by a shaded light and a short wireless message to Division H.Q. to report the position and thus the success of 25th Panzer Regiment. Every so often a look out of the hatch to assure myself that there was still no resistance and that contact was being maintained to the rear. The flat countryside lay spread out around us under the cold light of the moon. We were through the Maginot Line! It was hardly conceivable. Twenty-two years before we had stood for four and a half long years before this self-same enemy and had won victory after victory and yet finally lost the war. And now we had broken through the renowned Maginot Line and were driving deep into enemy territory. It was not just a beautiful dream. It was reality."

All roads in the area were jammed with refugees fleeing the front. Thousands of French and British troops trying to reach the front were caught up in the massive retreating mixture of civilians and military and were pushed back. German Stuka dive-bombers appeared and repeatedly strafed the masses on the roads.

In their headlong race to the seacoast, the German tanks and armoured vehicles were suddenly and mysteriously halted on 21 May by a High Command order. In this thrust they encountered and encircled thirty-five Allied divisions, including the British Expeditionary Force.

As the extremely mobile Germans efficiently threw the British and French troops back towards the Channel coast the British government chose to evacuate the British Expeditionary Force and several French Army units from the beaches at Dunkirk, an operation known as *Dynamo* which lasted from

27 May to 4 June. In the action, some 40,000 men, survivors of the French 1st Army, fought a desperate delaying action against seven German divisions—three of them armoured—which were attempting to block and destroy the Allied armies near Dunkirk. Of them Winston Churchill said. "These Frenchmen, under the gallant leadership of Molinié, had for four critical days contained no less than seven German divisions which otherwise could have joined in the assaults on the Dunkirk perimeter. This was a splendid contribution to the escape of their more fortunate comrades of the BEF."

Still outstanding in British memory is the amazing rescue effort mounted by the rapidly assembled fleet of some 700 merchant marine boats, pleasure craft, fishing boats, and Royal National Lifeboat Institution lifeboats, together with forty-two Royal Navy destroyers. By the final day of the evacuation, 338,226 soldiers (198,229 British and 139,997 French) were rescued from the beaches, the harbour mole, and from where they had waded out into shoulder-deep water. The various small vessels were mostly manned by civilians and the effort is today known as the "miracle of the little ships."

Following the Dunkirk evacuation, France was essentially on her own and on 5 June the Germans began the *Fall Rot* (Case Red) against the seriously depleted French armed forces. French resistance at the start was staunch, but the vastly greater enemy air superiority soon overwhelmed those resisting forces and their artillery. The vaunted Maginot Line defensive fortifications were smoothly outflanked by the well-organized, highly mobile German armoured forces and the French defence was nearly over. The German forces rolled into Paris meeting little real resistance on 14 June and their commanders soon met with French officials, the two sides talking about setting up an alliance. French president, Marshall Philippe Pétain sued for peace with the Third Reich. Pétain, who had led the French to victory at the Battle of Verdun in WWI, had to cede three-fifths of French territory to German control. Hitler insisted, too, that the Franco-German armistice agreement be signed in the same railway car in which Germany had been forced to formally accept defeat in that war. In only a few weeks the German Army had overwhelmed the army of the French Third Republic and in the process, caused a stunned Britain, France's ally, to withdraw the entire British Expeditionary Force from the European continent.

In the aftermath of that withdrawal, both the British and the French were left pondering how and why they had got it all so wrong. They had anticipated yet another long, drawn-out WWI-style defensive struggle in which they would prevail. They had seen themselves as being well-equipped, well-trained, and well-prepared to fight a modern war against the Wehrmacht. They hadn't banked on the Germans showing up with the blitzkrieg tactic. They had certainly counted on the Maginot Line along France's heavily fortified border with Germany, to their cost and embarassment. The British and

French had believed that the battle of this new war would evolve slowly and be fought traditionally, with infantry and artillery. Instead, they found in the Germans an enemy who came to fight an offensive war and with the equipment, skill and determination to win victory quickly.

In analyzing the defeat of the Allies in France and Belgium, Allied military observers ultimately attributed it to the blitzkrieg, the new type of warfare effectively implemented in the campaign by the German Wehrmacht. They pinned the success of the tactic to the enemy's brilliant use of the new technology of the tank and the dive-bomber.

Adolf Hitler issued a series of directives—his instructions and strategic plans—beginning in August 1939 and covered a wide range of topics, from the detailed direction of military units, to the governance of occupied territories. The subject of his Directive No. 6, issued 9 October 1939, was plans for the offensive in the west. His enduring interest had been in major military campaigns to defeat the countries of western Europe, preparatory to conquering much of eastern Europe. In doing so, he hoped to avoid a war on two fronts. His directive No. 6, though, appears to have been founded on the probability that several years would be needed before German military power would be capable of such adventures and that, for the present, only more limited objectives were realistic. Such objectives included an imminent conquest of the Low Countries, with the aims of improving Germany's ultimate ability to sustain and survive a protracted conflict, minimize the threat he perceived from neighbouring France, and prevent or minimize the threat of Allied aircraft bombing the vital Ruhr Valley industrial complex. Further, it was intended in part as a foundation for a German air and sea campaign against Britain. In the coming action he wanted to occupy as much of the area of northern France along the German border as possible. Ironically, on the same day he issued this directive, he discovered that his notion of implementing the action against the Low Countries and northern France within a few weeks was, in fact, illusory, as he learned that he been misinformed about the current strength of his forces. The Polish campaign had brought a heavy repair and servicing requirement for Germany's tanks and motorized infantry, and ammunition supplies were essentially depleted.

19 October 1939. Generalstabschef der Heeres (Chief of Staff of the German Army) Franz Halder, presented the initial plan for the Low Countries campaign, *Fall Gelb* (Case Yellow). It proposed a frontal attack in which upwards of a half million German soldiers might be sacrificed in order to shove the Allies back to the River Somme, and the consequence would include the depletion of the army's strength for upwards of two years, before Germany would be able to launch a main attack against France. Hitler and many of his principle military commanders were profoundly disappointed in the Halder plan. Hitler then wanted to attack, whether his forces were prepared

or not, on the basis that he might achieve a quick and easy victory by catching the Allies unprepared. Some of his commanders persuaded him to delay such a move while preparations were quickly advanced or the weather improved. Prinicipal among them was his commander of Army Group A, General Gerd von Rundstedt, who disagreed strongly with the Halder plan. He believed that the main body of the Allied forces had to be encircled and destroyed in the Sedan region, which just happened to be the main assignment area for Rundstedt's Army Group. He put his chief of staff, Generalleutnant Erich von Manstein, on the task of devising a new plan around his objective.

Manstein was headquartered in Koblenz where he was at work on the new plan and, at the same time, Generalleutnant Heinz Guderian, commander of the elite armoured XIX Army Corps, was also located in the city. Manstein's plan called for a powerful move north from Sedan to attack the rear of the main Allied forces in Belgium, and he invited Guderian to contribute ideas to the plan during informal discussions. Heinz Guderian offered a somewhat radical notion in which his own army corps, together with the majority of the Panzerwaffe tanks would be concentrated at Sedan. Rather than heading north, he proposed a rapid, deep-penetration strategic movement towards the English Channel, without waiting for the infantry divisions. Guderian thought that such an action might well cause a strategic collapse of the enemy forces and avoid the excessively high casualties projected for the German Army in such battles. Guderian's ideas, however, often met with considerable doubt among the German General Staff, and this was no exception. But Guderian knew his fundamentals well, including the terrain involved, and he was wholly confident in the Manstein plan.

Sensitive to the mixed reviews Guderian's ideas normally engendered in high Army circles, Manstein wrote a series of memos outlining aspects of his plan, while never mentioning Guderian's name as a contributor to it. The German High Command rejected all of this memoranda and did not forward the content to Hitler. In fact, Halder, supremely protective of his own plan for the campaign, relieved Manstein and reassigned him to command an army corps in Prussia on 27 January 1940, in order to reduce Manstein's influence over the campaign. Manstein's staff then informed Hitler of their commander's plan on 2 February. On 17 February, Hitler conferred with Manstein, High Command Chief of Operations General Alfred Jodl, and General Rudolf Schmundt, the German Army Chief of Personnel. At the end of the meeting, Hitler seemed in complete agreement with Manstein and was then hopeful of victory.

But Halder was determined not to allow the independent strategic penetration by the seven armoured divisions of Army Group A, and had that aspect of the new plan removed on 24 February, much to the anger of Guderian. As the plan continued to evolve, it drew intense criticism from many of the

German generals and much of the officer corps who thought it irresponsible and potentially catastrophic should the Allies fail to react as the plan anticipated. Halder ignored their objections.

The Netherlands and Belgium were still neutral in the autumn of 1939, though they had secretly arranged possible future cooperation with the Allies, should the Germans invade their territories. While the Germans were busy occupying Poland, Maurice Gamelin, Supreme Commander of the French Army, had suggested that the Allies take advantage of that fact and utilize the Low Countries as bases from which to attack Germany, but the French government chose not to pursue the suggestion.

Following the German invasion of Poland, French forces advanced along the Maginot Line into the Saar, fielding some 2,500 tanks and fully ninety-eight divisions, most of them reserve and fortress formation elements, against forty-three German divisions, thirty-two of them reserves, and no tanks. The French force reached what was then an undermanned *Siegfriedstellung*, the Siegfried Line, the Westwall defensive forts and tank defences along the German border with the Netherlands, Belgium, Luxembourg, France, and Switzerland. Had the French chosen to advance they probably would have readily penetrated the defences and continued their Saar offensive, but instead they elected to force the Germans into an offensive posture and withdrew to their own lines.

The Belgian consul-general in Cologne was receiving intelligence reports as the winter of 1939-40 set in. The reports indicated the direction of advance intended in the Manstein plan, as well as the expected concentration of German forces along the Luxembourg and Belgian borders. Persuaded by these reports, the Belgians believed that the Germans would push through the Ardennes and on to the English Channel, cutting off the Allied armies in northeastern France and Belgium. They believed too, that the Germans would use airborne and glider troops behind the Allied lines to neutralize fortifications in Belgium. When the Belgians passed the information on to the French and British governments, the warnings were ignored. By March, intelligence sources in Switzerland had detected up to seven panzer divisions on the German border between Belgium and Luxembourg, as well as additional motorized divisions. The French government was also informed then about German construction of pontoon bridges on the River Our along the German-Luxembourg border. The French were warned on 30 April that the German assault would come on the River Meuse at Sedan between 8 and 10 May.

Estimates of the German military strength in early May 1940 indicate 4,200,000 army, 1,000,000 air force, 180,000 navy, and 100,000 Waffen SS. Of these, the personnel then engaged in Poland, Norway, and Denmark had reduced the total of army men available for the coming offensive to about

3,000,000 and were set to be organized as 135 divisions for the offensive with forty-two divisions in reserve. The available German weaponry included 2,439 tanks and 7,378 artillery guns. Roughly half of all the soldiers had had only a few weeks of training and nearly half of the army at that time was at least forty years old. Popular belief is that the entire army was motorized at that point; in fact just ten percent was motorized then and amounted to 120,000 vehicles and many horse-drawn conveyances. The French Army then had 300,000 vehicles, and the British Army was well-equipped with vehicles. Of the German divisions available for the offensive, only about half were adequately equipped and actually combat-ready. The limited number of well-equipped and trained "elite" divisions were offset by the many second and third-rate divisions.

Organizationally, three principal groups comprised the German Army then. Gerd von Rundstedt commanded Army Group A: forty-five and a half divisions, of which seven were armoured. His assignment was to cut through the Allied defences in the Ardennes and his Group contained three Panzer corps, the XV allocated to the 4th Army, and XXXXI (Reinhardt) and XIX (Guderian) which were connected to the XIV Army Corps of two motorized infantry divisions, which were operationally independent as the XXII Corps (*Panzergruppe Kleist*).

Fedor von Bock commanded Army Group B comprised of twenty-nine and a half divisions, of which three were armoured. Von Bock's assignment was to advance through the Low Countries, drawing northern units of the Allied armies in traps. His force was made up of the 6th and 18th Armies.

Wilhelm Ritter von Leeb was in command of the eighteen divisions of Army Group C and his role was to prevent any flanking movement developing from the east, as well as the launching of small holding attacks against the Maginot Line and the upper Rhine. His force consisted of the 1st and 7th Armies.

Unlike the Allied armies, the German Army relied operationally on combined arms combat; on fast, very mobile offensive capability and well-trained infantry, artillery, engineering, and tanks combined as Panzer divisions. Good communications was key to the successful operation of the German land forces. This effective communication allowed the panzers to move into and exploit combat situations faster than their foes could react. The speed of the panzers enabled them to carry out vital reconnaissance, advance, defend, and attack vital or weak positions, after which the supporting infantry and artillery would hold the taken ground. While not meant for tank-against-tank action, these panzers were quite capable of luring enemy tanks into German anti-tank divisional attack. Supported by infantry and motorized divisions, these panzers could commonly be sustained in action logistically for three or four days of combat.

In 1940, the German Army was still two years away from possessing one of the most feared and best tank weapons of the Second World War, the *Panzerkampfwagen* Tiger. This heavy battle tank that mounted an impressive 88mm gun would engage in combat on all of Germany's battle fronts and was truly formidable, weighing in at just under fifty-seven tons, with a speed of twenty-four mph, and two 7.92mm machine-guns with 4,800 rounds, as well as between ninety-two and 120 rounds for its main gun. But the Tiger was not available in 1940, and the Germans had no match for the heavy tanks of the French, which were well-armed and armoured. The Germans did, however, possess certain significant advantages over their opponents, not least being the new radios with which the panzers were all equipped, enabling vital voice communication with other units. Such communication made it possible for the German tanks to be immediately responsive in a constantly changing battlefield environment, making possible quick changes in tactics; easier, more fluid action than that of the enemy operating without the benefit of radio communication. The Germans strived to take full advantage of the radio communicating capability, considering it at least as important as accurate firing capability. Proper utilization of radio communication enabled tank commanders to coordinate their formations, assembling for mass firepower when the attacking or defending situation required it. Having the radio communication capability was a decided advantage in battle for the Germans.

Not only did the radio capability greatly enhance the tank-to-tank communication on the battlefield, it importantly put the tanks in touch with Luftwaffe units, either in the air or on the ground, so that vital air support could be requested and quickly provided in support of an attack or defensive situation. Such air support was normally provided by Ju 87 Stuka dive-bombers and it is believed that, for example, in Guderian's famous dash to the Channel, his tanks never had to wait more than twenty minutes after calling the Luftwaffe for such support to arrive over the target area.

In the run-up to the offensive against the French, the German air force had 3,286 combat aircraft available in support of Army groups A and C, with 1,815 combat aircraft, 487 transport and fifty glider aircraft available in support of Army Group B. In 1940, the Luftwaffe, unlike the Wehrmacht, was operated without a central doctrine. Its facilities, equipment and personnel were then simply dedicated to the support of national strategy, including tactical and strategic bombing. More flexible in its usage, its applications included air superiority missions, strategic strikes, medium-range interdiction, and close support of ground forces. In 1939, less than fifteen percent of the Luftwaffe resources were given over to support of the German Army.

Fall Gelb actually began on the evening of 9 May with the occupation of Luxembourg by German forces. During the night, German Army Group B started a feint into Belgium and the Netherlands and the next morning, *Fallschirmjäger* (paratroopers) of the *7th Flieger* and the *22 Luftlande Infanteriedivision* under the command of Generaloberst Kurt Student, a fighter ace of the First World War, appeared in a series of surprise landings on a road to Rotterdam, at The Hague, and on the Belgian fort at Eben-Emael in support of the advance of Army Group B. The German action was met by the French with their 1st Army Group sent north, and their 7th Army which crossed the Dutch border. The Dutch were in retreat and the French pulled back into Belgium to protect Brussels.

In the thrust into the Netherlands, the Germans took full advantage of their great numerical and qualitative superiority over the Dutch Air Force, destroying half the Dutch combat aircraft in the first day of the operation. The 144 combat aircraft with which the Dutch began that day were no match for the 247 medium bombers, 147 fighters, twelve seaplanes, and 424 Junkers Ju 52 transports that the Luftwaffe brought. In the 332 sorties flown by the Dutch, 110 of its aircraft were lost, for the loss of only a few German combat planes.

For German forces, the operation was initially a mixed bag. The 18th Army readily captured all the strategic bridges within and around Rotterdam, but an effort by the Luftwaffe to take the Dutch seat of government in The Hague did not succeed and resulted in considerable losses for the Germans. The taking of three vital airfields near The Hague, Valkenburg, Ockenburg, and Ypenburg, cost the Germans 125 of their Ju 52 transport planes destroyed and a further 47 damaged. Losses among the German paratroopers in the offensive were more than 4,000, roughly half their paratrooper force, of which 1,200 became prisoners of war. An additional ninety-six German combat aircraft were lost to Dutch shell fire. In the battle, forty-two percent of the German Air Force officers were lost.

On the ground, the reinforced 9th Panzer Division rolled into Rotterdam on 13 May, overcoming relatively light resistance by the French 7th Army. The Dutch attempted a small counter-offensive, the Battle of Grebbeberg, to halt and contain German progress there, but the effort failed and the Dutch forces retreated. The next day brought a heavy bombing raid on Rotterdam by the Luftwaffe, in which Heinkel He 111 medium bombers destroyed the central part of the city and the Dutch Army surrendered that evening, in an attempt to stem the German destruction of other Dutch cities. The Dutch Queen, Wilhelmina, arranged the establishment of a Dutch government in exile in Britain. The combined Dutch army, navy, air force, and civilian casualties in the German offensive totalled more than 4,900.

In dealing with Belgium, the Germans had done their reconnaissance homework and rather easily destroyed nearly half of the Belgian Air Force in the first day of operations there and by the end of that day, the Luftwaffe had secured air superiority over the region of the Low Countries.

But the main Allied strongpoint in Belgium was Eben-Emael, the large, modern fortress blocking the advance of the German 6th Army, whose feint offensive was stalling. Eben-Emael was located at the junction of the River Meuse and the Albert Canal, and the problem for the Germans was that a serious delay in their advance at that position threatened the outcome of the campaign. For the German Army Group A to establish bridgeheads in the area, it was vital that the main body of Allied forces there be engaged and to that end, the Germans decided on a new approach to assaulting the fort. Early in the morning of 10 May, some 230 German gliders landed near the site, delivering dozens of combat teams whose job was to disable the gun cupolas of the fort, using hollow charges. German paratroopers, meanwhile, were engaged in seizing the bridges over the canal. In the action, the Belgians counter-attacked, but their effort was halted by attacks from the Luftwaffe. The Belgian Supreme Command had planned, if necessary, a withdrawal to a pre-determined point, but were so shocked by the failure of their key fortification to withstand the German airborne assault, they ordered the withdrawal five days earlier than they had anticipated. The Dutch did manage to slow German progress some by blowing up most of the key river bridges, stalling the advance of the German armour briefly.

Prior to the Belgian defeat at Eben-Emael, the Allies had been counting on strong Belgian resistance to provide several weeks for their preparation of a new defensive line near the Gembloux Gap, between Wavre and Namur, an area of flat terrain, ideal for tanks.

THE BATTLE FOR FRANCE

The British Expeditionary Force and the 1st French Army were rightly concerned about the Allied defeat on the Belgian border of 11 May. The battle had been a decisive victory for the Germans who had so effectively conducted a glider-born assault on the fortress of Eben-emael, using flame-throwers and explosives to disable the outer defences. They had killed many of the defenders within the fort, while other elements of the German assault force landed near the three bridges over the nearby Albert Canal to destroy many Belgian defensive positions and capture several Belgian soldiers. The German airborne troops incurred heavy casualties in the operation, but managed to hold the bridges until German ground forces arrived to assist the paratroopers in a second assault on the fort, during which the remaining Belgian forces surrendered the garrison. The access into Belgium provided by the bridges the German troops had captured enabled large numbers of German forces to advance into the Netherlands.

With the bridges in German control, the XVI Panzerkorps under the command of General Erich Hoepner, crossed and headed in the direction of Gembloux Gap, leading the French command to believe that the gap would be the scene of the coming main battle action, an area of flat terrain ideal for tank manoeuvring. In an effort to buy time to establish a dug-in defensive position in that unfortified section of the Allied line, the 1st French Army sent two light mechanized divisions ahead to engage and, hopefully, stall the advancing Germans near Hannut to the east of Gembloux. This resulted in the Battle of Hannut on 12-13 May, the biggest tank battle of the war to that date, involving more than 1,500 tanks.

In the action, ninety-one French Hotchkiss and thirty Somua tanks were destroyed or captured, for the loss of about 160 German tanks and armoured fighting vehicles. Then, with the withdrawal of the French, the Germans retained control of the battlefield, recovering and repairing all but forty-nine of their tanks. After the battle, the 1st French Army had indeed stalled the panzers long enough for the French troops to dig in and settle, thus creating a victory for the French. General Hoepner accomplished his primary assignment to that point—the diversion of the French First Army from Sedan, even though he failed to destroy it. Escaping the German encirclement, the French were then able to provide vital support to the BEF troops at Dunkirk a few weeks later.

General Hoepner, angry at having been held up by the light mechanized enemy divisions at Hannut, went against standing orders and attempted to break the French line a second time, an action that led to the Battle of Gembloux Gap on 14-15 May. Gembloux Gap was the last major prepared defensive position of the French on the Belgian front.

The Allied armies had wanted to halt the German advance into Belgium in the belief that it was the main German thrust of the offensive, and had committed the best of their armies to Belgium on 10 May. Unaware of the German intention to push through the Ardennes on to the Channel coast, the French army planned to stop the German advance at two defensive positions near the towns of Hannut and Gembloux. In a two-day battle that began on 14 May, the French forces repeatedly foiled German Sixth Army efforts to break through or circumvent French defences, knocking out more than 170 German tanks in the process. By the end of the second day though, the toll taken on the French side had forced them to withdraw from Gembloux and out of Belgium towards Lille in France.

French Général d'armée Maurice Gamelin had limited his reinforcement of the Meuse sector to rail travel by night, to avoid the attentions of the Luftwaffe. This delayed the reinforcement progress, but Gamelin was sure that the enormous build-up of German personnel, vehicles and equipment would be equally slow. He was confident about the French fortifications and artillery, if perhaps somewhat less so about the quality of his fighting men. He had no illusions about the strength of the enemy armour and infantry. What neither the French nor the Germans knew about each other was that they were both arriving in the combat area with extremely limited amounts of ammunition for their guns.

On the central front, the panzers of German Army Group A experienced delays as they attempted to advance into the Ardennes. A combination of French mechanized cavalry divisions and Belgian motorized infantry was slowing the progress of the German armour, but the French and Belgians were insufficiently armed with anti-tank weaponry to cope with the substantial number of enemy tanks they were encountering and were forced to retreat, unable to make much headway in their effort to block the advancing panzers. The Allied forces had to withdraw to behind the River Meuse. Now the problem for the huge German force was that of trying to advance their great number of troops, tanks, and various other vehicles and guns through the relatively poor road network of only four routes through the Ardennes. Generalfeldmarschall Paul Ewald von Kleist's panzer group alone contained more than 41,000 vehicles, and very soon the few roadways available to the massive German armada were heavily congested, a condition that would persist for several days. The German commanders were concerned about the threat of air attacks by the French, but they did not occur.

The German offensive heated up considerably on 13 May when Panzer divisions of the XIX Korps, reinforced by the *Grossedeutschland* infantry regiment made crossings of the River Meuse near Sedan. The French defensive line there was slightly less than four miles deep and defended by more than 100 pillboxes.

The French had anticipated a gradual assembly of German artillery near Sedan, but the Germans had something different in mind. XIX commander Generaloberst Heinz Guderian had conferred with the German Air Force chief Reichsmarschall Hermann Goering and Goering had assured him that the air force would provide an extremely powerful eight-hour air strike from early morning until dusk to blast a big opening in the French lines for Guderian's force to roar through on their way to the Channel coast. If anything, Goering had understated the effort. It turned out to be the heaviest and most intense air bombardment by the Germans in the war, with nine bomber wings of the Luftwaffe flying a total of 3,940 sorties against the Sedan target that day.

The bombing had affected the defenders in varying degrees, with some of the most forward pillboxes being unaffected. The personnel manning these particular defenses were able to repel the crossing efforts of some of the panzers. Some of the other pillbox defenders, however, were badly shaken by the air attacks, and the French gunners posted in artillery batteries in the immediate area simply fled their positions. By midnight substantial numbers of German infantry troops, though by no means the majority of them, had fought their way into the French defence zone. Morale problems were starting to permeate the length of the French lines. And by 7 p.m. the members of the French 295th regiment of the 55th Infantry Division, which were holding the final prepared defensive line on the Bulson Ridge about six miles behind the river, heard a false rumour that German tanks had already crossed the river and were now behind their position. The rumour panicked the infantry regiment soldiers who quickly fled, leaving a large gap in the French defences. In fact, the Germans were yet to cross the river and it would be a further twelve hours before the German artillery would begin shelling the Bulson position.

French Général Gaston-Henri Billotte, in command of the 1st Army Group which was then flanking Sedan, was then insistent that the bridges across the Meuse be destroyed by air bombardment immediately as he believed that "over them will pass either victory or defeat!" More than forty percent of the available Allied light bomber capability was lost that day in a failed effort to destroy the bridges.

German High Command, through Ewald von Kleist, ordered Guderian not to proceed in his panzer advance more than five miles beyond the Meuse crossing and, even though the order had been confirmed by von Rundstedt, Guderian managed to get agreement from Ewald von Kleist to go ahead with a "reconnaissance in force", a semantic means of circumventing the High Command order, which supposedly resulted from Guderian threatening to resign over it.

Guderian: "On the far bank of the river I found the efficient and brave commander of the 1st Rifle Regiment, Lieutenant-Colonel Balck, with his staff. He hailed me with the cheerful cry, 'Pleasure boating on the Meuse is forbidden!' I had in fact coined the phrase myself during the training we had had for this operation, since the attitude of some of the younger officers had struck me as too light-hearted. I now realized that they had judged the situation correctly.

"Once again to the 1st Panzer Division, where I found the divisional commander, Major Wenck; I asked him whether his whole division could be turned westwards or whether a flank guard should be left facing south on the east bank of the Ardennes Canal. Wenck saw fit to interject a somewhat slangy expression of mine *'Klotzen, nicht Kleckern'* [roughly translated, 'Boot 'em; don't spatter 'em'], and that really answered my question. 1st and 2nd Panzer Divisions received orders immediately to change direction with all their forces, to cross the Ardennes Canal, and to head west with the objective of breaking clear through the French defences. That I might co-ordinate the movements of the two divisions, I next went to the command post of the 2nd Panzer Division, which was in the Chateau Rocan, on the heights above Donchéry. From that vantage point a good view could be obtained over the ground across which the 2nd Panzer Division had advanced and attacked on the 13th and 14th of May. I was surprised that the French long-range artillery in the Maginot Line and its westerly extension had not laid down heavier fire and caused us more trouble during our advance. At this moment, as I looked at the ground we had come over, the success of our attack struck me as almost a miracle."

Having crossed the Meuse, the great mass of German armour was able to fan out as it raced west. Many dispirited French troops were cluttering the roads being used by the panzers. Some recalled the derisive shouts from German tankers: "Drop your rifles and get the hell out of here—we don't have time to take you prisoner."

Guderian: "I was pleased to have retained my freedom of movement when, early on the 16th of May I went to the headquarters of the 1st Panzer Devision. I drove through Vendresse to Omont. The situation at the front was not yet clear. All that was known was that there had been heavy fighting in the neighbourhood of Bouvellemont. So on to Bouvellemont. In the main street of the burning village I found the regimental commander, Lieutenant-Colonel Balck, and let him describe the events of the previous night to me. The troops were over-tired, having had no real rest since the 9th of May. Ammunition was running low. The men in the front line were falling asleep in their slit trenches. Balck himself, in wind jacket and with a knotty stick in his hand, told me that the capture of the village had only succeeded because, when his officers complained against the continuation of the attack, he had replied: 'In that case I'll take the place on my own!' and had moved off. His men had thereupon followed him. His dirty face and his red-rimmed eyes showed that he had spent a hard day and a sleepless night. For his doings on that day he was to receive the Knight's Cross. His opponents—a good Norman infantry division and a brigade of Spahis—had fought bravely. The enemy's machine-guns were still firing into the village street, but for some time now there had been no artillery fire and Balck shared my opinion that resistance was almost over.

"Now on the previous day we had captured a French order, originating if I am not mistaken, from General Gamelin himself, which contained the words: 'The torrent of German tanks must finally be stopped!' This order had strengthened me in my conviction that the attack must be pressed forward with all possible strength, since the defensive capabilities of the French was [sic] obviously causing their high command serious anxiety. This was no time for hesitancy, and still less for calling a halt.

"I sent for the troops by companies and read them the captured order, making plain its significance and the importance of continuing the attack at once. I thanked them for their achievements to date and told them that they must now strike with all their power to complete our victory. I then ordered them to return to their vehicles and to continue the advance."

As Guderian's tank forces advanced rapidly westward, higher-ranking German officers feared that his swift pace was laying his force open to the possibility of being cut off and trapped by the Allies as he continued to outrun his infantry units. Twice in the first few days after the breakthrough, they ordered his advance halted to allow the infantry time to catch up with the tanks. Guderian clearly disagreed and lobbied heatedly for the freedom to maintain his pace towards the coast. Incredibly, seventy-one German divisions were on the march westward, ten of them armoured.

When Guderian originally discussed the plan for the offensive with Manstein, Guderian had suggested the implementation of secondary attacks southeast, to the rear of the Maginot Line, in order to confuse the French. When Halder got hold of the Manstein version, he removed that aspect of the plan. But in the actual execution, Guderian elected to send the 10th Panzer division and the *Grossedeutschland* infantry regiment off on just such a feint thrust onto the only available southern route, across the Stonne plateau. 2nd French Army Commander Charles Huntziger had also planned to launch a counterattack at the same position in an effort to eliminate the bridgehead. Their separate actions ended in chaos with both units vying to gain the same ground between 15 and 17 May, and the village of Stonne being taken and re-taken seventeen times by both sides. For the French the occupation of Stonne and Bulson would have given them the desired high ground above Sedan, from which they might have disrupted the German bridgehead there whether or not Huntziger's forces had been able to take Sedan. But after all the back-and-forth activity, the village fell to the Germans for the last time on the night of 17 May. Guderian and Panzer divisions 1 and 2 departed rapidly towards the Channel coast.

Guderian: "After our splendid success on the 16th of May, it did not occur to me that my superiors could possibly still hold the same view as before, nor that they would now be satisfied with simply holding the bridgehead we had established across the Meuse while awaiting the arrival of the infantry corps. I was completely filled with the ideas that I had expressed during our conference with Hitler in March, that is to say to complete our breakthrough and not stop until we had reached the English Channel. It certainly never occurred to me that Hitler himself, who had approved the boldest aspects of the Manstein plan and had not uttered a word against my proposals concerning exploitation of the breakthrough, would now be the one to be frightened by his own temerity and would order our advance to be stopped at once. Here I was making a great mistake, as I was to discover on the following morning.

"Early on the 17th of May I received a message from the Panzer Group: the advance was to be halted at once and I was personally to report to General Kleist, who would come to see me at my airstrip at 07.00 hours. He was there punctually and, without even wishing me a good morning, began in very violent terms to berate me for having disobeyed orders. He did not see fit to waste a word of praise on the performance of the troops. When the first storm was passed, and he had stopped to draw breath, I asked that I might be relieved of my command. General Kleist was momentarily taken aback, but then he nodded and ordered me to hand over my command to the most senior general of my corps. And that was the end of our conversation. I returned to my corps headquarters and asked General Veiel to come to see me, that I might hand over to him.

"I then sent a message to Army Group Rundstedt by wireless in which I said that after I had handed over my command at noon I would be flying to the Army Group headquarters to make a report on what had happened. I received an answer almost at once: I was to remain at my headquarters and await the arrival of Colonel-General List, who was in command of the Twelfth Army that was following behind us and who had been instructed to clear this matter up. Until the arrival of Colonel-General List all units were to be ordered to remain where they were. Major Wenck, who came to receive these orders, was shot at by a French tank while returning to his division and was wounded in the foot. General Veiel now appeared and I explained the situation to him. Early that afternoon Colonel-General List arrived and asked me at once what on earth was going on here. Acting on instructions from Colonel-General Rundstedt he informed me that I would not resign my command and explained that the order to halt the advance came from the Army High Command (the OKH) and therefore must be obeyed. He quite understood my reasons, however, for wishing to go on with the advance and therefore, with the Army Group's approval, he ordered: 'Reconnaissance in force to be carried out. Corps headquarters must in all circumstances remain where it is, so that it may be easily reached.' This was at least something, and I was grateful to Colonel-General List for what he had done. I asked him to clear up the misunderstanding between General Kleist and myself. Then I set the 'Reconnaissance in force' in motion. Corps headquarters remained at its old location in Soize; a wire was laid from there to my advanced head-quarters, so that I need not communicate with my staff by wireless and my orders could therefore not be monitored by the wireless intercept units of the OKH and the OKW."

In a little over a day, the French suffered defeats when the motorized infantry of Guderian routed the 6th French Army west of Sedan. The 9th French Army collapsed and surrendered, and the French 102nd Fortress Division was surrounded and destroyed at the Monthermé bridgehead by Panzerdivisions 6 and 8, operating without air support. Breaking through the defences of the 9th French Army, Erwin Rommel's 7th Panzerdivision, driv-en by him day and night without rest, pushed on some thirty miles in only twenty-four hours.

Rommel lost communication with the headquarters of his superior, General Hermann Hoth, and decided to disobey his orders and maintain his advance northwest to Avesnes-sur-Helpe, ahead of Panzer divisions 1 and 2. Encountering the bivouac of the 5th French Motorized Division along his route, Rommel's tanks rolled through them and was soon joined by the tanks of the 5th Panzer division. Severely disadvantaged by lack of speed, lack of communications capability and overloaded crews, the French were quickly overwhelmed by the German armour which came in fast and attacked them at close range. In the rout, the French lost all but three of their tanks. They managed to knock out fifty of the 500 German tanks.

Rommel's force had taken 10,000 French prisoners by 17 May and he and Guderian were pleased with the rate of their progress, ordering their forces to keep on towards the Channel until they exhausted their fuel.

In his diary entry of 17 May, Halder commented on Hitler being worried about the pace of the German advance being too quick: "Führer is terribly nervous. Frightened by his own success, he is afraid to take any chance and so would pull the reins on us . . . [he] keeps worrying about the south flank. He rages and screams that we are on the way to ruin the whole campaign." It seems that Guderian and Rommel were maintaining their advance through selective interpretation of orders as they continued their trip to the coast.

That very pace, though, now threatened the plans of Guderian and Rommel. The tank crews were exhausted from the punishing effort, they were running low on fuel and had lost several of their number to break-downs. Worse, a large and dangerous gap had opened between the Panzer divisions and their supporting infantry. They were at risk of a large enemy attack that could cut them off completely from the infantry. But the French had serious problems of their own at this point. Their command was hopelessly stuck in a traditional warfare methodology and, somewhat shocked by the speed of the German offensive and the degree of success the enemy was achieving, an air of defeatism was spreading among the French forces. In a telephone call in the morning of 15 May, the French Prime Minister Paul Reynaud spoke to the British PM Winston Churchill: "We have been defeated. We are beaten. We have lost the battle."

The next day, Churchill flew to Paris and he was greeted with the sight of French government officials burning documents in preparation for the imminent evacuation of the capital. Churchill is said to have received the greatest single shock of his life when, in a meeting with the French commanders, he asked Général Gamelin about the state of their strategic reserve and was told: "There is none." When Churchill pursued the point, asking Gamelin when and where he proposed to counterattack against the Germans, the Général replied: ". . . inferiority of numbers, inferiority of equipment, inferiority of methods."

In extremes of contrast, the character of the offensive primarily saw the Germans utilizing the combination of their tanks and fighting vehicles, and operational infantry formations to good effect in their main efforts, while the French had scattered the bulk of their armour and had lost one of its key divisions when it ran out of fuel. Another of their more capable armoured divisions had missed a ripe opportunity to attack and probably destroy the enemy bridgeheads at Sedan. The scattered companies of the only other French armoured division still in reserve, the 2nd Division Cuirassée de Réserve, were strung out along a thirty-seven mile front and, while desperately trying to form up, were overrun and destroyed by the tanks of 8 Panzer division, all of this despite the French having a numerical advantage over the Germans in these situations.

Then-Colonel Charles de Gaulle was commanding the 4th DCR. On 17 May he initiated an attack on the 1st Panzer Division from Montcornet in the south and to the rear of the Germans. Early in the action, Guderian swiftly brought his 10th Panzer Division up against de Gaulle's flank and the French attack was soon broken up by Luftwaffe planes of the VIII Fliegerkorps. In the action the French lost thirty-two tanks and armoured vehicles. By 19 May Colonel de Gaulle had received substantial reinforcements and tried a second attack, with the loss this time of eighty out of 155 vehicles. Once again, the French effort was halted mainly by the cooperative participation of the VIII Fliegerkorps. De Gaulle's attempts, while valiant, had not altered the German advance.

Exhilarated by their achievements of recent days, and the evident inability of the Allies to halt or escape from their continuing advance, the Panzerkorps paused on 17-18 May to rest, refuel, eat, sleep, and service their vehicles. And in an all but incidental gesture, Rommel's armoured force made a feint towards the city of Cambrai which led to it surrendering to the Germans.

Worryingly for the British, when General Edmund Ironside, Chief of the Imperial General Staff, met with BEF commander General Lord Gort at Gort's headquarters near Lens on 19 May, he discussed the possibility of the BEF launching an attack to the southwest towards Amiens. Gort said that he could only commit two of his nine divisions to such an attack and, when Ironside asked Gort about Général Billotte, commander of the 1st French Army, Gort told him that Billotte had issued no orders for eight days. When Ironside than went to see Billotte about the situation, Ironside felt that the French general was evidently incapable of decisive action, leaving Ironside believing that the fate of the BEF was probably already sealed. Ironside went back to Britain and called for urgent anti-invasion preparations.

Guderian: "On the 19th of May we crossed the old Somme battlefield of the First World War. Until now we had been advancing north of the Aisne, the Serre and the Somme, and those rivers had served to guard our open left flank, which was also covered by reconnaissance troops anti-tank units and combat engineers. The danger from the flank was slight; we knew about the French 4th Armoured Division, a new formation under Général de Gaulle, which had been reported on the 16th of May and had first appeared, as already stated, at Montcornet. During the next few days de Gaulle stayed with us and on the 19th a few of his tanks succeeded in penetrating to within a mile of my advanced headquarters in Holnon wood. The headquarters had only some 20mm anti-aircraft guns for protection, and I passed a few uncomfortable hours until at last the threatening visitors moved off in another direction. Also we were aware of the existence of a French reserve army, some eight infantry divisions strong, which was being set up in the Paris area. We did not imagine that Général Frére would advance against us so long as we kept on moving ourselves. According to the best French formula, he would wait until he had exact information about his enemy's position before doing anything. So we had to keep him guessing; this could best be done by continuing to push on."

The German lightning strike was producing better results than even Hitler had expected. Guderian's panzers had reached Abbeville and Amiens by 20 May and nearly one million Allied troops were isolated in the north by the Panzer units racing to the Channel coast. The best elements of the British and French armies, and all of the Belgian army, were cut off and could not be resupplied except through a few of the Channel ports.

In the last days of the blitzkrieg on France, she was also subjected to a short but noteworthy procession of staggeringly inept generals in top command roles. Elderly, exhausted, and essentially devoid of any practical ideas for turning back the evaders, this little parade contributed nothing but more confusion to the sad situation; all soon lost their will, the plot, and finally the fight.

The advance of the panzers continued unabated to the French coast. With the end of May came the end of the Battle of France and the most powerful and impressive armoured sweep the world had ever seen.

Trapped at the French seaside town of Dunkirk, 338,000 troops, mostly from the British Expeditionary Force, along with some French and Belgian units, now faced likely annihilation at the hands of the German invaders. Field Marshal Rundstedt sat behind the town with his five Army Group A armoured divisions, poised to destroy the massive Allied congregation which was gathered mainly on or near the beaches. He certainly had the firepower and the will to complete the task, but it was not to be. Rundstedt: "If I had had my way the English would not have got off so lightly at Dunkirk. But my hands were tied by direct orders from Hitler himself. While the English were clambering onto the ships off the beaches, I was kept uselessly outside the port unable to move. I recommended to the Supreme Command that my five Panzer divisions be immediately sent into the town and thereby completely destroy the retreating English. But I received definite orders from the Führer that under no circumstances was I to attack . . ."

It seemed that Hitler believed that his panzers had been severely strained in their race across France. He dared not risk them in a direct assault over the difficult terrain around Dunkirk when he needed to deploy them against the remaining French armies to the south. So he gave the job of wiping out the beach-bound BEF to Hermann Goering's Luftwaffe which he felt could easily destroy the enemy forces by bombing them. His misjudgement allowed most of the British troops to be evacuated from the beaches when the Royal Navy, together with an improvised fleet of vessels including coasters, paddle steamers, fishing boats, colliers, yachts and other craft, managed to rescue them. British losses during the evacuation amounted to 68,111 killlled, wounded or taken prisoner.

Rested and somewhat revived, Guderian's armoured forces and infantry received permission to continue their advance to the Channel coast. The pressure was on the Germans to move quickly again and not give the Allies sufficient time to reorganize for their defence. Guderian's forces rolled easily through the British defences at the Somme, took Amiens, and a key river bridge at Abbeville, all of which served to block the British, Belgian, Dutch and French forces to the north. In the massive panzer race to the Channel, an advance unit of 2nd Panzer Division arrived in Noyelles-sur-Mer on 20 May, having established a pocket containing huge numbers of men from the British, French, and Belgian armies. From there the Germans were within sight of the Somme estuary and the Channel.

French Général d'armée Maurice Gamelin ordered his armies that were trapped in Belgium and northern France to break out on 20 May, head south and join with the French forces that were moving north from the Somme. Gamelin, however, had already been sacked the preceding evening by French Prime Minister Paul Reynaud for Gamelin's inability to halt the German offensive. Reynaud replaced Gamelin with Maxime Weygand, a man with no grasp of the urgency at hand. Weygand wasted several days in courtesy calls on dignitaries in the French capital before finally proposing a counter-offensive similar to that planned by Gamelin.

The Germans, meanwhile, had been able to bring up additional infantry divisions into the "corridor" through which they were pushing toward the coast. That corridor was relatively narrow, and theoretically, the French were sufficiently manned and equipped to make an effective counter-offensive against the German divisions, but Weygand had wasted too much time and the opportunity to act when his action might have succeeded.

In conversation with King Leopold III of Belgium, and Général Billotte, Wegand learned that the Belgian Army was unable to operate offensively as it lacked both tanks and aircraft and was established solely for defence. Free Belgium, what remained of it, according to the King, was within two weeks of starvation. He told them that a continuing offensive action by the British and involving the Belgian Army would soon bring the collapse of his army. The King then urged the British and French to set up a beachhead at Dunkirk and the Belgian channel ports.

Général Billotte died in a road accident on 23 May and no one was left in charge of the Allied First Army Group in the "pocket" for the next three days. And no one else had been fully briefed on the details of Weygand's plans. The other notable event of the 23rd was the decision by the British to evacuate their men from the channel ports.

There followed a failed attack by the British at Arras on the afternoon of 21 May, in which the tank battalions of Major-General Harold Franklyn incorrectly assumed that he was to relieve the garrison at Arras and cut German communications in that area, and into the action he sent eighty-eight tanks including seventy-four Matildas. Franklyn did gain some early success, but again, as so often had been the case with the French, the British field communications and arms coordination had been poor compared with those of the Germans, and the heavier 88mm and 105mm guns of the Germans soon stopped the attack. Only twenty-eight of the British tanks survived the engagement.

One unexpected effect of the Arras battle was spreading panic in the German High Command where it was thought for a short time that their elite Panzerkorps was in genuine danger of being wiped out. Somehow the Germans came to believe that the Allies had massed hundreds of tanks to smash their own tank force. By the next day the panic was over, confidence was restored and the High Command was issuing orders for Guderian's Panzer Divisions to push on to the Channel ports. From this point, only rather meagre attempts were made by the British and the French to attack the onrushing enemy forces. In each case the Allies were beaten back, suffering considerable losses.

In one of the most controversial events of the war, Generalfeldmarschall Günther von Kluge proposed that the German Army "halt and close up" on 23 May when it was ready to make the final push and attack the Allied forces trapped at Dunkirk. Generalfeldmarschall Gerd von Rundstedt, commander of Army Group A, concurred with Kluge, who then issued the order that on 24 May "the army will, in the main, halt tomorrow in accordance with Colonel-General von Rundstedt's order. General Walther von Brauchitsch, Commander-in-Chief of the German Army, did not agree with Kluge and Rundstedt, wanting to pursue the attack against Dunkirk. He wanted to put Army Group B, under the command of General Fedor von Bock, in charge of the attack. Halder then entered the controversy on the side of Kluge and Rundstedt, at which point the argument went to Hitler, who agreed with halting the action against Dunkirk, and overruled Brauchitsch. The "halt" order remained in effect. In what would ultimately come to be seen as a mistake by the triumvirate of Hitler, Rundstedt, and Hermann Goering, a delay of three days occurred, 24-27 May, during which Goering entered the fray to persuade Hitler that his Luftwaffe would prevent an evacuation from Dunkirk. The delay gave the Allies time to establish some sort of defence of the approaches to Dunkirk.

In the morning of 23 May General Lord Gort called a retreat from the battlefield of Arras. Having become disenchanted with the Weygand plan, and more so in Weygand's notion of trying to hold a pocket of resistance on the Flemish coast, Gort was well aware of the heightening German threat to the channel ports the British would need for a re-supply effort. Later that day, the 2nd Panzer Division attacked Boulogne and the British garrison there was finally forced to surrender. While the Royal Air Force was able to maintain air superiority over the port, the Royal Navy managed to evacuate nearly 4,300 men from the garrison facility.

The next day, the 10th Panzer Division under the command of General der Panzertruppen Ferdinand Schaal, launched an assault on Calais. Cruiser tanks of the 3rd Royal Tank Regiment, together with vehicles of the 30th Motor Brigade were quickly brought in ahead of the German attack, enabling the Allied defenders to hold the port for as long as possible. They were trying to stall the advancing German units from reaching Dunkirk. The British units fought determinedly, frustrating Guderian who stated that if Calais had not fallen to the German forces by 2 p.m. on 26 May, he would order the withdrawal of 10th Panzer Division and request that the Luftwaffe destroy the city. Just before that deadline, the British and French units ran out of ammunition, allowing the Germans to enter and take the fortified city. The British, though, managed to hold control of the dock area until the morning of 27 May. For the cost of nearly sixty percent of the participating Allied personnel, 440 were evacuated from Calais.

On 26 May, Operation Dynamo was launched by the Allies, to evacuate the encircled troops of the British, French, and Belgian armies from the Channel coast of France. Général Weygand, in failing to withdraw the bulk of the remaining French 1st Army from Lille, had condemned it to fight a lengthy, futile defence of the city, in which 50,000 French soldiers would finally surrender on 31 May. Their defensive action at Lille pulled thousands of German troops away from the town of Dunkirk, enabling some 70,000 additional Allied soldiers to escape.

Dynamo was the inspiration of British Vice Admiral Bertram Ramsey, operating from his headquarters in tunnels underneath Dover Castle. It was in the dynamo room which provided electricity for the the castle that Ramsey devised the evacuation scheme, and thus the name for the operation. He had been given a week to organize and direct the evacuation of up to 400,000 British and French troops who were facing virtually constant attack from German forces. Ramsey assembled a force of destroyers, corvettes, mine-sweepers and naval trawlers to protect and escort a small fleet of passenger ferries that his staff had gathered in order to embark troops from the quays at Dunkirk. The protective vessels were to be augmented by a wide variety of cargo ships, coasters, and the addition of some forty self-propelled Dutch barges.

The Small Vessels Pool of the Admiralty in London, meanwhile, was busy signing up the services of all possible seaworthy pleasure craft which would be manned by volunteer crews, most of whom had never sailed out of sight of land before. These "captains" were assembled at Sheerness Dockyard, checked in and sent on to Ramsgate where they were to await final sailing orders. The first convoy of the "little ships" departed Ramsgate at 10 p.m. on 29 May. By the next day they were crossing the Channel in great numbers. The courage of these civilians was breathtaking as they repeatedly endured attacks by the aircraft of the Luftwaffe, coastal batteries, and the threat of randomly-placed mines. Luckily, most of their great adventure was blessed by relatively calm seas. For the most part, the crewmen of the little ships operated them as tenders, ferrying troops directly from the beaches.

Arthur Divine skippered one of the little boats that participated in the evacuation: "It was one of the queerest, most nondescript flotilla that ever was, and it was manned by every kind of Englishman, never more than two men, often only one, to each small boat. There were bankers and dentists, taxi drivers and yachtsmen, longshoremen, boys, engineers, fishermen and civil servants . . .

"It was dark before we were well clear of the English coast. It wasn't rough, but there was a little chop on, sufficient to make it very wet, and we soaked the Admiral to the skin. Soon, in the dark, the big boats began to overtake us. We were in a sort of dark traffic lane, full of strange ghosts and weird, unaccountable waves from the wash of the larger vessels. When destroyers went by, full tilt, the wash was a serious matter to us little fellows. We could only spin the wheel to try to head into the waves, hang on, and hope for the best.

"Even before it was fully dark we had picked up the glow of the Dunkirk flames, and now as we drew nearer the sailing got better, for we could steer by them and see silhouetted the shapes of other ships, of boats coming home already loaded, and of low dark shadows that might be enemy motor torpedo boats.

"Then aircraft started dropping parachute flares. We saw them hanging all about us in the night, like young moons. The sound of the firing and the bombing was with us always, growing steadily louder as we got nearer and nearer. The flames grew too. From a glow they rose up to enormous plumes of fire that roared high into the everlasting pall of smoke. As we approached Dunkirk there was an air attack on the destroyers and for a little [while] the night was brilliant with bursting bombs and the fountain sprays of tracer bullets.

"The beach, black with men, illumined by the fires, seemed a perfect target, but no doubt the thick clouds were a useful screen.

"The picture will always remain sharp-etched in my memory—the lines of men wearily and sleepily staggering across the beach from the dunes to the shallows, falling into little boats, great columns of men thrust out into the water among bomb and shell splashes. The foremost ranks were shoulder deep, moving forward under the command of young subalterns, themselves with their heads just above the little waves that rode in to the sand. As the front ranks were dragged aboard the boats, the rear ranks moved up, from ankle deep to knee deep, from knee deep to waist deep, until they, too, came to shoulder depth and their turn.

"The little boats that ferried from the beach to the big ships in deep water listed drunkenly with the weight of men. The big ships slowly took on lists of their own with the enormous numbers crowded aboard. And always down the dunes and across the beach came new hordes of men, new columns, new lines.

"On the beach was a destroyer, bombed and burned. At the water's edge were ambulances, abandoned when their last load had been discharged.

"There was always the red background, the red of Dunkirk burning. There was no water to check the fires and there were no men to be spared to fight them. Red, too, were the shell bursts, the flash of guns, the fountains of tracer bullets.

"The din was infernal. The 5.9 batteries shelled ceaselessly and brilliantly. To the whistle of shells overhead was added the scream of falling bombs.

Even the sky was full of noise—anti-aircraft shells, machine-gun fire, the snarl of falling planes, the angry hornet noise of dive-bombers. One could not speak normally at any time against the roar of it and the noise of our own engines. We all developed 'Dunkirk throat,' a sore hoarseness that was the hallmark of those who had been there.

"Yet through all the noise I will always remember the voices of the young subalterns as they sent their men aboard, and I will remember too, the astonishing discipline of the men. They had fought through three weeks of retreat, always falling back without orders, often without support. Transport had failed. They had gone sleepless. They had been without food and water. Yet they kept ranks as they came down the beaches, and they obeyed commands.

"We stayed there until everybody else had been sent back, and then went pottering about looking for stragglers. While we were doing that, a salvo of shells got one of our troopships alongside the mole [pier]. She was hit clean in the boilers and exploded in one terrific crash. There were then, I suppose, about 1,000 Frenchmen on the mole We had seen them crowding along its narrow crest, outlined against the flames. They had gone out under shell fire to board the boat, and now they had to go back again, still being shelled. It was quite the most tragic thing I have ever seen in my life. We could do nothing with our little park dinghy.

"Going home, the Jerry dive-bombers came over us five times, but somehow left us alone though three times they took up an attacking position. A little down the coast, towards Gravelines we picked up a boatload of Frenchmen rowing off. We took them aboard. They were very much bothered as to where our 'ship' was, said quite flatly that it was impossible to go to England in a thing like ours. Too, too horribly dangerous."

In the action of Operation Dynamo, the German Air Force attacked the Allied evacuees and the vessels trying to rescue them, as often as the weather permitted. The town of Dunkirk was reduced to rubble in the bombing, and the Luftwaffe managed to destroy 235 vessels of all types and sizes, and 106 Allied aircraft, as well as more than 5,000 Allied soldiers. In addition to the combined evacuation of British, French and Belgian troops from the beaches and quays of Dunkirk, a further 220,000 Allied troops were saved by British ships from the ports of Brest, Cherbourg, Saint Malo and Saint Nazaire, making a total of Allied personnel evacuated of 558,000. On 4 June, in a speech to the House of Commons, Churchill hailed the evacuation as "a miracle of deliverance."

For the sake of national security, censorship in wartime Britain was such that the press and radio news put out relatively little information about the dramatic situation of the British and French armies at Dunkirk. King George VI, however, issued a call for a week of prayer in the churches and synagogues of Britain beginning 26 May, underscoring the desperate plight of the servicemen. The Archbishop of Canterbury also led prayers for the soldiers in dire peril in France.

Under the guidance of British naval vessels, the great armada of small ships, pleasure craft, and fishing boats had made repeated crossings of the English Channel from Dover and the Thames estuary to shuttle the stranded Allied troops from the French beaches and ports out to the waiting larger ships or back to the English shore.

Through the evacuation effort, the Luftwaffe attempted to thwart the operation, flying 1,882 bombing sorties and 1,997 fighter sorties. In the air action, sixty R.A.F. fighter pilots were lost. The Luftwaffe was unsuccessful in its effort to prevent the evacuation, but did destroy eighty-nine merchant vessels and twenty-nine of the forty Royal Navy destroyers participating in the operation. German air losses were more than 100 aircraft destroyed, against the loss of 106 R.A.F. aircraft. The total Luftwaffe aircraft losses in the Dunkirk area during the operation came to 240.

Left behind in the wake of the successful British evacuation at Dunkirk, were nearly 65,000 military vehicles, 20,000 motorcycles, nearly 2,500 guns, more than 400,000 tons of supplies, 68,000 tons of ammunition, and 147,000 tons of fuel. Between 30,000 and 40,000 French soldiers were captured by the Germans. Many small vessels were sunk, from ferries to pleasure craft and several merchantmen.

Of the evacuation that he had referred to as a "miracle of deliverance", Churchill had to warn: "We must be very careful not to assign to this deliverance the attributes of a victory. Wars are not won by evacuations." Psychologically, the British public morale got a lift from the events of Dunkirk and, while the army had lost much of its equipment and vehicles at that French port, most of its soldiers had been saved and, when the threat of German invasion ended, many of those same soldiers were sent overseas to fight in other campaigns including the great Allied invasion landings of June 1944.

Extraordinary praise for the staunch resistance of the British forces came from Generalfeldmarschall Erwin Rommel, who complimented them despite their being under-equipped and virtually without ammunition for much of the fighting.

The fate of most of the French soldiers evacuated to England from the Dunkirk beaches was quite different. They were soon repatriated on British ships to ports in Brittany and Normandy, where about half were deployed again briefly before the armistice when most became prisoners of the Germans. Of the total brought to Britain, about 3,000 joined Charles de Gaulle's Free French army in London.

In the wake of the offensive and the Dunkirk evacuation, lies the assumption which has persisted for many years since the war, that it was Hitler who ordered the German Army to stop its assault on the Allies there, as he preferred to allow Goering's Luftwaffe to complete the operation with bombing.

However, according to the official War Diary of German Army Group A,

Generalfeldmarschall Gerd von Rundstedt, Chief of the General Staff, had been concerned about the vulnerability of his flanks and the supply capability to his forward troops, and he ordered the halt. Hitler had simply rubber-stamped the order. At the same time, Luftwaffe chief Hermann Goering talked Hitler into letting the Luftwaffe destroy the trapped British and French forces, to the great displeasure of the High Command Chief of Staff, Franz Halder, who questioned the decision and was concerned about the Luftwaffe's dependency on the weather conditions at Dunkirk. The German dithering and delay gave the British the time they needed to set up and carry out the bulk of the evacuation. Supposedly, Rundstedt's order to halt of 23 May was confirmed by Hitler on the 24th, but on the afternoon of the 26th Hitler ordered the armoured forces to resume their advance, the delay having enabled the Allies sufficient time to establish the defences needed to support the evacuation.

In the opinions of various high-ranking German commanders, including Admiral Karl Dönitz, and Generals Erich von Manstein and Heinz Guderian, the failure of the German High Command to eliminate the BEF and French forces at Dunkirk was one of the greatest errors the Germans made on the Western Front. General Günther von Kluge, who had originally proposed the "halt", and committed suicide in August 1944, left the following note for Hitler: "When you receive these lines I shall be no more. I cannot bear the reproach that I have sealed the fate of the West through faulty measures, and I have no means of defending myself. I draw a conclusion from that and dispatching myself where already thousands of my comrades are. I have never feared death. Life has no more meaning for me, and I also figure that I'm on the list of war criminals who are to be delivered up. Our applications were not dictated by pessimism but by sober knowledge of the facts. I do not know if Field Marshal Model, who has been proved in every sphere, will still master the situation. From my heart I hope so. Should it not be so, however, and your cherished new weapons do not succeed, then, my Führer, make up your mind to end the war and put an end to a hopeless struggle when necessary. The German people have received such untold suffering that it is time to put an end to this frightfulness. There must be ways to attain this end, and above all, to prevent the Reich from falling under the Bolshevist heel."

The period of the *Fall Gelb* (Case Yellow) offensive and the Battle of France was a bitter, humiliating one for the French and British. When the cream of the French armies had been sent north, they, along with their best armoured formations and heavy weaponry, had been lost in the enemy encirclement. With a depleted army, Général d'armée Maxime Weygand had to defend a front line that ran from Sedan to the Channel, without much Allied support. The Allies had lost sixty-one divisions in *Fall Gelb* and Weygand had only sixty-five remaining, while the Germans still retained 142 divisions.

Almost incredibly, the French somehow managed to regroup and rejuvenate through the last three weeks of June, putting up strong resistance when the Germans restarted their offensive after 5 June. In the period, the French were able to replace much of the equipment lost earlier in the offensive, all of which contributed to a heightened overall morale among the French Army. It seemed to stem from the recent tactical experience gained by the French officers against the German armoured forces, and greatly increased confidence in the French weaponry and tanks after comparing them to the those of the enemy. They now knew that the French tanks of the day were better armed and armoured than their German counterparts.

Tactically, Weygand seemed to have taken hold of his forces and was now getting much more from them. The forty-seven divisions of German Army Group B, meanwhile, were making little progress in their attacks around Paris. The XVI Panzerkorps of Erich Heopner, now with more than 1,000 armoured fighting vehicles, was achieving even less at Aisne where, in its initial attack it lost eighty of the AFVs and the Germans struggled to cross the river there, frustrated by the deep defence that Weygand had established in the area. And the stiff artillery defences he had set up at Amiens were consistently driving the Germans back. It took fully three days of the renewed offensive before the German land forces, with considerable help from the Luftwaffe, were finally able to force some river crossings. A German comment on the action: "[it was] . . . hard and costly in lives, the enemy putting up severe resistance, particularly in the woods and tree lines, continuing the fight when our troops had pushed past the point of resistance." Then the French forces began to weaken. To the south of Abbeville, the 10th French Army was forced to retreat to Rouen. It provided the opportunity for Erwin Rommel and his 7th Panzer Division to roll west across the River Seine through Normandy where they captured the port of Cherbourg on 18 June, accepting the surrender of the 51st British Highland Division on 12 June along the way to Cherbourg. The continuing attentions of the Luftwaffe were adding greatly to the problems of the French, dispersing their armoured forces and undermining their ability to function under the frequent air attacks.

By 10 June Paris was being seriously threatened by the 18th German Army and, finally, on the 14th, the French resistance gave way and the city fell to the German invaders. Throughout June the German armies were launching new offensives in the west. German Army Groups A and C were involved in a combined effort to encircle and capture the French forces on the Maginot Line and take the fortifications of the Metz region in order to stave off a possible French counter-offensive from the Alsace against the German front line on the Somme. The assignments had Guderian's XIX Corps rolling to the French border with Switzerland to encircle the French forces in the Vosges Mountains. The XVI Corps was to attack the Maginot

Line, approaching it from the west and its more vulnerable rear. They were to take the cities of Verdun, Metz and Toul. The French had recently repositioned their 2nd Army from Alsace to the Weygand Line along the Somme. They had left only a small force to guard the Maginot Line. Army Group B, meanwhile, was undertaking its offensive against Paris and from there on to Normandy. Army Group A began its advance on the rear of the Maginot Line, and Army Group C then began a frontal assault across the River Rhine into France.

Prior to these efforts, the Germans had had no success in trying to break into the Maginot fortifications, but now on 15 June, they greatly outnumbered the French. This time the determined Germans literally brought up their big guns, 88mm, 105mm and several railway batteries. Added to this was the air force's V Fliegerkorps for air support.

Gradually, the Germans attacked and overcame the resistance offered by the French as each of the major Maginot fortresses was targetted. Progress was made on 17 June when the French 104th and 105th Divisions were pushed back into the Vosges Mountains elements of the VII Army Corps, and that same day Guderians XIX Corps arrived at the Swiss border. By then much of the Maginot defences had been cut off from the rest of France, most of the fortress units surrendering by 25 June. The Germans claimed to have taken some 500,000 prisoners of war in the actions.

By mid-June the Luftwaffe had achieved complete supremacy of French airspace. Goering's Luftwaffe, still smarting after the failure to destroy the BEF and French forces in the Dunkirk rescue, was determined to prevent any further evacuation attempts by the Allies. In a mini-campaign to that end beginning 9 June, the Germans bombed Cherbourg, Le Havre and various Allied shipping including the liner RMS *Lancastria* out of Saint Nazaire, resulting in the loss of 4,000 Allied personnel. Still, despite the efforts of the Luftwaffe, nearly 200,000 additional Allied personnel were successfully evacuated from France.

On 16 June, French Prime Minister Paul Reynaud resigned when he became convinced that he no longer had the support of his ministers, and his cabinet had reacted angrily to a British proposal that France and Britain unite to avoid surrender. Reynaud was succeeded by Marshal Philippe Pétain. Pétain promptly addressed the people of France to announce that he intended to ask the Germans for an armistice.

Germany's humiliating defeat in the First World War had been consumated on a railway carriage in the Compiégne Forest in 1918. Hitler chose to have the signing of this new armistice in the same rail car. He would even sit in the same chair in which Marshal Ferdinand Foch had sat when watching the defeated German representative sign at the end of WWI. France capitulated on 25 June 1940.

With the German occupation, France became a divided nation. The

Germans held the north and west of the country, and a so-called independent state, Vichy France, was located in the south. From his new London headquarters following the surrender of France, Charles de Gaulle, who had been made Undersecretary of National Defence by Paul Reynaud, declined to recognize the Vichy government of Marshal Pétain and set about organizing the Free French Forces.

The French Admiral Francois Darlan had promised the British government that he would not let the French fleet based in Toulon become part of the German fleet, but the British did not trust the promise, concerned that the Germans would simply seize the fleet, then docked at Toulon and at Mers-el-Kébir in what was then French Algeria, and use it in an invasion of Britain, which Hitler would soon call Operation Sea Lion. On 3 July, a British naval force bombarded the French fleet at Mers-el-Kébir, sinking a battleship, damaging five other vessels, and killing nearly 1,300 French servicemen. The British needed military aid and financial assistance from the United States and the attack on the French fleet was also meant to show the U.S. that Britain intended to continue the war with Germany despite the French capitulation. In 1942, when the Germans tried to take control of the French fleet in Toulon, the French crews scuttled the warships—this, after Churchill had ordered that the French fleet either join forces with the Royal Navy or be neutralized somehow to prevent it from falling into German or Italian hands.

With Operation Torch, the Allied invasion of northwestern Africa in November 1942, the Germans moved to safeguard southern France by occupying the Vichy state. Among the most significant events of the war was the Allied invasion of the European continent on 6 June 1944, the D-Day landings at Normandy, leading to the liberation of France. By then, more than 580,000 French people had been killed, of whom 92,000 were military personnel. It is believed that upwards of 49,000 Germans were killed in the offensive for France and in the occupation period. British casualties have been estimated at about 68,100 killed, wounded or missing. By August 1940, more than 1.5 million Allied military personnel had become prisoners of war of the Germans.

BARBAROSSA

The name for Operation Barbarossa, the code-name for the German invasion of the Soviet Union in the Second World War, came from the medieval Holy Roman Emperor Frederick Barbarossa, a leader of the Third Crusade in the 12th century. The invasion by Adolf Hitler's armoured and infantry forces opened on 22 June 1941. It was the largest operation in military history, an epic undertaking involving more than four million troops on the German side alone, and their 600,000 motor vehicles and 750,000 horses. They came in to make war along an 1,800-mile front. The adventure would finally cost the German Army ninety-five percent of all its casualties in the war. In the action the Germans took more than three million Soviet prisoners of war. They were not protected by the conditions of the Geneva Conventions on the treatment of prisoners of war and most of them never returned alive, having been systematically worked and starved to death by their captors, a part of the Nazi plan to reduce the Eastern European population. The ultimate failure of Barbarossa would turn the tide of the war against Germany.

Sunday morning. 22 June 1941. Just as the early morning raid by aircraft of the Imperial Japanese Navy on the ships and facilities of the American fleet at Pearl Harbor, Hawaii, on Sunday, 7 December 1941 would surprise the men of the U.S. Navy, the arrival of German Panzer divisions surprised the Russians. The German forces overran the Soviet positions and advanced a substantial distance before the Russians were able to react.

While serving a prison sentence in 1924, Hitler was at work on his two-volume *Mein Kampf* (My Battle), in which he wrote of the German people's need for *lebensraum* (increased living space, land and raw materials) and how this should be accessed in the East. His National Socialist ideology identified the people of the Soviet Union as *untermenschen* or subhuman. He claimed that it was Germany's destiny to end the Jewish domination of Russia and how, through an inescapable battle against Pan-Slav ideals, German victory would lead to a permanent mastery of the world. Nazi policy, according to Hitler, included the killing, deportation or enslavement of the the Russian and other Slavic peoples and the repopulation of their eastern lands with Germanic peoples.

Hitler believed that the Nazis would achieve their concept of the new world through depopulating the Soviet Union and eastern lands in a four-part policy beginning with a German blitzkrieg victory in the summer of 1941, leading to the collapse of the Soviets, as they had with Poland in 1939. This was to be followed with a campaign of starvation against the thirty million people inhabiting Russia, the Ukraine, Poland, Belarus, and the Caucasus through the winter of 1941-42 as the Germans diverted food from those regions to Germany and western Europe. This was to be followed by implementation of the Nazi plan to eliminate all Jews from the Soviet Union, Poland, and all of Europe in a 'Final Solution' programme. And finally, the completion of the Nazification of Europe and the East would follow with the deportation, enslavement, murder, or assimilation of all remaining peoples and the resettlement of eastern Europe by German colonists.

The Molotov-Ribbontrop Pact, a non-aggression treaty between the Soviet Union and Germany was signed just prior to the German invasion of Poland in 1939, the invasion that started the Second World War in Europe. The pact came as a great surprise to the world at large due to the obviously conflicting ideologies of the two, and their essential hostility towards each other. For awhile anyway, they maintained diplomatic and trade relations and the Germans received oil, wheat and other raw materials from the Soviets in exchange for military and industrial equipment. Behind the scenes, however, both were deeply suspicious of the other.

Into the late 1930s, Germany's appetite for raw materials was increasing dramatically and her territorial interest in the Balkans seemed to indicate an ever greater likelihood of a German invasion of the Soviet Union in the offing. In the summer of 1940, Hitler is said to have told one of his generals that the recent victories in western Europe had "finally freed his hands for his important real task—the showdown with Bolshevism." He was anticipating a number of benefits that would accrue from the German occupation of western Russia. They would include, but not be limited to the Ukraine becoming a reliable source of agricultural products, the Soviet Union a source of forced labour under German rule, reduction of the labour shortage in Germany through the demobilization of many German soldiers, further isolation of the Allies—especially Britain, through the defeat of the Soviet Union, and access to additional oil through German control of the Baku oilfields.

Hitler received and approved the military plans for Operation Barbarossa on 5 December 1940. The plan called for launching the assault in May 1941 and he signed his War Directive No. 21 on 18 December saying: "The German Wehrmacht must be prepared to crush Soviet Russia in a quick campaign."

At that time, according to German historian Andreas Hillgruber, the majority of Germany's leading generals believed that the German Army was ill-informed about the Soviet Union, especially about the military and the economy; due to the limited information available to it then, German Army thinking about the Soviet Union was based on traditional German stereotypes of Russia as a primitive, backward country that lacked the strength to stand up to a superior opponent; the leadership of the German Army saw the prospect of war with the Soviets from an extremely narrow military viewpoint with little consideration given to politics, the economy or culture, and the industrial capacity of the Soviet Union was not considered at all as a factor that might influence the outcome of a German-Soviet war; the average Red Army soldier was thought of as brave and tough, but the Red Army officer corps were held in contempt; The German Army leadership after the victory over France in 1940 was in a state of hubris with the Army being seen as more or less invincible; it was assumed that the Soviet Union was destined to be defeated, that it would likely take Germany between six and eight weeks to defeat the Soviets.

Meanwhile, in the Soviet Union, Joseph Stalin was telling his key generals of Hitler's references to the Soviet Union in *Mein Kampf,* and that they must always be prepared to repulse a German attack. He told them that Hitler thought the Red Army would need at least four years to ready itself for such a confrontation, so they must be prepared for such an attack much earlier.

"We have only to kick in the door and the whole rotten structure will come crashing down." —Adolf Hitler

The main intent of Barbarossa was the combining of a northern assault on Leningrad, a symbolic capture of Moscow, and the seizure of the oilfields in the south beyond the Ukraine. Hitler held many planning sessions with his generals on the offensive in which considerable disagreement was aired as to which of the aims should take priority. He was impatient to get on with the invasion, believing that Britain would sue for peace when the Germans had won victory in the Soviet Union, and Generaloberst Franz Halder wrote a diary notation that, by destroying the Soviet Union, Germany would destroy Britain's hope of victory.

Now Hitler was captivated by the hubris of his lightning victories in France and western Europe and spurred on by the seeming ineptitude of the Red Army's recent efforts. He appeared to genuinely believe that the campaign he was so eager to begin against the Soviets would be yet another example of the quick and the dead—quick and relatively easy success for him, and dead for the Russians. This perspective and his overconfidence would cause him to send his massive armies off into a hellish struggle, disgracefully underequipped and improperly prepared for the protracted, punishing winter campaign that awaited them, against a greatly underrated enemy force. He assumed that the Russians would face up to their hopeless odds and quickly throw in the towel. "When Barbarossa commences, the world will hold its breath and make no comment."—Adolf Hitler

The German Army was still involved in a Balkans campaign when it was ordered to start massing huge numbers of troops, weaponry, vehicles and equipment along the Soviet-Romanian border and by February 1941, there were more than 480,000 Wehrmacht troops waiting there. In the months leading up to the June invasion, he had positioned 3.2 million German and 500,000 Axis soldiers on the Soviet border, had Goering's Luftwaffe fly dozens of aerial reconnaissance sorties over the area, and stockpiled a record supply of war materiél to be ready for his big moment.

Stalin was convinced that, while he didn't trust the Germans, he could, for the time being, rely on the Molotov-Ribbontrop agreement which had been signed only two years earlier, and the fact that the Germans were still involved in war with Britain, to keep the peace between the two powers for awhile at least. He gave no credence to reports from his own intelligence service about the massive Nazi troop build-up along his border, considering much of what he heard along those lines to stem from British misinformation intended to set off a war between the USSR and the Germans. For several months prior to the 22 June German invasion of the Soviet Union, the British intelligence resources processing Ultra intercepts at Bletchley Park, as well as American intelligence reports, had been warning the Russians about an impending invasion by the Germans. Seeming substance to the notion that the Germans were, in fact, preparing to invade Britain, rather than the Soviet Union, was indicated through the apparent evidence of German training exercises, reconnaissance flights and ship concentrations in areas that might confirm such an intention. By 5 May, however, Stalin had accepted the reality of Hitler's intentions. In an address to military academy graduates in Moscow he said: "War with Germany is inevitable. If comrade Molotov can manage to postpone the war for two or three months that will be our good fortune, but you yourselves must go off and take measures to raise the combat readiness of our forces."

After a number of brainstorming sessions with his generals, agreement was reached on the specific goals and assignments of the three German army groups that would be making the assault on the Soviets. Army Group South was assigned to hit the heavily populated agricultural area of the Ukraine with the intention of capturing Kiev before moving east across the Steppes of the southern USSR to the River Volga where it was to take and control the oilfields of the Caucasus region. Army Group North was ordered to march through the Baltic states to northern Russia and either capture of destroy Leningrad. And the job of Army Group Centre was to roll on to Smolensk and then Moscow and take the capital. There was, however, still disagreement among Hitler and the generals about exact priority of these goals. The German High Command wanted to lead with a direct thrust at Moscow. Hitler much preferred to give priority to seizing the resource-rich Ukraine and the Baltics before going for the Soviet capital. The argument took time and brought a substantial delay to the launch of the offensive.

In the run-up to the invasion of the Soviet Union, Hitler and German High

Command persisted with the view that, in general terms, the Soviets were relatively weak and poorly prepared for the conflict coming their way. Their intelligence appears to have failed in that they didn't seem to have realized how quickly the industrialization and industrial output of the Soviets had grown during the 1930s, placing them equal to that of Germany and second only to the United States. Throughout that decade, the continuous growth of the Soviet economy leant towards production of military equipment.

Troop availability for the Soviets amounted to 2.6 million in the west, 1.8 million in the far east, and about 600,000 in training or deployed elsewhere. The total of German and Axis forces available for the offensive against the Soviet Union came to about 3.9 million. In terms of organized units available for combat operations on 22 June 1941, the Germans were prepared to field ninety-eight divisions, of which twenty-nine were armoured and motorized divisions, for an allocation of approximately ninety percent of the German Army's total mobile forces. They were to be deployed along a 750-mile front from the Baltic Sea to the Carpathian Mountains. From the start of the campaign, the German and Axis forces had a slight numerical advantage in manpower, but that ratio changed throughout the course of the war. In weapon systems, the Soviets had a significant numerical advantage. The Red Army possessed more than 23,000 tanks, of which more than 12,700 were positioned in the five Western Military Districts, three of which faced the German invasion front. It is also true that, in June 1941, Red Army maintenance standards for this equipment were poor, ammunition and radio equipment were in short supply, as were the trucks needed to bring in supplies. Following their observation of the German offensive against France in 1940, though, the Soviets soon began to reorganize their armoured equipment along the lines of Germany's large armoured divisions and corps. That reorganization, however, was only partially implemented by the beginning of Operation Barbarossa.

Germany's armies were equipped with approximately 5,200 tanks and of these, about 3,350 were prepared and committed to the offensive against the Soviets in June 1941. The ratio of armour then was to be 4:1 in the Soviet's favour, numerically. In terms of quality, only slightly more than seven percent of the Soviet tank force on that date was made up of the superior T-34 and KV-1 tanks. The numerical advantage of the Soviets, it must be said, was offset at that moment by the superior training and the readiness of the Germans. In the period 1936-38, Stalin had purged his officer corps and, of ninety generals who were arrested, only six survived the purge; just thirty-six of the 180 divisional commanders survived it, as did only seven of the fifty-seven army corps commanders. In that nightmarish time, some 30,000 personnel of the Red Army were executed, largely for being "politically unreliable." By the summer of 1941, seventy-five percent of the Red Army officers had been in their posts for less than a year, and the average Soviet corps commander was twelve years younger than the average German division commander. The majority of these Soviet officers lacked the proper training for their jobs and were, in many cases, reluctant to use initiative.

In the beginning of Barbarossa, the Soviet Army was dispersed rather than properly concentrated, largely unprepared for the action to come, and lacking the transport capability to become appropriately concentrated before the start of combat operations. While their artillery units were equipped with good guns, many had little or no ammunition, and lacked the transport capability to move their guns as needed. With inadequate maintenance standards, the Soviet tank units were mostly ill-equipped and their training and logistical support was also sub-standard. When combat began, these units were frequently sent into battle with no fixed provision for the resupply of ammunition, refueling, or even the replacement of dead, wounded, or captured personnel. Thus, one combat engagement could and often did mean the elimination of the Soviet unit. The Red Army then, was frequently at a significant disadvantage in the early days of the Barbarossa campaign. Before the beginning of the campaign, the Soviet border troops were not put on full alert and were clearly not prepared for the on-rushing Germans when the attack came.

With the fall of France in the German blitzkrieg offensive of 1940, the Soviets began the reorganization of their armoured and infantry divisions, concentrating the bulk of their forces into large formations and the majority of their tanks into twenty-nine mechanized corps, with more than 1,000 tanks in each. The Soviet plan, should the Germans attack, was to have their mechanized corps eliminate the German armoured spearheads. The Soviet mechanized corps would then work with their infantry armies to halt the advancing German infantry and shove them back. The left side of the Soviet force in the Ukraine was to be greatly reinforced in order to execute a giant envelopment. After destroying the German Army Group South, that huge Soviet force would then move north through Poland, behind the German Army Groups North and Centre, to completely encircle and annihilate them. All this would be followed by a major Red Army offensive into western Europe.

Operation Barbarossa started at 03:15 Sunday morning, 22 June 1941, when the German Air Force began dropping bombs on the cities of Soviet-occupied Poland. This precipitated the advance of nearly three million troops of the Wehrmacht toward nearly that many of their opposite number on the other side of the Soviet border. At a few minutes after midnight, a small number of Russian border troops were warned that a German attack was imminent. Relatively few of the Soviet border units were alerted before the attack began. As the offensive began, some 500,000 Hungarian, Croatian, Slovakian, Romanian, and Italian troops joined with the Germans in the assault, along with members of the Army of Finland and a division of volunteers and Nazi sympathizers from Spain.

Even though it managed to destroy more than 2,000 planes of the Soviet Air Force on the first day of the campaign, the Luftwaffe failed to achieve the total destruction of the SAF, its objective for the early part of the offensive. It did achieve air superiority over the three main sectors of the front, destroying 3,922 aircraft in the first three days of the conflict—eliminating enough of enemy air power for the German pilots and air crews to devote much of their efforts to the support of German ground forces.

The German 4th Panzer Group with its 600 tanks found itself between two Soviet armies. The objective of the 4th was Leningrad and to get there it would have to cross two major obstacles, the Neman and Daugava rivers. The Germans were able to get across the Neman on the first day of the offensive, and rolling fifty miles into the interior to a point near Raseinai. There they ran into a counterattack by 300 tanks of the 3rd and 12th Soviet Mechanized Corps. In the ensuing four day battle, the German armour surrounded and destroyed most of the Soviet tanks, which by then were out of fuel and ammunition. More than ninety percent of the entire Soviet Mechanized Corps equipment and personnel had been lost by the end of the first week of the campaign. Soon the Germans had crossed the Daugava and were closing in on Leningrad, but they had outrun their supply line and the GermanHigh Command ordered them to halt and hold their position until their infantry caught up with them. The wait lasted more than a week, giving the Soviets ample time to establish an effective defence around Leningrad and the nearby Luga river.

To the detriment of the Soviets, though, a huge anti-Soviet uprising was getting started in Lithuania. Within one day an independent Lithuania was proclaimed and more than 30,000 Lithuanian rebels clashed with Soviet soldiers and were quickly joined in the action by ethnic Lithuanians from the Red Army. The resistance soon spread to neighbouring Estonia, adding considerably to the problems of the Soviets, as the German advance proceeded northward.

There were four Soviet armies on the salient opposite German Army Group Centre. The salient thrust into German-occupied Polish territory; its centre was Bialystok and just beyond that was the city of Minsk, a primary railway junction and the capital of the Byelorussian Soviet Socialist Republic. The mission of the two panzer groups of Army Group Centre was to join up at Minsk to prevent the Red Army units escaping from the salient. In the ensuing action, the infantry of AG Centre stormed the salient and encircled the enemy troops at Bialystok, while the 2nd Panzergruppe crossed the Bug river to the south to attack the Soviets; the 3rd Panzergruppe crossed the Neman and hit the balance of the enemy forces.

And, in a seemingly hopeless gesture from Moscow, Marshall Semyon

Timoshenko directed that all Soviet forces were to launch a general counter-offensive against the invading Germans. It appeared to be a futile response as his communications system was all but inoperative, his supply capability marginalized and his ammunition dumps destroyed. Without properly functioning communications, these uncoordinated attacks were bound to fail. Marshall Georgy Zhukov had been required by Stalin to sign the Directive of People's Commissariat of Defence No. 3, ordering the Red Army to begin the major offensive with the seizure of the Suwalki region by 26 June, encircling and destroying the enemy grouping there. The effort collapsed and much of the Red Army that was involved in the action was destroyed by the Wehrmacht forces.

By 27 June the 2nd and 3rd Panzergruppes had joined up and advanced nearly 200 miles into Soviet territory on their way towards Moscow. To the south, the advancing German Army Group South, under the command of Gerd von Rundstedt, encountered three Soviet armies which put up fierce resistance, but the 600-tank spearhead of the 1st Panzergruppe slashed through one the enemy armies. This was followed by one of the most intense and violent battles of the entire offensive, a four-day action involving more than 1,000 Soviet tanks in a major counter-attack against the tanks of 1st Panzergruppe, which suffered very heavy losses, but prevailed in the final outcome.

The counter-offensive of the Soviets collapsed and commitment of the only remaining Russian tank forces in Ukraine soon forced the Soviets onto the defensive amd into a strategic withdrawal. Though a major victory for the Germans, it also resulted in a significant delay to the offensive against Moscow, hampering German progress toward the capital by eleven weeks. German General Kurt von Tippelskirch, Staff Intelligence: "The Russians had indeed lost a battle, but they won the campaign." When the campaign was a week old, each of the three German army groups had hit their prime objectives, but the Soviets were still actively and effectively resisting, especially in the areas around Minsk and Bialystok, and the Germans were suffering heavy casualties.

It was not until 3 July that Hitler finally ordered the German armoured units to roll east again, as their infantry forces caught up with them. Once again, however, a delay brought on this time by a torrential rainstorm reduced the progress rate of the panzers. The delay allowed the Russians time to reorganize and mount a massive counter-attack against Army Group Centre, whose objective was then Smolensk on the way to Moscow. Heading there, the German AGC encountered no less than six Soviet armies in a defensive line. It required the great air superiority of the Luftwaffe for the Germans to overwhelm and defeat a huge Soviet counter-attack with 700 tanks, after which the 2nd and 3rd Panzergruppes closed on Smolensk from the north and south, trapping three Soviet armies between them. Finally, on 26 July, the German armoured and infantry units prevailed, capturing some 300,000 soldiers of the Red Army, of which roughly 100,000 managed to escape and take up in the defense of Moscow.

The harsh reality of their situation was starting to become meaningful to the Germans as Barbarossa entered a second month. They now knew they had greatly underestimated the strength, resourcefulness, and determination of their enemy. The German armies had rapidly gone through the supplies they had brought with them and had not achieved the swift rate of progress they had anticipated. They now had to slow their pace and await resupply which would bring yet another substantial delay. The German High Command, spurred by Hitler, shifted to a new approach to defeating the Soviet enemy; taking away their industrial capacity for making war, through the capture of facilities such as the oilfields of the Caucasus, the Donets Basin, and the industrial complex of Kharkov, as well as Leningrad which was a centre of war production in the north. Hitler's generals in the field, however, strongly favoured maintaining a top-priority drive against Moscow which they saw as the main prize. Moscow was not only a primary arms production centre and a principal hub of communications and transportation; it was important psychologically as the capital, and the largest part of the Red Army was positioned there for the defence of the city.

Still, Hitler was insistent and ordered Generaloberst Guderian to drive the tanks of Army Group Centre towards the industrial targets and, for the time being, stop the drive on the capital.

The Germans approached to within a few kilometres of Kiev, the capital of Ukraine on the Dnieper river in mid-July. One element then turned east, encountering and trapping three Soviet armies. German tanks went north across the Dnieper and the panzers and infantry soon trapped four additional Soviet army groups.

Between 30 August and 8 September, the Germans suffered a major tactical loss, their first since the start of Barbarossa, the Yelnya Offensive, in a major retreat and the worst reversal for the Germans in the Soviet war to date. The setback refocused Hitler on the German Army Group Centre and the drive on Moscow. Shortly, the 3rd and 4th Panzer Armies were ordered to support Army Group Centre in its assault on Moscow.

In the beginning of a final push on Leningrad, an armada of tanks from Army Group Centre linked up with the 4th Panzer Army and, on 18 August, smashed their way through Soviet defences while the German 16th Army struck from the northeast. Shortly after this, an order came through from Hitler calling for the total destruction of Leningrad with no prisoners taken. The Soviets mounted a fierce defence of the city and, after a nine-day struggle, the

Germans were stopped within seven miles of their objective, with mounting casualties. At that point, the impatient German leader demanded that Leningrad should be starved into submission rather than stormed. Capturing the city was simply going to be too costly to the Germans, so heavy was Soviet resistance there. The ensuing German blockade then started the Siege of Leningrad. The Soviet troops there were able to hold out against several attempts by the enemy to break through the defences using air power and artillery, and despite the desperate shortages of food and fuel. Finally, early in 1944 they drove the Germans back from the city which had suffered the loss of more than one million people in the long siege.

The new focus on Moscow was linked to repositioning the bulk of Army Group Centre and Army Group South, to encircle the Soviet force in Kiev, which occurred on 16 September. The German forces ended a ferocious ten-day battle there with the loss to the Soviets of more than 450,000 men and nearly 600,000 captured.

In their focus on Moscow, capital city of the USSR and the largest Soviet city, the Germans launched Operation Typhoon, the Battle of Moscow, on 2 October 1941. In an attack that took the Soviets completely by surprise, the 2nd Panzer Army came up from the south to capture Oryol, a federal subject of Russia located on the Oka river, and roughly seventy-five miles to the south of the first main line of defence for the capital. The tanks then pushed on to take Bryansk, 235 miles southwest of Moscow as the German 2nd Army attacked from the west. In the north, the 3rd and 4th Panzer Armies assaulted Vyazma, in the Smolensk district, trapping four more Soviet armies. At this point in the Barbarossa campaign, the Germans had taken more than three million prisoners of war. For the final defence of Moscow, the Soviets were down to 90,000 men and 150 tanks.

By 13 October, the 3rd Panzer Army was within ninety miles of the capital and in Germany the government was predicting the imminent fall of Moscow, where Martial law had been declared. And, as the fortunes of the Soviets appeared to be in freefall, the weather in the Moscow region also took a severe turn for the worse. As the temperature dropped, heavy rains soon reduced the largely unpaved road network to mud, which slowed the German advance on the city to no more than two miles a day. The German Army supply situation in the Soviet Union had now deteriorated to the point that High Command in Berlin had to call a temporary halt to the activities of Operation Typhoon while the German armies were reorganized. The Soviets, whose own supply lines were functioning reasonably well, were able to use the German down-time to reorganize their own situation, calling up many new reservists and consolidating their positions in and around the capital. Incorporating thirty new divisions of Siberian troops, they organized eleven entirely new armies in less than a month, and with the Siberians came an additional 1,000 tanks and more than 1,000 aircraft.

The German advance on Moscow resumed on 15 November, but the weather was now becoming extreme and the ground rock-hard. Exhausted, cold and with little improvement to the resupply situation, the men of the German Army proceeded in an agonizing effort towards the capital. The plan of attack called for the 3rd and 4th Panzer Armies to cross the Moscow Canal and circle the city from the northeast, while the 2nd Panzer Army would run an attack on Tula, an industrial city 120 miles south of Moscow on the Upa river, and move in on Moscow from the south, and the 4th Panzer Army would attack the centre of Moscow. But without the necessary fuel and ammunition resupply, the Germans were unable to maintain more than a crawling pace of advance over the next two weeks. And in the south, the 2nd Panzer Army was routed by the Soviet Siberian troops. The 4th Panzer Army, though, was successful in crossing the Moscow Canal and starting the planned encirclement.

The first horrendous blizzards of the coming winter began on 2 December as part of a German infantry division approached within fifteen miles of Moscow. A single German battalion on a reconnaissance mission was able to advance to the town of Khimki, just five miles from the Soviet capital. It was the closest the Germans would get to Moscow. In the preceding three weeks of warfare, the German toll in dead and wounded came to 155,000, with disease and frostbite accounting for more casualties than actual combat. The combat-ready strength of many German divisions had by now been reduced to fifty percent or less, and the severity of the cold was taking a massive toll of the guns, tanks, and equipment in the German ranks, as well as grounding the Luftwaffe with increasing frequency. The growing, rejuvenated Soviet forces in the Moscow area had reached more than half a million men and they came at the Germans in a huge counter-attack on 5 December, driving the enemy back some 200 miles. To date, the invasion of the Soviet Union had cost the Germans 210,000 killed and missing, and 620,000 wounded, more than a third of whom had become casualties since 1 October.

Originally, the planning for Barbarossa had called for the capture of Moscow within four months, but, despite substantial early gains, the Germans met with unexpected resistance from the Soviets. By September, when Moscow was relatively vulnerable to attack, Hitler ordered his forces to change course and head south and eliminate the Russian forces at Kiev and Leningrad. This diversion significantly delayed the push on Moscow and threatened any possibility of success in Barbarossa. In their slow-paced advance on the Soviet capital, the Germans were handicapped by the heavy, gluey mud that resulted from the incessant rains that had arrived, and by the thick forests around Moscow, in which only narrow trails existed which were easy enough for the Soviet defenders of the city to block. At the same time, the slow pace of the enemy enabled the Russian infantry to manoeuvre behind the German columns to lay mines and ambush the German supply vehicles.

An example of what befell the German forces in their approach to the Soviet capital occurred on 6 October as the 4th Panzer Division under command of Generaloberst Heinz Guderian ran into a Soviet ambush near Mtsensk. The Soviet 1st Guards Rifle Corps, commanded by Major-General D.D. Leliushenko, had appeared in order to block the advance of the 2nd Panzer Army. His force included two tank brigades and two airborne brigades. One of the tank brigades, under the command of Colonel M.E. Katukov, was equipped with new T-34 tanks and was hidden nearby in the forest as an advance guard of Germans passed. Suddenly, Leliushenko's forces moved up to block the tanks and troops of the 4th Panzer Division as Katukov's troops came around to ambush the German force from the sides. When the German Mark IV tanks then tried to break out of the trap by turning out from Katukov's forces, they were stopped in brief counter-attacks. By day's end, many of the 4th Panzer Division tanks had been destroyed.

When the chill of the Russian winter began to arrive in October, the Germans had not been provided with proper winter uniforms. More than 100,000 of them developed frostbite and other cold-weather health problems. Many of their vehicles were no match for the severe cold and developed cracks in their engine blocks. The tank crews were forced to light and maintain small fires under their vehicles to hold a minimum temperature in them. And the aircraft of the vaunted Luftwaffe were grounded for much of the time.

The Battle of Moscow was particularly significant in that it was the first occasion since the German Army began its programme of blitzkrieg victories in 1939 that it was forced into a retreat from which it would not recover the initiative.

Of all the major battles of the Second World War, Stalingrad is among the most important and decisive. By the summer of 1942, Hitler's main goal for Barbarossa had become the Caucasus oilfields. He hoped to capture them, depriving the Russians of their primary fuel supply and securing an alternative oil source for Germany. To achieve this, the German 6th Army had been ordered to capture and occupy Stalingrad and, in so doing, isolate and neutralize this key enemy manufacturing and communications centre in southwestern Russia.

The battle for Stalingrad took place between 23 August 1942 and 2 February 1943. It was easily one of the bloodiest battles in the history of warfare, resulting in nearly two million casualties, both military and civilian, and nearly constant close-quarter combat.

The Soviet determination to defend Stalingrad was absolutely total and not to be questioned. Every Russian soldier was ordered "Not one step backwards" by Joseph Stalin. The battle was the major Soviet victory of the war and proved to be the turning point in the war with the Germans. Hitler himself sealed the fate of his Caucasus campaign in July when he diverted much of the army intended to occupy the oilfields, to the already futile struggle at Stalingrad. General Zhukov, meanwhile, had amassed a force of nearly a million men which attacked and encircled the German troops in a pincer movement on 19 November. The Germans ran out of food and ammunition and were freezing. In the battle, 70,000 German soldiers died and 91,000 became prisoners. Near the end of the fight, Hitler's commander there, General Friedrich von Paulus, was asked by the Russians to surrender. He had been forbidden by Hitler to attempt to break out of the encirclement and now was urged by the Führer not to be taken alive. On 2 February, Paulus gave himself up to the Russians. The German advance in the south was halted and thereafter the Russians were virtually always on the offensive and on the move towards Berlin.

The Battle of Stalingrad began with a brief campaign of intensive bombing by the Luftwaffe that turned much of the city to rubble. No matter how much of the city came under control of the German Army, they were never able to completely overrun and destroy the remaining defenders who resisted the Germans determinedly in building-to-building fighting.

With the horrors of the winter of 1941-42 behind them, Hitler's armies in the Soviet Union prepared for the spring / summer offensive that he was determined would be completed before the Americans, who had recently entered the war, could become really active in it. Stalin, meanwhile, was expecting the Germans' main effort of the new year to be against Moscow once more. If the nature of the coming combat was to be primarily in large urban areas, the emphasis would be on small arms weaponry rather than on armoured and mechanized units, which would favour the Soviets who, at that stage, were still less capable in heavily mobile operations than the Germans.

Generalfeldmarschall Wilhelm List commanded German Army Group South and was chosen to take his forces in a dash through the steppes into the Caucasus to grab the oilfields there in the new offensive code-named *Fall Blau*, or Case Blue. The new offensive was scheduled to open in May 1942, but various delays caused it to be deferred until 28 June when Army Group South headed into southern Russia. They encountered little resistance from Soviet forces as they rolled eastward across the broad steppes region. The Soviets tried several times to establish new defensive lines, but were readily outflanked by the Germans. In early July, an enormous armoured traffic jam occurred when Hitler, flushed with the initial success of Fall Blau, assigned the 4th Panzer Army to join with Army Group South. The small road network in the region could not support the thousands of vehicles coming through and a week-long delay resulted as the various commanders struggled to free up the mess.

At the end of the month, the Germans had advanced east across the Don river and had left their supply depots west of the river. The German 6th Army had come within ten miles of Stalingrad as the 4th turned north to join in the assault on the city. Down south the effort of Army Group South (A) slowed significantly in its push towards the Caucasus when it greatly overextended its supply lines.

Once the Russians realized that the main object of the new German offensive was Stalingrad rather than Moscow, Stalin put Marshal Andrey Yeryomenko and Commissar Nikita Khrushchev in charge of planning the defence of Stalingrad. The 62nd Soviet Army was to be a key force in the defence of the city. It was newly formed and deployed across the Volga river which formed the eastern border of Stalingrad. Marshal Yeryomenko had just appointed Lieutenant General Vasily Chuikov in command of the 62nd from 11 September 1942 and, when told of the role for his forces in the coming assault on the city, Chuikov said, "We will defend the city or die in the attempt." His leadership in the defence would ultimately earn him one of the two Hero of the Soviet Union awards he would receive in his career.

The Russians knew that the Germans were coming to Stalingrad. They had ample warning and were able to load and ship nearly all of the grain, cattle, and railroad rolling stock of the city across the river to safety. The action, of course, depleted the food supplies of Stalingrad, which left the citizenry in dire need even before the enemy attack began. Determined to prevent the Germans from having the use of any buildings, farmhouses, and grain storage facilities, the Soviets followed a scorched-earth policy in the outlying areas, burning such sites whenever they were forced to retreat.

The first German action against the city itself took place in the early morning of 23 August. The Soviet leadership knew the bombing was coming, but resisted evacuating the citizens of Stalingrad because of urgently needed production output of the city's factories for the war effort. One effect of this raid was the creation of a firestorm, similar in nature to that which one year later would result from combined and sustained attacks on the city Hamburg, Germany, by British and American bombers. In the Stalingrad raid, thousands of residents were killed.

For five days the Heinkel He 111s of Generaloberst Wolfram von Richthofen's Luftflotte 4 rained bombs on the city, starting numerous fires and killing many civilians. Additionally, the effect of this bombing reduced much of the city to rubble. Production of T-34 tanks, however, continued at the Stalingrad Tractor Factory, some of whose workers were fighting the fires. Tanks built at STF were manned by volunteer factory worker crews when shortages of manpower required. Often they were driven right from the assembly line to the fighting front line, some of them without paint and lacking certain equipment.

Prior to these raids, the Luftwaffe had conducted a series of bombing attacks to sink thirty-two Soviet ships on the Volga river, making the river unusable to Soviet shipping. Also destroyed in the attacks were the ferries and barges that had been used to move troops and civilians across the river.

The Soviet Air Force lost a considerable number of aircraft in the period between 23 and 31 August; the Luftwaffe having secured and maintained air supremacy over the Stalingrad area. The massive relocation of Soviet war production industry in 1941 to areas that were unreachable by the planes of the Luftwaffe, enabled the production of Soviet military aircraft in the second half of 1942 to reach 15,800. That production, together with the military aircraft being provided to the Soviets by Britain and, through the Lend-Lease programme, by the United States, would soon overwhelm the inventory of the Luftwaffe.

Late in August, Army Group South (B) got to the Volga north of Stalingrad. The Germans maintained a nearly constant bombing by aircraft and shelling by artillery of the river to hamper or prevent vital resupply crossings by the Soviets. In a major attack by Junkers Ju 87 Stuka dive-bombers against Soviet infantry and tank divisions trying for a breakthrough near factories, forty-one Soviet tanks were destroyed.

The fierce, savage fighting in the urban area gave rise to a clever new tactic by General Chuikov, called "hugging the Germans." In a counter to the Germans own familiar tactics of combined-arms teams, close cooperation between the armoured units, infantry, engineers, artillery and ground-attack aircraft, the Soviet commanders tried to always keep the front lines as close to the German positions as possible. This forced the German infantry to either fight on their own or risk casualties from their own support fire. It also tended to neutralize the Luftwaffe's close air support and weakened the supporting artillery fire.

The intense street-fighting combat in the city led to the establishment of Soviet strongpoints throughout the residential and business neighbourhoods, from office blocks to high-rise apartment buildings, basements, penthouses, corner offices and residences, factories, and warehouses. All such locations were furnished with mortars, machine-guns, anti-tank rifles, barbed wire and submachine guns. They served as hideouts for the hundreds of snipers holed up against the enemy and helped the locals to retain the bits of ground they took. The many ruined buildings were turned into ideal nests for snipers, some of whom were expert in the business of killing. One such was Vasily Zaytsev, who was credited with 225 confirmed kills in the battle. As the tutor and mentor of more than thirty "students", Zaytsev groomed them to the extent that, by the end of the campaign for the city, they had accounted for more than 3,000 sniper kills of German soldiers.

One position of special note was the unusual hill known as Mamayev Kurgan, overlooking the city. The hill was taken and lost many times by both

sides. As high ground, it provided an excellent vantage point and firing position, and was always a high-priority objective for both Soviet and German forces.
And in an action to retake Mamayev Kurgan, nearly one-third of the Soviet
13th Guards Rifle Division soldiers were killed in the first twenty-four
hours. Of the original 10,000 men in the division, only 320 survived the battle for Stalingrad.

Another site of great notoriety throughout the battle and since is a former
apartment building that was turned into a virtually impenetrable fortress by
the Soviet platoon leader Sergeant Yakov Pavlov. Located near an important
square, the building, which became commonly known as Pavlov's House,
was surrounded with a minefield set up by the men of Pavlov's platoon, who
established key firing positions for their machine-guns at the windows. The
members of the platoon had to hold out in the building for two months without relief or reinforcements. Through the course of the lengthy battle for the
city, the bodies of German soldiers kept accumulating, forcing the men of
the Pavlov platoon to run out and shove them out of the way in order to keep
their firing lines across the square clear. For his amazing achievements in
the battle, Sergeant Pavlov, too, was honoured with the award of Hero of the
Soviet Union.

From the start of the battle for Stalingrad, some 75,000 local women and
girls who had completed military or medical training would serve in various
capacities. Some would staff the hundreds of anti-aircraft gun batteries which
were used against the German tanks, as well as the planes of the Luftwaffe.
Those with medical training were not only pressed into service treating the
thousands of wounded troops; they were frequently required to come under
fire when retrieving the wounded from the vivid scenes of the fighting. Those
women with technical training, wireless and telephone operators and others,
were exposed to combat fire in the command posts where they worked and
suffered many casualties there. A great many Soviet women and girls, while
not infantry-trained, served in infantry units as mortar operators, machine-
gunners, and scouts, and many were snipers. The Soviet Air Force organized
three entirely female air regiments that flew in the Stalingrad campaign, and
a number of women drove or were a part of tank crews, three of them receiving the award of Hero of the Soviet Union as tank drivers.

As the battle ground on, with both sides giving and taking ground, fighting and fighting again for the same small gains, the Germans began moving
up their heaviest artillery pieces, among them the huge 800mm railroad gun
they called Dora. Still, they did not try to mount a force to cross the Volga,
which let the Soviets establish many effective artillery battery positions along
the east side of the river from which they could readily bombard the German
positions. As the shells of both sides continued to rain down on the city, and
enormous mounds of rubble accumulated everywhere to a height of eight to
ten meters, much of the area became virtually impossible for the operation

of the German tanks. The battle wore on and both the Soviet and German leaders perceived Stalingrad as symbolically important, more so perhaps, than her actual strategic value. Stalin had the strategic reserves of the Red Army brought into the lower Volga region and had thousands of aircraft flown from all over the Soviet Union to the Stalingrad area.

By October, the German Air Force had dramatically increased its presence and activities in the Stalingrad area. On the 5th, the Stuka dive-bombers of Luftflotte 4 flew 900 sorties targetting the crucial Soviet positions at the Dzerzhinskiy Tractor Factory complex, completely destroying several Soviet infantry regiments there. The Stukas dropped 540 tons of bombs on the Volga west bank positions of the Soviets on the 14th of the month, as units of German infantry encircled the three factories. The Stukas then turned their attention to eliminating the Soviet artillery positions on the eastern bank of the river before returning to the job of attacking enemy reinforcement and supply shipping on the river. The ships were being used in support of the Soviet 62nd Army which was being held to a standstill there by the German forces. What remained of the 62nd, some 47,000 men and only nineteen tanks, was confined to a narrow 1,000-yard strip along the west bank of the river. Though under the additional intense bombardment of 1,200 Stuka sorties, the Soviets somehow prevented the German 6th Army and 4th Panzer Army from capturing the west bank.

While the Luftwaffe continued to hold air superiority in the skies over Stalingrad, it had lost nearly half of its aircraft in the more than 20,000 sorties it had flown by the end of October, with more than half of its bomber force destroyed. Eighty percent of the entire German Air Force was committed to action on the Eastern Front. Despite the German air superiority there, the Luftwaffe was unable to halt or slow the rapid growth of the Soviet Air Force to this point. The Soviets would soon outnumber the Germans in the air. Qualitatively, however, for now, the Soviet aircraft, training and tactics were still largely inferior to that of the Germans and they had sustained huge losses against the Germans, to the extent that they were restricted to night operations which were achieving relatively little.

But with November came ever increasing challenges for the German Air Force. The great Allied invasion in North Africa starting on the 8th suddenly required the withdrawal of several important units of Luftflotte 4 to combat the landings. The German Air Force was becoming badly overstretched across Europe and the Soviet Union. At the same time, the Soviets were starting to receive enormous shipments of Lend-Lease aid from the Americans— 230,000 tons of aviation gas, 450,000 tons of steel, 45,000 tons of explosives, 11,000 Jeeps, 60,000 trucks, and two million pairs of boots.

The winter cold set in in November, freezing the Volga and preventing further use of the river for the resupply of the Soviet defenders of Stalingrad. Finally, following three months of agonizingly slow advance, the Germans moved to the river banks and managed to take ninety percent of the the ruined city. The action shoved the Soviet defenders into two tight pockets of resistance. Still, they fought on as fiercely as before, within the factory complex area and on the sides of the Mamayev Kurgan hill, from the Dzerzhinskiy Tractor Factory, from the Barrikady gun factory, and from the Red October Steel Factory. The Soviets were well aware of the condition of many of the German troops in the treacherous winter that was building in intensity and severity daily. They knew that the Germans were poorly prepared to cope with extreme and unrelenting offensive operations in winter as they launched into an unprecedented winter campaign on 19 November, fielding fifteen armies on several fronts.

With the coming of the Russian winter and the Soviet winter offensive campaign, the exhausted, war-weary and ill-equipped Germans were stymied in Stalingrad, effectively halted by the unbelievably stubborn resistance of the Red Army defenders, together with the extreme weather.

Early in their new winter offensive, the Soviets identified and exploited a major weakness in the enemy force. Soviet generals Alexsander Vasilevsky and Georgy Zhukov, who were handling the strategic military planning for the Stalingrad battle, assembled huge army forces in the steppes areas north and south of the city. The generals were aware that the German northern flank was especially vulnerable as it was defended largely by Romanian and Hungarian units with inferior equipment, morale and leadership problems. The Soviet generals planned to crash through the weakly-defended German flank and encircle the German forces within Stalingrad. Soon, in that city, the Germans would experience one of their greatest defeats of the entire war.

Approximately 250,000 German and Axis soldiers were effectively surrounded in the city. The Soviet offensive ended the German hopes for taking Stalingrad. By the third week of January, the German forces in the city were starving and nearly out of ammunition, their resupply efforts having largely failed. In the belief, though, that any Germans who surrendered would be executed by the Soviets, most of the beleaguered German troops continued to resist. The Germans had few tanks left within the city and those that remained were only usable as pillboxes.

Generalfeldmarschall Friedrich von Paulus was in command of the German 6th Army's assault on Stalingrad as his forces were encircled and defeated in the massive Soviet counter-attack. The Soviets sent a small envoy to Paulus with an offer: If Paulus would surrender within twenty-four hours, the Soviets would guarantee the safety of all prisoners, medical care for the sick and wounded, normal food rations, and repatriation to any country after the war. Paulus had been ordered by Hitler not to surrender and he did not respond to the Soviet offer.

On 22 January Paulus requested that he be allowed to surrender in order to save the lives of his troops. Hitler denied the request, telegraphing the 6th

Army that it had "made an historic contribution to the greatest struggle in German history and that it should stand fast, to the last soldier and the last bullet." As no German Field Marshal had ever been taken prisoner, Hitler assumed that Paulus would either fight on or take his own life. As Soviet forces closed in on Paulus' headquarters in the ruined GUM department store building the next day, the German commander surrendered, and on 2 February the remains of the starving, demoralized Axis forces in Stalingrad surrendered.

Nearly 110,000 Germans became prisoners of the Soviets at Stalingrad. Of these, fewer than 6,000 ever returned. Of the others, the causes of death were many; wounds, cold, starvation, overwork, malnutrition, mistreatment, typhus and other diseases. Slightly less than 1,300,000 Red Army soldiers were casualties (killed, wounded, captured or missing) in the campaign for Stalingrad.

Today a massive monument, The Motherland Calls, overlooks the city of Stalingrad (now Volgograd). Other war memorials abound in the city including the heavily damaged remains of the buildings left just as they were at the end of the battle, as well as the old apartment building called Pavlov's House where a small group of Red Army soldiers held out for two months until they were finally relieved.

T-34

"The finest tank in the world."—Generalfeldmarschall Ewald von Kleist

The arsenal of armour in the Soviet Union by mid-1941 included more than 22,000 tanks—more tanks than in all the armies of the world combined; more than four times as many as the Germans had. But the majority of these tanks were obsolete and the supremely confident Germans knew it. What they apparently didn't know was that the Russians had designed, built and tested two new and considerably better tanks: the KV heavy and the T-34 medium. They also didn't know that a number of these new tanks were already operational and serving in front-line Soviet Army units. These new tanks were very good fighting weapons, well-designed, each mounting a big gun and protected with thick armour. They were good, but they were not miracle weapons, and they had their faults. They were both relatively simple, low-technology vehicles. Their crew habitability and visibility was on the poor side, and their rates of mechanical breakdown on the high side. But the T-34, for its faults, is now often referred to by tank experts and historians as possibly the best tank of the war.

Of the T-34, noted author / historian / tank expert Douglas Orgill wrote: ". . . the effectiveness of a weapon is directly equal to its ability to get itself properly into position to deal decisive blows without being harmed by the blows it is itself receiving." When the German invaders entered the Soviet Union in the summer of 1941, they would have been amazed by the T-34 tank then being fielded in large numbers by the Russians. Flushed with their successes in the Battle of France, they came into the Eastern Front expecting to roll over the opposition as they had already done with relative ease in the Low Countries, Poland, and France. Nazi doctrine had been working overtime to instill in them the notion of German superiority. Now, in the new T-34 weapon system, they were facing up to the fact that the Russians—a people they had been led to believe were Untermenschen, or subhuman, were capable of producing an armoured fighting vehicle more advanced in some ways, and more threatening than their own panzer tanks.

How did the Germans react to their experience of the T-34? Field Marshal Ewald von Kleist: ". . . it was the finest tank in the world." Major-General F. W. von Mellenthin: "We had nothing comparable . . ." And Colonel-General Heinz Guderian: "Very worrying . . . up to this time we had enjoyed tank superiority, but from now on the situation was reversed. The prospect of rapid, decisive victories was fading in consequence . . ."

Initially, the surprise attack by the Germans was quite effective. With all the great numerical superiority of the Russian tank force, only about twenty-five percent of their tanks were in good operating condition. The bulk of their operational armoured units was then being reformed; their service equipment and spare parts in short supply. And the majority of their officers and men were short on experience of driving and operating their tanks.

On the German side, there was disagreement about the approach to take with the Soviets. Guderian, Erich von Manstein and some of the other army leaders strongly advocated using powerful force to quickly destroy the Red Army as the chief obstacle to their achievement in the campaign. But Hitler and others in the German government believed it vital to begin by paralyzing the Russian government through the seizing of poilitical and economic objectives. Ultimately, Hitler agreed to the "destruction of the Red Army in western Russia by deep penetration of armoured spearheads."

The German forces began the operation with rapid panzer attacks which appeared to result in somewhat sluggish, though brave, and rather uncoordinated responses from the Soviet armoured units. The essential policy of the German armoured corps was, at all costs, to keep up their momentum and the pressure on the enemy force with speedy thrusts culminating in effective encirclements to seal off the other side in defeat. Manstein: "The farther a single Panzer corps ventured into the depths of the Russian hinterland, the greater the hazards became. Against this it may be said that the safety of a tank formation operating in the enemy's rear largely depends on its ability to keep moving. Once it comes to a halt it will immediately be assailed from all sides by the enemy's reserves."

At the start of the action the panzers rolled swiftly through the shocked Soviet tank and artillery units, doing great damage. Quite soon, though, the German tanks, which were apparently superior in quality and capability, were faced with the harsh reality of their dependency on the vital re-supply of fuel, munitions, and rations, their security and ability to keep fighting depending heavily on their preventing the enemy from interferring with the German supply routes. The other main fear was the weather; if heavy rain came the German supply trucks would wallow in the great sticky swamps of Russian mud.

In the earliest days of the campaign, the Germans had momentum and the priceless advantage of better organization. What they discovered almost immediately, however, in their early encounters with the heavy KV tank and then with the T-34 medium, was the genuine and terrible threat posed by the 76mm gun mounted in those vehicles. The big distinction between the panzers and those two Russian tanks was the ability of the KV and T-34 to lie back beyond 1,000 yards, shoot and penetrate the thickest German armour with those 76mm rounds, while the Germans had to close to within 200 yards before firing to kill a T-34 or KV.

In the beginning of the offensive, the Germans faced far fewer examples of the T-34 and KV tanks than the sort of numbers that they would soon be up against. They were able to destroy the Soviet armour with relative ease for a while, thanks to that limited number of opposing quality weapons, the better German training, organization, leadership, and, of course, the aerial reconnaissance which gave them ample early warning of likely Soviet attack, strength and positioning of the enemy forces. In those early days of the campaign, there was little indication of the enemy being able to compile the elements needed for successful opposition to the German onslaught. The enemy the Germans were up against then seemed greatly disadvantaged by incompetent leadership, inadequate training, and tank crews inept in handling their vehicles. The Soviet tanks seemed to be plagued with breakdowns, due at least partly to the way in which the tanks were handled. The Soviet tank crews then were exhibiting poor tactics, inconsistent shooting accuracy and, because it was still early days in the offensive, an insufficient supply of the formidable T-34 and KV tanks to make an appreciable difference on the battlefield. In the period beginning with the opening of the German offensive in the Soviet Union in June, through December 1941, the Soviets lost more than 15,000 tanks and one million men to the German invader.

Soon, however, the Germans were up against the reality of war with the Soviets. The losses they were experiencing were half again as great as they had been in their earlier campaigns in the west. Perhaps more significantly to the future of the offensive, Guderian and the other German panzer leaders were plagued with re-supply and repair problems, radically diminishing the level of success they had been accustomed to in their previous, spectacular blitzkrieg adventures. After the initial months at war in the USSR, the German panzers were being slowed dramatically by logistics, the mechanical realities, the actions of the enemy, and soon, by the arrival of the horrific winter months. With the coming of the cold, the effectiveness of the tanks of both sides was lessened considerably, resulting in greatly increased pressure on the infantry units to consolidate the gains of the tank units and to fight off enemy tank actions.

The German plan for Operation Barbarossa required that the southern-most sector of the Southern Front be under the watchful eyes of the Hungarian and Rumanian armies while the Army Group South, under the command of Field Marshal von Rundstedt, and led into battle by Kleist's panzer division attacked Kiev. Field Marshal von Bock's Army Group Cental, meanwhile, was meant to bring a primary attack aimed at Moscow, via Smolensk and Minsk, utilizing the two most powerful and effective panzer groups, those of Guderian and Hoth, and Field Marshal Leeb's Army Group North, including Hoepner's panzer group, was to attack and take Leningrad. Lesser emphasis appears to have been placed on the capture of the key Soviet industrial areas and the destruction of the Russian field armies, this despite the view of the German military command that by far the most important objective was the destruction of the Russian Army by the panzer groups.

top: Driver training aboard a British Mark III 'male' tank at Bovington Camp in 1917; above: A French '37' in firing position on a second-line trench, awaiting an enemy tank. All photographs from the collections of the author.

top: Production of the 28-ton Chrysler M-3 tank began in late 1940, employing up to 10,000 workers; above: Members of a Canadian armoured division and their M-3 American tanks in wartime training during 1942.

above: The skipper and gunner of an American Whippet tank northwest of Verdun, France, in 1918.

below: A Mark I male tank attacking at Thiepval on the Somme in September 1916; bottom: Mass production of British Valentine tanks in Montreal, Canada, 1942.

below: Chrysler-built Grant tanks and their crews on training manoeuvres in southern California early in the Second World War.

above: Generaloberst Heinz Guderian, considered the father of modern tank warfare and Germany's Panzer force, commanded the XIX Corps in the invasion of Poland, and was known as 'Fast Heinz' for his rapid, blitzkrieg advances through France and Belgium. He commanded Panzer Group 2 in Operation Barbarossa, the German invasion of the Soviet Union from June 1941; right: A German Panzer III tank in France during the 1940 invasion.

left: Generalfeldmarschall Erwin Rommel, known as 'The Desert Fox', was respected by his own men and the enemy; top: British Field Marshal Bernard Montgomery led the Eighth Army in North Africa from August 1942; A Panzer III afire in Egypt.

top: A Panzer III of Rommel's Afrika Korps in Libya; above: British soldiers rushing from a German Panzer III tank on which they have just placed an explosive charge.

above: A still from the 1967 war film *Tobruk* which starred Rock Hudson, Nigel Green, George Peppard, and Guy Stockwell.

top left: A Panzer crew in North Africa, 1942; left: German armoured and infantry forces in the Battle of Rostov, Operation Barbarossa, in autumn 1941; above: An 18-ton Skoda-built Hungarian Turan tank of the Second World War.

above: A British Valentine tank towing a disabled Mark IV cruiser tank in mud-recovery trials during the Second World War; top right: An American half-track driver attempts a shave in the field with assistance from South Korean children in August 1950; right: Long-serving M-4 Sherman tanks, referred to by the Germans as 'Tommy Cookers', seen here in U.S. Marine version, having lost their footing on icy roads in Korea, November 1950.

below: U.S. Marines crouching for cover behind an M-26 Pershing tank that is firing on enemy troops in the Korean War; bottom: One of the best main battle tanks in the world, the Israeli Merkava. Its uncoventional design provides good crew protection.

From the outset of Eastern Front activities, Hitler wanted and expected the prize of Moscow to be in hand by the end of October. With the autumn his already exhausted armoured units were expected and required to mount a new campaign aimed at taking the Russian capital. Guderian's armoured and infantry forces did pile up sizeable gains at Vyazma and between Sevsk and Bryansk, but then they became bogged down on the new front with the coming of the great rains. Road surfaces there had been poor and inadequate for tank operation to begin with, and with the heavy rains became virtual quagmires.

From the Soviet standpoint, General Georgy Zhukov, by far the most powerful and successful Russian commander of the entire war, was attempting to rebuild the crews and equipment of his armoured forces to make them into the sort of fighting force able to perform on the same level as that of the German adversary. In his favour, the seemingly endless rains created masses of thick, glue-like mud which increasingly prevented the Germans from advancing any closer than 150 miles from Moscow. These troubles for the Germans that came with the mud allowed Zhukov time and opportunity to fight a delaying action and reinforce his own armour units, both of which added appreciably to the problems of the Germans.

By this point, the creeping, rather ineffectual movements of the German forces displayed their loss of momentum and, when they finally came within sight of the capital, they simply could go no further.

J. Kugies was a panzer platoon leader and tank commander on the Russian Front in the Second World War: "At Tilsit in East Prussia I led a section of five tanks. In the lead tank we were only able to advance at about 12-14 km/h over the soft, marshy roads. Our riflemen marched ahead of us in a wide front to deal with any resistance that I could not break through. Just behind the Russian-Latvian frontier, we encountered Soviet soldiers. Our section had been ordered to halt, but, due to my defective wireless set, I did not receive the order in our tank and continued to drive on alone. The road soon became blocked by Soviet trucks and my driver had to take us through open terrain. He couldn't stop because of the marshy ground. The Russian truck convoy was escorted by many of their tanks and, before they could turn their turret toward me I began to fire on them. Their aiming was bad and I managed to shoot nine of them out of action. With their tanks burning, and the crews fleeing, I was then able to destroy an anti-tank battery and an artillery position. I crossed a bridge and then closed my hatch-cover to prevent any enemy shells from coming in. By this time my cannon ammunition supply was exhausted and I could only shoot with my machine-gun. We now stayed where we were, alone, for about thirty minutes until our following tanks reached us. After such a dangerous situation, we all had a sip of vodka which, unfortunately, was warm for having been under our gear. Later, we learned that the tanks behind us had stopped often, as ordered, on the marshy ground. They incurred many losses.

"While trying to aid a German infantry reconnaissance patrol which was fighting in a lost cause on 13 August 1941 at the Luga bridgehead, I was wounded. I was nearly out of ammunition and a Russian machine-gun was only five metres ahead of us. I ordered us forward to try and save the reconnaissance patrol. Standing in the hatch, I was pointing in the direction of the Russian machine-gun, which was now firing at us. I was shot three times through my right hand and forefinger and got a graze on the side of my head. My cap was torn to pieces but I was hardly bleeding. As I sank into the tank, I was fired on from a nearby house. I was hit in the right shoulder by splinters and my uniform jacket was torn up. My chief took me immediately to the doctor at a nearby field unit where my wounds were bandaged. I was then flown by Ju 52 aircraft to a field hospital near Dünaburg followed by a two-day train trip to a military hospital in Germany. I always remember hearing infantrymen say to us again and again: 'I wouldn't like to go in your deathboxes', and we always answered: 'And we don't like to walk.'"

Now the German tank commanders were within sight of Moscow and the weather was becoming substantially worse. The temperature was falling like a stone and a deep, unyielding freeze was setting in, paralyzing the battle-weary panzers. Their oil froze as did the grease in their guns, and the heavy, sticky mud froze and had to be chipped away with pickaxes.

As bad as the conditions were, for both sides in the conflict, the rather small but very effective T-34 and KV tank force of General Zhukov was out-performing Hitler's tanks in the appalling conditions to this point. While Zhukov lacked sufficient numbers of those excellent tanks to actually over-whelm the German opposition, he did have a large, highly-effective and effi-ciently positioned concentration of anti-tank obstacles which gave him an important capability in defending Moscow. This was proving to be the worst winter in 140 years, and as it continued, the German troops suffered horrif-ically in the bone-chilling cold. The sucking, clogging mud suppressed all movement, mechanical and human, to a bare minimum. In the punishing conditions, the Russians seemed both more fit and better able to contend with the brutal weather. The normally flawless standards of performance and serviceability of the German forces began to falter as the snows and bitter cold intensified.

The German armoured and infantry forces had entered Russia believing that they would simply fight a brief, efficient summer campaign to victory. They were utterly unprepared and ill-equipped for fighting and surviving in the extremes of winter in the region. They had brought summer-weight uni-forms. Their tanks and other vehicles were not properly winterized and were soon suffering frozen engine blocks. The men were suffering frostbite, trench

foot, shock, exposure, and exhaustion on a nearly unimaginable scale. Each
day the German units were achieving less; the initial successes virtually forgotten in their dismay. Worse, their commanders were quickly losing confidence in and respect for the directions coming to them from Berlin.

In spite of the suffering and problems they had to endure, the Germans
somehow were able to regroup and recover to the extent of effecting a partial
re-supply, repair, and re-organization. They had not recovered their initial
momentum, but were now able to repel most of the Russian penetrations they
were receiving, and to promptly hit back with short, rapid tank and infantry
assaults which, though they failed to gain them much, enabled them to retain
their positions. This reaction—action approach was to become their operating policy for most of the remaining campaign on the Russian Front.

As the offensive ground on, by early 1943 the German tank force in Russia
was in very bad shape. Their deteriorating morale, operational inefficien-
cies, confusion, and indecision at the command, supply and manufacturing
levels were rampant. For both the Russians and Germans, the efficient,
effective use of tanks was key to success in the offensive. Tanks provided the
ability to penetrate the enemy front line and bring vital support to one's overextended infantry, and they could powerfully defend against penetrations by
the enemy forces. The Germans were losing the battle to field, fight and
maintain tanks in this unrelenting, unforgiving situation. They were forced
to continue their reliance on the PzKpfw III and IV tanks, of which the III
was utterly outclassed by the Soviet T-34, a fact not lost on the panzer commanders in the field. When the commanders then prevailed upon the German
Ordnance Office to quickly design produce a copy of the T-34 for their use,
the designers instead went to work on an entirely new general purpose tank,
the forty-five ton Panther.

From its introduction in 1940, the T-34 was a tank with exceptionally
well-balanced attributes: mobility, protection, firepower, and ruggedness.
On the downside, it lacked good crew habitability characteristics, had a
scarcity of radios in the early production runs, and was limited by a two-man
turret capability, requiring the commander to aim and fire the gun (an
arrangement inferior to that of most German panzer tanks of the day). Still,
when the technicians at the Aberdeen Proving Ground in Maryland evaluat-
ed a T-34 that had been sent over by the Russians, they found it to have,
among other very positive aspects, the best optics of any tank they had
analysed there to date in 1942.

Over the course of its production, 84,070 T-34s were built between 1940
and 1958. Operated by a crew of four, the 26.5-ton tank mounted a 76mm
main gun and two 7.62mm machine-guns. Its twelve-cylinder diesel 500hp
engine powered it to a high speed of 33 mph and it had an operating range
of 250 miles.

Through the war years, the T-34 was gradually and continously refined to improve its capability and effectiveness and lower its manufacturing cost, which enabled the Russians to build it in greater numbers and deploy ever more on the battlefield. Its versatility, capability, and cost-effectiveness meant that it could replace many light and heavy tanks then in service. The tank was initially produced by the KhPZ factory of Kharkov, Ukraine, and was the standard tank of the Soviet armoured forces throughout the war. It was, by any measure, the most-produced tank of the Second World War and the second most-produced tank ever, after its successor, the T-54.

When the T-34 first came out, it was considered by many to be one of the best tank designs ever achieved. It boasted a range of impressive characteristics, from the greatly increased protection of its sloping armour, to its new V-2 diesel engine (much safer than previous and highly flammable petrol engine), to the Walter Christie suspension allowing it to roll fast over rough ground, and its wide tracks and low ground pressure for excellent mobility in snow and mud. True, it did have some reliability and manufacturing issues that would take a long time to resolve. But, overall, it certainly proved to be the right tank at the right time for the Russians.

The design of the T-34 began in 1937 when an assistant engineer, Mikhail Koshkin, was assigned by the Red Army to head a design team working on a replacement tank for the old BT model. In the course of the project, Koshkin was able to convince Joseph Stalin to leapfrog to the development of a newer tank design he had in mind, which would become the T-34. He called it T-34 after the year in which he first started planning the revolutionary design.

In the beginning, T-34s were produced at the Stalingrad Tractor Factory and, immediately after the German invasion started, production began at the Krasnoye Sormovo Factory in Gorky where major problems soon plagued the assembly process. Defective armour plating was discovered and a shortage of the new V-2 diesel engine was slowing the assembly line there. A critical shortage of the costly radios for the T-34 required that the sets be allocated to the tanks built for the company commanders only, thus all other tank commanders were required to signal to one another using flags. Problems with the main gun led to a new 76mm gun originating from the Grabin design bureau at Gorky, but no official production order was actually issued until after Russian troops used the weapon on the battlefield and praised it, after which the Stalin State Defense Committee gave official permission for its manufacture.

With the German invasion in June 1941, the Soviets froze further development of the T-34 and dedicated its assembly lines to full production of the tank at its current stage of evolution. As the German armies rapidly advanced into Soviet territory, their presence forced the evacuation of the major Russian tank factories to relocation sites in the Ural Mountains, a huge undertaking that had to be achieved in great haste. Main manufacturing facilites were quickly set up at Dzherzhinski Ural Railcar Factory in Nizhny Tagil, which was renamed the Stalin Ural Tank Factory. The Kirovsky Tank Factory and the Kharkov Diesel Factory were relocated to Chelyabinsk which was soon nicknamed 'Tankograd' and the Voroshilov Tank Factory of Leningrad was incorporated into a new Ural factory at Omsk. A number of small ancillary supply factories were absorbed into the Ordzhonikidze Ural Heavy Machine Tool Works in Sverdlovsk. By the end of this whirlwind set of relocations, some forty percent of all the T-34 production was occurring at the Stalingrad Tractor Factory, and during the heavy fighting in the Battle of Stalingrad of 1942, material and spares shortages developed causing critical manufacturing problems and resulting in some quality-control difficulties and in some tanks being rolled out and delivered to the battlefields unpainted. Even through the turmoil of battle in and around Stalingrad, however, full production was maintained through September 1942.

Throughout the inevitable shortages, disruptions, and difficulties of the lengthy combat periods of the German offensive in the east, the Soviets maintained a policy of no significant product changes on the assembly lines apart from measures to reduce and simplify production and the associated costs. Certain innovations did figure in the manufacturing process, including a plate-hardening procedure and the introduction of automated welding. The design of the 76mm main gun for the tank was refined to produce the weapon from 614 parts instead of the 861 previously required. And over the course of two years' manufacturing, the unit cost of the tank was reduced from 269,500 rubles to 135,000, and the actual production assembly time was reduced fifty percent by the end of 1942; this in spite of major changes to the workforce building the tanks. Roughly half the workers had been sent to fight on the battle front and they had been replaced by a mix of women, boys, older men, and invalids. The manufacturing fit-and-finish standard dropped some from what had previously been "beautifully crafted machines with excellent exterior finish, comparable or superior to those of Western Europe or America." Now the T-34 was more roughly finished, but its quality and reliability was not compromised in the process.

In addition to building up the Red Army's inventory of the tank and replacing battlefield losses, a prime goal was the improvement of tactical efficiency of the weapon. The main emphasis was put on quickly increasing the rate of production. A new, larger, more user-friendly turret was designed and added to the production line in 1942, along with the addition of a commander's cupola for 360 degree visibility. At the same time, the desirable rubber rims for the road wheels had to be sacrificed in favour of steel-rimmed road wheels due to rubber shortages in the Soviet Union. The engine and five-speed transmission were improved and a new clutch was added. By 1943, production of the T-34 had reached 1,300 a month and, like the Spitfire fighter to Britons, the T-34 had become iconic for the Russians, symbolizing the power and effectiveness of the Soviet counterattack against the Germans.

In its manufacture, particularly in the war years of 1942-1944, various innovations were gradually introduced to the design and the assembly process of the T-34. By 1944, the tank had evolved into the T-34-85 version, with a larger turret that mounted an 85mm gun. The new turret overcame the two-man limitation problem of the earlier T-34. Many of these tanks were also fitted with appliqué armour made from scrap steel of differing thicknesses and welded onto the hull and turret.

The soldiers of the German Army by this time had come full circle in their peception of the Russian tank. In the T-34-85 especially, they came to a collective recognition that they were dealing with technical superiority and a genuinely formidable weapon that they respected and feared. That respect was shared at a higher level in the person of Germany's most renowned tank leader, Heinz Guderian. So impressed was he by the qualities he saw in the T-34 that he ordered a special commission with representatives of the army ordnance office, the armaments ministry, the tank designers and manufacturers, to visit the front lines in Russia to examine, evaluate and study captured T-34s. Part of his reason was to determine what would be required in the high-priority design and manufacture of a new anti-tank gun capable of destroying the state-of-the-art Soviet tanks.

The then-planned improvements to the design / manufacture of the existing Mark III Panzer tank would, Guderian knew, achieve little towards making it comparable to the T-34, and the German tank designers and builders were greatly concerned about the challenge. The only possible quick solution was the Mark IV, which was also not equal to the Russian tank, but would be improved with a better gun over the course of the war. The aim of the Germans was, clearly, not just equality with the T-34, but a tank which would be reliably capable of destroying the Russian tank. The pressure on the German tank industry was significant and it responded by rushing a new design into production, the Mark VI, which had been tested with promising results. The big Mark VI weighing fifty-six tons, was armed with an 88mm gun. Its turret had 100mm armour on the front, which made it virtually invulnerable to the gun of the T-34 except when at close range. Its manufacture was hurriedly begun in July 1942. They called it the Tiger.

Basically, the Tiger was mainly a defensive weapon, an assault tank to be employed in support of infantry. In performance it did not compare particularly well with the T-34, having an open-country speed of just over twelve mph and a range of less than sixty-five miles. Its great size and weight would make it a handicap when it broke down—as it frequently did—for it would normally require another Tiger to tow it off for repairs. To the German commanders on the Eastern Front, and their tankers, the Tiger was not the anwer to the T-34. To the irritation of the German tank designers, the field commanders wanted them to essentially copy the T-34 and give the result better armour protection and a better gun. When their proposal reached those in authority for German tank production it was soon rejected, primarily because their industry was not then equipped for the rapid mass production of an aluminium tank engine like that of the Russian tank. That rejection led immediately to the start of design work on a new tank, the Mark V Panther, a weapon more like the T-34. The Panther weighed forty-five tons, had a road speed of twenty-eight mph and was designed with sloped and angled armour, like the Russian tank. It was armed with a high-velocity version of the 75mm L70 gun and had turret armour extended to 120mm in thickness. The Panther may well have been the best German tank of the war, but by spring 1943, when it was being introduced in German armoured units, like nearly all new weapon systems, it arrived with problems.

As good as the T-34 had proven itself to date, the Soviets were well aware that it had serious problems of its own which needed resolution. The chaos of having to relocate factory production of the entire Soviet tank industry to the Urals early in the Barbarossa campaign had meant the deferral of the more important changes planned for the T-34. The changes had to wait as they could not be allowed to interrupt the vital tempo of massive production. With the appearance of German tanks armed with a superior long 75mm gun on the battlefield in 1942, the Soviet Morozov design bureau started a priority project to develop an advanced T-43 tank, a weapon with greatly improved armour protection, a three-man turret, and torsion-bar suspension. Their goal was a relatively universal design intended to replace both the T-34 medium and the KV-1 heavy. It would be developed in direct competition with the KV-13 project, a Chelyabinsk heavy tank design.

By 1943 Soviet tank crews had gone up against the new German Tiger 1 and Panther tanks and believed that the 76.2mm gun of the T-34 was now inadequate. The Soviets had an existing 85mm anti-aircraft gun that could be adapted for tank use against the new German tanks. The armour of the new Soviet T-43, however, was found to be less effective than anticipated against the 88mm gun of the Tiger and, even before installation of the 85mm gun, the T-43's mobility was less than that of the T-34. These factors, together with the slowed production that would have resulted from a commitment to manufacturing the T-43, led to its cancellation. That decision then caused the Soviets to retool the production lines of the T-34 to upgrade the tank. The primary changes for the new model were an enlarged turret ring to accommodate a three-man turret with radio (prior to the upgrade the radio had been located within the hull) and the 85mm gun, a truly significant improvement. A quick adaptation of the T-43 turret design for the T-34 was made at the Krasnoye Sormovo Factory. This enabled the tank commander to command, with operation of the gun left to the gunner and the loader. A further addition to the T-34-85 was the Mark 4 observation periscope mounted on the turret roof (a copy of a British design), giving the tank commander a 360-degree viewing field.

When the Soviets decided to add these improvements to the T-34 to create the T-34-85, rather than retooling from scratch to build an entirely new tank, the saving in time enabled them to manufacture the new T-34-85 in huge numbers, thereby negating the qualitative differences between it and the Panther (which still had the edge, but an edge that was not seen as greatly significant). By May 1944, the Germans had produced only about 300 Panthers, against the Soviet T-34-85 production which had risen to 1,200 a month.

In comparison with the Panther, the 85mm gun of the T-34-85 could fire a 21.5 lb shot at a 2,600-foot-per-second muzzle velocity, while the Panther 75mm gun could fire a 15 lb shot, but at a much higher muzzle velocity of 3,068 feet-per-second. The overall weight of the T-34-85 rose from the twenty-seven tons of the T-34, to thirty-two tons, reducing its operating flexibility somewhat and its range from 280 miles to about 190. The top operating speed of both the T-34-85 and the Panther was virtually the same at about thirty mph. When full production of the T-34-85 began during the winter of 1943, it was generally believed that, while it was probably the best and most formidable tank then being produced and fielded by any Allied army, the Panther was, in fact, marginally better. Russian tank crews operating the T-34-85 on the front lines, however, when given the opportunity to evaluate and compare captured Panthers, preferred the Soviet tank, seeing it as an effective adversary for the newer German tanks, and it achieved that capability without its makers having to reduce the numbers or production rate of the tank. The Panther, by contrast, was rapidly gaining a reputation for its tendency to catch fire easily.

German tank production was much less numerous. With roughly 5,400 Panthers built by the end of 1944, and only 1,347 Tigers by the end of August that year, the Russians had a substantial production lead. With more than 9,000 Mark IVs alone built by war's end, clearly, the Mark IV, in its many upgunned variants remained the basis of German armoured forces throughout the war. The German tank manufacturing industry was never able to keep pace with the Russians.

In a new-found confidence and their pride of accomplishment in creating and fielding the Tiger and Panther tanks, the German High Command requested in early 1943 that all tank production be halted, except for that of the Tiger and Panther, in order for the industry to focus entirely on those two machines. Guderian: "This new plan contained only one major weakness: with the abandonment of the Mark IV, Germany would until further notice be limited to the production of twenty-five Tigers a month. This would certainly have led to the defeat of the German Army in the very near future . . . the Russians would have won the war even without the help of their Western allies. No power on earth could have stopped them." As it happened, Hitler then appointed Guderian to be Inspector General of Armoured Troops, giving him the responsibility for organizing and training the panzer forces, and Guderian immediately set out to build up the quality and quantity of the panzers.

The T-34-76 had proven a tremendous challenge to destroy on the battlefield in 1941. The conventional anti-tank equipment of the Germans was simply not up to the task. The Soviets deployed a considerable number of the medium T-34s in five of their twenty-nine mechanized divisions at that time, along with the heavy KV tanks.

It must be recognized too, that the T-34 in those early days of the war was a very considerable challenge for its crews, who, when deployed on a lengthy road march, tended to lose many of their number to mechanical breakdown, an early problem that plagued the Soviets to a greater extent than it did the Germans. And the upside of the T-34 was diluted to some extent for the crews by its internal layout, poor crew comfort and vision devices.

Testing of the T-34 at the Aberdeen, Maryland, proving ground by the Americans resulted in their unconditional rejection of the Christie suspension system for tanks. The Russian tank utilized this coil-spring system, designed by the American engineer Walter Christie, which enabled considerably longer movement than conventional leaf springs systems and greater cross-country speed. The Christie system employed large, rubber-rimmed road wheels which, when less rubber was available due to wartime shortages, meant a reduced amount of rubber on the wheels. The contact with the tracks at high speeds set up noisy, unpleasant harmonics for the crews. The harmonics could also damage the tank by loosening parts. Certain deficiencies in the tracks resulted from the lightness of their construction. They were subject to damage by small-calibre weapons and mortar rounds. Basically, the pins used were made of poor quality steel and were poorly tempered, causing them to wear out quickly and the tracks to break. Russian crews often brought spare parts and tracks with them into combat situations. One Russian tanker recalled: "The caterpillars used to break apart even without bullet or shell hits. When earth got stuck between the road wheels, the caterpillar, especially during a turn—strained to such an extent that the pins themselves couldn't hold out."

Other conclusions from the Aberdeen evaluation were: In their tank production, the Russians were apparently not very interested in careful machining or finishing, or the technology of small parts and components, a negative aspect of what is otherwise a well-designed tank. In comparison to the then-current American tanks, it was found that the Russian tank had many good features, good contours in the design, diesel power, good and reliable armament, thick armour, wide tracks and more. But it was thought inferior to the

American tank in manoeuvring, speed, ease of driving, firing muzzle velocity, mechanical reliability, and ease of maintenance. The Aberdeen technicians found many problems with improper radio installations and shielding
in the 1941 T-34. Commenting on the turret design: "The main weakness of
the two-man turret of the T-34 of 1941 is that it is very tight. The electrical
mechanism for rotating the turret is very bad. The motor is weak, very overloaded and sparks horribly, as a result of which the device regulating the
speed of the rotation burns out, and the teeth of the cogwheels break into
pieces. We recommend replacing it with a hydraulic or a simple manual system."

The uneven build-quality is called into question when considering the
armour of the T-34, in particular on the plating joins and welds. The use of
too-soft steel and the shallow surface tempering was also noted by the
Aberdeen technical personnel. They noted too, that the various chinks and
cracks resulting from relatively careless build-quality tends to admit a lot of
water when it rains, which can disable the electrical system and negatively
affect the ammunition.

What was operating the T-34 like for the crewmen? The driver sat either on
a hard bench seat or on shell storage containers, an arrangement that
adversely affected his operation of the tank due to the frequently severe
vibration and shocks in combat situations over rough terrain for extended
periods. Other negative aspects included poorly made transmissions that
were prone to mechanical failure and whose operation could be nightmarish-
ly difficult. The Russians' use of low-quality, poorly finished steel side
clutches further contributed to the breakdown rate of the tank. But the main
complaint of those who had to take the T-34 into battle was the low-set, very
cramped two-man turret. It could only accommodate the commander and the
loader, thus making the job of the commander far more labour-intensive and
distracting him from his primary role. A further restriction imposed by the
design meant that the turret gun could not be depressed more than three
degrees, creating a shooting problem at close range or on a reverse slope.

Another somewhat disfunctional arrangement in the T-34 was that of the
ammunition storage for the main gun, making the job of the loader more difficult and less efficient than it should have been. The turret lacked a rotating floor that would move as a part of the turret when the turret was rotated.
The small spare ammunition boxes were stowed on the floor under the turret
and covered with a rubber mat. Nine rounds of ammunition were stowed on
the sides of the fighting compartment and when these rounds had been used,
the loader and / or commander had to pull up more ammunition from the floor
boxes. The floor was then left littered with open boxes and and rubber mat-
ting, impairing the crew performance.

For the tank commander of the T-34, his vision of the field and his situational awareness was disadvantaged by the forward-opening hatch and the lack of a turret cupola, requiring him to view the field of battle through a small vision slit and a traversable periscope. This method was inferior to the German tank method where the commander fought in a heads-up position with his seat raised, giving him a full field of view, something not possible in the T-34. Russian crews took a dim view of the turret design with its heavy hatch that was difficult to open and, should it jam, would trap the crew inside. Their objections to this situation led to the manufacturer changing to a two-hatch turret in August 1942. In the matter of gun-sighting and ranging, the system of the T-34 was comparatively crude in relation to that of the Germans, which was particularly disadvantageous to the Russian crews when operating at longer ranges. One German commented on the combination of T-34 fighting characteristics, including the two-man turret, poor vision devices and weak optics: "T-34s operated in a disorganized fashion with little coordination, or else tended to clump together like a hen with its chicks. Individual tank commanders lacked situational awareness due to the poor provision of vision devices and the preoccupation with gunnery duties. A tank platoon would seldom be capable of engaging three separate targets, but would tend to focus on a single target selected by the platoon leader. As a result T-34 platoons lost the greater firepower of three independently operating tanks." German tankers generally felt that T-34 crews were slower in locating and engaging their targets, while Panzers normally were able to shoot about three rounds for every round fired by the T-34.

Another impression of the early T-34s in a battlefield environment was that of the difficulties involved in arranging for repairs due to a crippling shortage of recovery vehicles and repair equipment. The impact of the Soviet tank on the enemy forces initially was one of poor Russian leadership, tactics, and crew training, which many attributed to the effects of Stalin's purges of his officer corps in the 1930s, together with heavy losses by the Red Army in 1941 that took the lives of some of their best armoured personnel.

In the combat arena, by 1942 the T-34-76 was the Soviet main battle tank in the field. The key German tanks to that point were the Panzer III and the Panzer IV. By mid-year, the improving German tank armament had evolved to the extent of making the T-34 vulnerable to it and T-34 losses in that year were substantial, much worse than in the previous year. Of a total of 15,100 armoured fighting vehicles in the Red Army front line, 6,600 T-34s were lost to combat or mechanical problems. But through the difficult winter of 1941-42, the wide-tracked T-34 proved superior to the German tanks in being able to manoeuvre over deep mud and snow without bogging down; conditions in which the German tanks frequently were halted.

Into 1943, armoured battlefield momentum was with the Soviets. Soviet AFV losses were higher than ever, including those of 14,700 T-34s, but so was their tank production. And strategically, the Germans were mainly on the defensive and in retreat. Throughout 1943 and well into 1944, for the most part the T-34 with its 76mm gun was outclassed by the guns of both the Tiger and Panther, and even with the upgrade of the 85mm gun, the T-34-85 was really not the equal of those two German tanks, though the Soviet 85mm gun could penetrate the armour of both German tanks at distances up to 550 yards; the Tiger and Panther could still destroy the T-34-85 at 1,600 yards or more.

In the beginning of Barbarossa, the T-34 made up only about four percent of the Soviet armoured forces, but at war's end it made up at least fifty-five percent. With the gradual progression of the Eastern Front campaign, the original design advantages the T-34 held over the German tanks were gradually overcome and the Russian tank became an ever easier target for the German tankers. Still, over the course of the war, and the greatly increasing manufacture of the T-34 (even with the increasing weight resulting from the many improvements made to it), its top speed held up, while both its turret frontal armour thickness and its main gun armour penetration nearly doubled.

While it cannot reasonably be claimed that the T-34 was the equal of the Panther or Tiger tanks of the Germans, its design simplicity, wide tracks, low silhouette, innovative armour layout, its ease and quantity of production—despite its faults and heavy losses—made it a strategic war winner. In all, 55,550 T-34s were produced during the war years. Of the 96,500 fully-tracked armoured fighting vehicles produced during the war by the Soviets, 44,900 T-34s were lost to combat and other causes.

Following the end of the Second World War, various client-states of the Soviets operated the T-34-85 in their armoured arsenals. When the North Koreans invaded South Korea in June 1950, the spearhead of their assault force was comprised of 120 T-34-85s and were joined later in the incursion by additional T-34s. In the early going, the American M24 Chaffee light tanks in opposition were hopelessly outclassed by the Soviet tank. By August, however, the United Nations forces opposing the North Koreans there were equipped with the M26 Pershing medium / heavy tank, the M4 Sherman, and the British Centurion, Churchill and Cromwell tanks, all of which inflicted major losses on the North Koreans. In September, the American landings at Inchon led to the U.S. troops cutting off North Korea's supply lines, leading to the end of fuel, ammunition and other supplies and the retreat of the North Koreans who had to abandon many of their T-34s. The Chinese entered the conflict on the North Korean side in February 1951 bringing four tank regiments, mostly equipped with T-34-85s, but relatively few tank-to-tank battles occurred throughout the war. In such actions as did occur, ninety-seven T-34-85s were knocked out in engagements with American M26s and M46

Patton tanks. The Patton was a definite overmatch with the T-34, its 90mm high-velocity armour-piercing round able to penetrate all the way through the T-34 from front to rear.

THE DESERT FOX

The news of Field Marshal Sir Bernard Montgomery having invited his prisoner of war, General Wilhelm von Thoma, Field Commander of the Afrika Korps, to dine with him in his General Headquarters trailer in North Africa shocked and infuriated many Britons. But Prime Minister Winston Churchill reacted: "I sympathize with General Thoma. Defeated, humiliated, in captivity, and . . . dinner with Montgomery."

Erwin Rommel came from Heidenheim, Germany, in thepleasant kingdom of Württemberg. He was born on 15 November 1891, the second child of the Protestant headmaster of a secondary school at Aalen. It was his father's wish that the boy have a military career and in 1910 Rommel attended the Officer Cadet School at Danzig, graduating in November 1911. He was commissioned a lieutnant in January 1912. While a cadet, he met his future wife, Lucia Mollin and they were married in November 1916. Two years later their son Manfred was born.

Young Rommel fought in France and was a member of the Württemberg Mountain Battalion of the Alpenkorps in the First World War. He served with distinction, was wounded three times, and received the awards of the Iron Cross, First and Second Class, as well as the order of the Pour le Mérite. In 1937, his book, *Infanterie greift an* (Infantry Attacks) was published and impressed German Chancellor Adolf Hitler who put Rommel in charge of War Ministry liaison with the Hitler Jugend (Hitler Youth).

In a previous chapter, *The Battle for France*, references are made to Rommel's command of a panzer division during the German invasion of France. He had requested that Hitler give him such a command and when that request was granted, it sparked a reaction in some other army officers who resented it due to Rommel's lack of experience in armoured command. But Rommel had been inspired by the effective use of German armoured forces in the Polish campaign and began educating himself with enthusiasm and intensity about the advanced uses of mobile infantry and armoured warfare techniques, with enthusiasm and intensity. Giving him that command proved to be sound. His division, the 7th Panzer, would become so adept at the application of the blitzkrieg method that it was referred to as the "Ghost Division" due to the speed of its advances and its rapid attacks. They were often so far ahead of the rest of the German army that they were out of communication with it. While he was mindful of the risks to his flanks, Rommel rarely hesitated to drive forward at a staggering pace. He believed that the shock to the enemy by his rapid advances served to neutralize the enemy attacks to his flanks as the 7th rolled over the French countryside. When he did run into enemy resistance, he would counter by increasing the pace of his tanks and ordering them to advance with all guns firing. Frequently his technique not only quashed the enemy attack but brought on their surrender. Amazingly, his approach in such situations served to equalize the fact that the heavier tanks of the enemy forces had better armour and higher-calibre guns than those of the Germans, yet they often lost in such encounters, terrorized and giving up without really exploiting the advantage they held. Rommel's method also served to help the division eliminate the possibility of prolonged fights which could impede his progress and subject his forces to greater casualties.

Rommel captured Cambrai on 18 May 1940, but was halted by a resupply problem resulting in a lack of fuel for his tanks and other vehicles. Not having received radio reports from Rommel, his chief of staff, who was then in Belgium with an unmotorized element of the division, had decided that Rommel's group had been lost in combat and he had not arranged for the fuel to be dispatched to the commander. The problem was soon overcome and on the 20th Rommel's force rolled on to Arras where his aim was to cut off the British Expeditionary Force from the coast. As units of the 7th with the support of Stuka dive-bombers, forced their way across the canals near the town, the enemy launched a counter-attack on 21 May. In this, the Battle of Arras, the Germans were up against British Matilda tanks which were unphased by the 37mm guns of the panzers. Rommel's answer was to have some 88mm guns brought up, whereupon he personally directed their fire. It was following the Arras engagement that Rommel was ordered to hold his position and take a few days rest, something his force sorely needed at that point. In that period the British launched Operation Dynamo to evacuate the BEF and French troops from Dunkirk.

On 27 May Rommel rushed on to Lille and, to the increasing ire of his fellow armoured officers, Rommel was awarded the Knight's Cross of the Iron Cross. They further resented what they perceived as Rommel's close relationship with Adolf Hitler and the preferential treatment they thought he was getting. Though under intense fire from the French artillery at Lille, Rommel persevered, capturing the city and keeping half the French army there from retreating to Dunkirk. The 7th Panzer Division reached the French coast on 10 June.

By the 16th, the 7th Panzer Division had captured Cherbourg and then rolled on towards Bordeaux. With the signing of the armistice with the French on the 21st, however, Rommel's forces were redirected to the Paris area to prepare for Operation Sea Lion, the invasion of Britain. The operation was called off a few months later when it was clear that Goering's Luftwaffe was not going to achieve air superiority over the R.A.F.

For his French campaign efforts, Rommel had been the subject of considerable praise and considerable criticism. Generaloberst Hermann Hoth, who would later command the 3rd and 4th Panzer Divisions in Operation Barbarossa, had public praise for Rommel's achievements, but privately he said that Rommel should not be given command of a corps unless he "gained greater experience and a better sense of judgement." He also thought Rommel unwilling to acknowledge the contributions of others to his victories, a statement echoed by Generalfeldmarschall Günther von Kluge, who would command the German 4th Army and Army Group Centre, and claimed that Rommel both misrepresented the advances of his neighbouring units to his own advantage, and failed to give proper credit to the Luftwaffe for its contribution to his successes. Hitler, though, still thought highly of Rommel, rewarding him well for all his achievements in France with a promotion to Generalleutnant and the appointment to command what would become the *Afrika Korps*, which was sent to Libya in 1941 to help the troops of Germany's ally Italy, following their severe loss to British Commonwealth forces there under the command of General Richard O'Connor in the December 1940 Operation Compass.

Rommel was put on the defensive by German High Command, ordered to simply hold the front line until the start of a limited offensive they were planning against Benghazi and Agedabia for May. At that point Rommel argued that Cyrenaica would have to be captured in its entirety in order to hold the front lines against the enemy. The little Libyan territory remaining to the Italians after the defeat by O'Connor seemed in itself nearly impossible to hold in the face of the losses that had been inflicted on the Italians— 130,000 troops captured and nearly 400 tanks lost.

The *Afrika Korps* had been established as a kind of stopgap organization to aid Germany's Italian Fascist allies in North Africa, but shortly developed into what was then perceived as possibly the most formidable land warfare units of all time. Many historians have credited the innovative Rommel's tactics and clever application of psychological warfare techniques with much of that reputation. Such a high-achiever was he in the early North African campaign that he was soon being called "the Desert Fox" by friends and foe alike.

Pending the opening of the Benghazi-Agedabia offensive in the spring, Rommel launched a small offensive utilizing the 5th Light Division and the support of two Italian divisions. He anticipated taking command of the 15th Panzer Division in time for the planned May offensive. He was now going up against a partially depleted British army force as many in their ranks had been withdrawn to fight in Greece. The British had to retreat to Mersa el Brega where they began building defensive positions. To take full advantage of the situation and hamper that enemy effort, Rommel pressed his attacks on the new defences. After achieving success at Mersa el Brega, he decided against delaying until May for the action against Agedabia.

Meanwhile, General Archibald Wavell, Commander-in-Chief, Middle East Command, was determined not to be cut off by Rommel's new advance. He tended to overestimate the actual strength of the German's forces and in early April ordered the British troops to withdraw from Benghazi. That act led Rommel to believe that the British were either unwilling or unable, or both, to fight such a decisive action then. He now brashly determined to take his admittedly light forces and seize all of Cyrenaica.

To that end he sent his Italian Ariete armoured division after the retreating British force while ordering his 5th Light Division, under the command of Generalmajor Johannes Streich, on to Benghazi. Streich argued against the order saying that his vehicles were no longer in condition for such an operation, but Rommel brushed aside the objection, "One cannot permit unique opportunities to slip by for the sake of trifles."

General Italo Gariboldi, the Italian Commander-in-Chief, was also trying to stop Rommel's rapid advance, but could not contact him. The Italian GHQ protested vehemently against Rommel's disregard of his orders, and concurrently, Rommel received an order from the German High Command not to advance beyond Maradah. He ignored that order, as well as a number of complaints and protests from some of his own staff and divisional commanders. His imagination was captivated by what he saw as a real opportunity to destroy much or all of the Allied forces in North Africa and go on to capture Egypt. To do it he needed to increase the pressure on the retreating British by starting an outflanking offensive against the vital port of Tobruk. In so doing, he captured the Military Governor of Cyrenaica, Lieutenant-General Philip Neame, along with General Richard O'Connor, who was then an advisor to Neame.

Rommel's Italian force was actively engaged along the coast and he elected to use his 5th Light Division in a power sweep south to attack the harbour from the southeast, in the hope of trapping much of the British force there. Supply and logistical problems, however, doomed his plan to failure. But the Germans completed the encirclement of Tobruk by 11 April and began attacking. By the 15th, they had secured Libya.

There were 25,000 Allied troops, including the garrison with the Australian 9th Division under the command of Lieutenant-General Leslie Morshead, defending the port city of Tobruk when Rommel began a series of small attacks on it. The Italians had built the pre-war port facilities and he looked to them to provide him with the blueprints for the fortifications— which they failed to do—to his disappointment. Actually, his forces had advanced so quickly and so far beyond their agreed stopping point, that the Italians had not had time to produce the plans.

From *The Rommel Papers*, edited by B.H. Liddell Hart: "The Brescia Division, which had meanwhile taken over the western front of Tobruk, opened the attack in the afternoon. The 5th Light Division was not too happy about its orders for the attack and raised a number of objections which I had to brush aside. It was a day of driving sand and there was no need to concern ourselves about aimed British artillery fire. The 5th Light Division's attack finally got under way at about 16.30 hours. I drove north in my Mammoth behind the tanks. Enemy artillery scattered shells over the area as the tanks approached, but caused few casualties. The 5th Panzer Regiment halted when they arrived at the break-in point and, of course, came under heavy artillery fire. Finally, the tanks were brought to a standstill in front of an anti-tank ditch, which we were not then in a position to blow in. Tobruk's defences stretched much farther in all directions, west, east and south, than we had imagined. We had still not been able to get hold of any of the plans of the defences, which were held by the Italians.

"After the failure of this attack, I decided to renew the attempt a few days later when more artillery and the Ariete had arrived. In no circumstances was the enemy to be allowed time to complete the organisation of his defence."

Now Rommel was so intent on securing Tobruk that he tended to ignore the critical responses of his subordinate officers to his continuing strategy. As those relationships were deteriorating he started a series of courts-martial (though, in fact, he signed few of the verdicts.) In the wake of this, the chief of the German Army, Walther von Brauchitsch, wrote to Rommel to suggest that "instead of making threats and requesting the replacement of officers who, hitherto, had excelled in battle, rather . . . a calm and constructive debate might bring better results." The letter made no impression on Rommel.

Rommel's relationship with the German High Command Chief of Staff Franz Halder, never a warm one, soured further when he requested of Halder reinforcements to sustain a renewed attack on Tobruk. Rommel was refused on the grounds that the High Command was then involved in preparations for Operation Barbarossa and had no forces to spare. Halder, never a fan of Rommel, is said to have remarked of him: "Now at last he is constrained to state that his forces are not sufficiently strong to allow him to take full advantage of the 'unique opportunities' offered by the overall situation. That is the impression we have had for quite some time over here." Halder's anger with Rommel led him to send Generalmajor Friedrich von Paulus out to North Africa to "head off this soldier gone stark mad."

When Paulus arrived on 27 April, Rommel convinced him to approve another Tobruk attack, to which Halder responded, "In my view it is a mistake," but he deferred to Paulus on the decision. When Rommel launched the attack on 4 May, it did not go well and appeared to be failing as Paulus ordered a halt to it. Paulus now ordered Rommel not to commit any forces or mount any new attacks on Tobruk. No new assault was to be launched without specific High Command approval. Now it was Rommel who was angry, but he agreed to at least defer any further attacks, at least until the detailed

Italian plans for the Tobruk port fortifications could be produced, the 15th Panzer Division could be brought in to participate in the offensive, and his current troops could be given more training.

While deferring attacks on Tobruk, Rommel used the delay to construct defensive positions in the area and secure the strategic Halfaya Pass. His Italian infantry units consolidated the positions they held at the Solum-Sidi Omar line and Bardia, and motorized German and Italian units were in reserve pending any British attacks out of Egypt. But the British continued to believe that Rommel possessed greater strength in men and equipment than he actually possessed and the British Lieutenant-General Sir Leslie Morshead declined to launch any major action against the Germans. Had he then assaulted Rommel's forces in an effort to get to El Adam, his troops might well have cut the German supply and communications lines at Bardia, Sollum and Halfaya covering the Egyptian frontier.

In February, British General Archibald Wavell, who had previously mounted successful operations against Axis forces in Libya, Ethiopia, and Eritrea, had been ordered to halt his moves into Libya and divert many of his troops to Greece to contend with new German and Italian operations there. Wavell opposed the sending of part of his forces there, but obeyed the order, resulting in the Germans being allowed time and opportunity to reinforce the Italians in North Africa with the *Afrika Korps*. By late April Rommel's forces had shoved the British Western Desert Force right back to the Egyptian border, and Tobruk was left under a siege that would last 240 days.

There were two failed efforts by General Wavell in mid-May and mid-June—Operations Brevity and Battleaxe—to relieve the pressure on Tobruk, but in both cases the Germans readily put them down. Both of these British operations were too quickly mounted due to heavy pressure from Prime Minister Churchill for action. The Halfaya Pass was briefly recaptured and then lost again on 27 May by the British forces during Operation Brevity. Wavell was having doubts about Battleaxe, as stated in his report of the 28th: "Our infantry tanks are really too slow for a battle in the desert, and have been suffering considerable casualties from the fire of the powerful enemy anti-tank guns. Our cruisers have little advantage in power or speed over German medium tanks." And in the four-day armoured battle of Operation Battleaxe on the flanks of Halfaya and Sollum passes, the British lost eighty-seven tanks for a German loss of twenty-five. British forces could not take the passes from Rommel's heavily-fortified forces. Rommel was appointed commander of Panzer Group Africa, which incorporated his former *Afrika Korps* (the 15th Panzer Division and the 5th Light Division, now redesignated the 21st Panzer Division) under the direct command of Generalleutnant Ludwig Crüwell, with Generalleutnant Fritz Bayerlein as the chief of staff. Rommel's Africa command also included the German 90th Light Division, six Italian divisions, the Italian XX Motorized Corps comprised of the Trieste and Ariete Divisions, and four infantry divisions at Bardia and Tobruk.

The events in Greece were going from bad to worse for the British forces there, which were not able to defend the mainland and had to evacuate to Crete. They experienced 15,000 casualties and the loss of most of their artillery and heavy equipment. The actions in Greece then inspired pro-German and pro-Italian factions in Iraq to overthrow the government there. Wavell's forces were being stretched on various fronts and he could not divert any to Iraq, which Churchill thought vital to Britain's strategic interests. By early May, heavy pressure from Churchill forced Wavell to send a division over the desert from Palestine to relieve the British air base at Habbaniya, leading to a much more successful outcome for the British. But Churchill was not pleased by Wavell's prior reluctance to move against the German enemy, and on 20 June, Churchill relieved Field Marshal Wavell, replacing him with General Claude Auckinleck, who was at that time the Commander-in-Chief, India, and who promptly reorganized and enhanced the Allied forces in North Africa into the XXX and XIII corps which then became the British Eighth Army under the command of General Alan Cunningham.

Sunday, 23 November, was the German Day of Remembrance for those who died in the First World War. The orders of the day called for the destruction of the British main striking force by a concentric attack of all German-Italian mobile forces. General der Panzertruppe Ludwig Crüwell, lacking Rommel's direct verbal orders, decided to act on his own initiative and left his headquarters in the early morning to personally lead his forces in what the Germans would later refer to as the Battle of Totensonntag (Memorial Sunday). From *The Rommel Papers*: "The enemy armour was thought to be lying on the extensive desert plateau of Sidi Muftah and Bir el Haiad, divided up into several combat groups.

"General Crüwell's plan was to attack the enemy in the rear, but he first intended to join up with the Ariete, who were moving up from Bir el Gobi, in order to bring all the available armour to bear in one united effort. At about 07.30 hours, the 15th Panzer Division moved to the south-west where they discovered and immediately attacked a strong force of enemy armour round Sidi Muftah. Violent tank fighting developed. More enemy groups with vast vehicle parks, numerous tanks and guns were discovered north of Hagfed el Haiad and General Crüwell accordingly embarked on an even wider outflanking movement. By the early afternoon, after continuous fighting, he reached a point south-east of Hagfed el Haiad, deep in the enemy's rear.

"The Ariete's assault spearheads had meanwhile arrived with 120 tanks and General Crüwell now launched the combined German and Italian armoured forces northwards into the enemy's rear, with the object of bottling him up completely and forcing him back against the 21st Panzer Division's front at Sidi Rezegh.

"The attack started well, but soon came up against a wide artillery and anti-tank gun screen, which the South Africans had formed at a surprising speed between Haiad and Muftah. Guns of all kinds and sizes laid a curtain of fire in front of the attacking tanks and there seemed almost no hope of making any progress in the face of this fire-spewing barrier. Tank after tank split open in the hail of shells. Our entire artillery had to be thrown in to silence the enemy guns one by one. However, by the late afternoon we had managed to punch a few holes in the front. The tank attack moved forward again and tank duels of tremendous intensity developed deep in the battle-field. In fluctuating fighting, tank against tank, tank against gun or anti-tank nest, sometimes in frontal, sometimes in flanking assault, using every trick of mobile warfare and tank tactics, the enemy was finally forced back into a confined area. With no relief forthcoming from a Tobruk sortie, he now saw his only escape from complete destruction in a break-out from the ring surrounding him.

"At one moment during this confused battle, the *Afrika Korps*' Mammoth containing General Crüwell and his staff, was suddenly ringed round by British tanks. The German crosses on the sides of the vehicle, which had been originally captured from the British, were not easy to identify. The hatches were shut. The British tankmen, who had fortunately fired off all their ammunition, had no idea whom they had met. A number of them left their Mark VI, walked across to the Mammoth and knocked on the armour plate, whereupon General Crüwell opened the hatch and found himself looking into the face of a British soldier, to the great astonishment of both. At that moment gunfire started to spray into the neighbourhood. The occupants of the Mammoth threw themselves on the thin wooden flooring, but the vehicle escaped undamaged. A German 20mm anti-aircraft gun had opened fire on the dismounted British tank crews, who promptly jumped back into their tanks and disappeared as fast as they could to the south, thus releasing the staff of the *Afrika Korps* from a highly precarious situation.

"The wide plain south of Sidi Rezegh was now a sea of dust, haze and smoke. Visibility was poor and many British tanks and guns were able to break away to the south and east without being caught. But a great part of the enemy force still remained inside. Twilight came, but the battle was still not over. Hundreds of burning vehicles, tanks and guns lit up the field of that Totensonntag. It was long after midnight before we could get any sort of picture of the day's events, organise our force, count our losses and gains and form an appreciation of the general situation upon which the next day's operations would depend. The most important results of this battle were the elimination of the direct threat to the Tobruk front, the destruction of a large part of the enemy armour and the damage to enemy morale caused by the complete ruin of his plans."

With the support of nearly 800 tanks and 1,000 aircraft, Auckinleck began Operation Crusader on 18 November 1941, a major offensive for Tobruk. He faced two Rommel armoured divisions, the 15th and 21st with 260 tanks, the 90th Light Infantry Division, three Italian corps, five infantry and one armoured division with 154 tanks. The British attack, however, did not go according to plan. Their armour was overwhelmed by enemy tank and anti-tank resistance. British armoured thrusts in the next two days were largely ineffective and, on 23 November, Rommel sent his powerful, though numerically inferior, armoured force against the British in a concentrated effort. The 21st Panzer Division retained their Sidi Rezegh positions, and the tanks of the 15th Panzers and the Ariete Division struck at the flanks of the British armoured forces in one of the largest tank battles of the entire North African campaign. The German and Italian tanks surrounded the British armoured force, destroying nearly two-thirds of it. The remaining British tanks managed to fight their way from the trap and head off south to Gabr Saleh.

Finding himself and his staff behind the Allied lines a number of times during the confusion in Auckinleck's Operation Crusader offensive, on one occasion Rommel came upon a New Zealand Army field hospital still under Allied control. Rommel asked a doctor there if anything was needed there in the way of supplies. The visit over, the German and his staff drove off. Later, he arranged for the delivery of various medical supplies and equipment to the little hospital.

Looking to exploit the misfortune of the British enemy, Rommel then launched a counterattack on the British rear areas in Egypt, hoping to take advantage of chaos and confusion there to cut the enemy supply lines. He launched the attack in the belief that the enemy forces would be likely to abandon their border defences under the threat of the German force to their rear. And, as Rommel had anticipated, General Cunningham did indeed elect to withdraw the British Eighth Army into Egypt, but before he could do so, Auckinleck, who had been away in Cairo, returned to intervene, cancelling the withdrawal.

In the operation, with only 100 tanks remaining to him, Rommel's force was halted when it outran its supply line and into growing enemy resistance. The operation then brought down a storm of criticism on Rommel, from German High Command and several of his staff officers, all of whom thought the attack unwise and wasteful in light of the considerably reduced German tank force now available to him. Generalmajor Friedrich von Mellenthin: "Unfortunately, Rommel overestimated his success and believed the moment had come to launch a general pursuit." In fact, the attack by Rommel would probably have been successful had Auckinleck not arrived in time to cancel the British withdrawal.

And as Rommel took his limited force into Egypt, his Chief of Staff, Oberstleutnant Siegfried Westfal, who had for several days been trying without success to contact his commander, had withdrawn the 21st Panzer Division to use it in support of the siege of Tobruk. British and Commonwealth forces east of the city were then threatening the relatively weak German / Italian lines there. Now, having suffered significant losses, Rommel was forced to regroup and reorganize the divisions he had used in the attack into Egypt. By 7 December Rommel was somehow able to establish a new defensive line to the west of Tobruk, at Gazala, even though his forces were under persistent harassment by aircraft of the Royal Air Force.

London. Under a headline TANKS IN RUNNING BATTLE WITH ROMMEL, *The Daily Telegraph* on 21 December: "The Eighth Army was reported last night to be pressing its pursuit of Rommel's army, which was still in full flight and showing no signs of making a stand.

"A running fight was in progress between the fast armoured British vanguard and German rearguards west of Sultan, thirty miles east of the tiny port of Sirte, and about 150 miles west of El Agheila. Algiers radio stated yesterday that the Eighth Army was now only eight miles from Sirte.

"The main body of the Axis army is believed to have reached Buerat el Sun, a point on the coast 50 miles west of Sirte where big salt marshes force the road to take a curve inland. It is in this area, which has strong natural defences, that Rommel must fight if he intends to defend Tripoli. Italian troops were reported to be leaving Tripoli for Tunisia.

"Allied fighter-bombers continued their non-stop attacks, almost unopposed, on enemy transport retreating along the coast road, destroying many vehicles and silencing anti-aircraft batteries.

"Twenty German tanks were destroyed, 500 prisoners taken and 30 guns captured from the enemy in the battle of the 'squeeze' which took place last Wednesday.

"Rommel's rearguard was then surprised by the out-flanking force which interposed itself at Wadi Matratin, west of the panzer force and the British armour advancing along the Libyan coast road. The out-flanking force was the New Zealand Division in command of the famous V.C., Gen. Freyberg.

"Our casualties in men and material were comparatively slight.

"The success of Gen. Montgomery's move is even greater than was supposed when it became known that some of the enemy tanks had been able to escape westwards in the confused fighting which took place.

"Moreover, the suddenness with which our unexpected spearhead was plunged into his flank accelerated his rate of retreat westward.

"Advance forces were last night reported to be in the Sultan area. This represents an advance of nearly 150 miles in just under a week, an extraordinarily satisfactory rate of progress in view of the heavy mining carried out by the enemy to slow up the pursuit of our forces.

"Details are available of the battle which developed in the pocket created by the New Zealanders when they reached Wadi Matratin after their chase over the rough country to the south and cut off strong elements of one panzer division.

"The New Zealanders took up positions at Matratin and in the long Wadi el Ridel, which curves to the south-east, then to the south-west.

"British armour and infantry were following up from behind. The enemy had sown mines in such profusion that the infantry could make only slow progress, so the tanks advanced through them and, moving westwards from the south of Suera, near Marsa Brega, came into contact with the enemy rearguard south of El Agheila. A running fight ensued, and, pushing forward, our armour attacked the enemy wherever he tried to make a stand.

"The heaviest engagement occurred on the causeway where the Marada road joins the main road. Here the Germans offered fierce resistance before being driven from their position.

"When the panzer elements found themselves trapped between the New Zealanders and our armour they split up into small scattered groups, which battled desperately to find loop-holes.

"In extremely confused fighting prisoners were taken and retaken by both sides. German tanks received a severe mauling from our armour and anti-tank guns, but some succeeded in bursting through gaps in the New Zealanders positions.

"The New Zealanders had been compelled to thin out at the end of their long and difficult trek and could not hold the west jaw of the clamp in sufficiently compact formations to ensure annihilation of the trapped enemy.

"But by the time the pocket between our forces had been closed the Axis, in addition to heavy casualties in guns, tanks and personnel, had left behind hundreds of wrecked transport vehicles and large numbers damaged.

"The New Zealanders, before occupying their positions at Wadi Matratin, were in sharp conflict by moonlight with enemy occupying the hilltop. They charged the height with fixed bayonets and routed the enemy, taking prisoners, all German. When the Germans attempted counter-attacks they were beaten off; further casualties were inflicted.

"One column of six enemy tanks which came into conflict with our light armoured forces broke its formation and made off upon being engaged. Such was the surprise of the meeting that the Germans were sitting on the tops of some their tanks' turrets, which were open.

"An indication of the extent of the mining which is being carried on by the enemy before retreating was provided by the fact that we had to move 2,000 mines from one landing ground. In forty-eight hours it was clear. Then our fighter-bombers were flown on to the abandoned airfield. At dawn on Friday a fleet of transport aircraft, carrying personnel, petrol and bombs, accompanied by fighter-bombers, took off from the rear landing ground.

"It landed on the cleared airfield according to schedule, and two hours later R.A.F. and R.A.A.F. fighter-bombers had been bombed-up and took off and caught the unsuspecting enemy rear columns off their guard."

The situation, for both sides, was deteriorating, both being exhausted and somewhat disorganized. Rommel's forces were suffering sufficiently to require their retreating all the way back to El Agheila, the position they had been holding at the start of their effort in March. Through the course of the retreat, Rommel worried about being outflanked on the south and he employed the *Afrika Korps* to protect his southern flank during the movement. The Axis position at Bardia was lost on 2 January when the German-Italian garrison there surrendered.

Then, in a reversal of fortune, Rommel's *Afrika Korps* was resupplied and re-equipped with fifty-five new tanks on 5 January. By the 21st, he had launched a very effective counterattack in which 110 Allied tanks and other heavy vehicles were destroyed and Benghazi and Timimi were retaken by the Axis forces on 29 January and 3 February respectively. The actions forced the Allies back to the area around Tobruk to build their new defensive positions around Gazala.

The British now held strong points at Gazala, but Rommel's forces were now finally being resupplied, for the first time, at the rate he required. His tank situation, however, was still insufficient, with just 320 German panzers available, fifty being the obsolete Panzer II, together with 240 Italian tanks of about the same quality and capability as the Panzer II. The British had 900 tanks in the Gazala area, of which 200 were new M3 General Grant models with 75mm guns. Rommel was also greatly outnumbered by the British in infantry and artillery. In terms of air power support, both sides were roughly equal at this stage. Rommel would have to rely on bringing up a number of 88mm guns to destroy the British tanks, and the 88s were also in relatively short supply. But he had reason to expect a new summer offensive from the British and thought his forces could outflank the British positions around Gazala, get around behind and destroy them.

Rommel opened the Battle of Gazala on 26 May 1942 with a blitzkrieg outflanking manoeuvre, while sending his Italian infantry units in a head-on assault on the enemy fortifications. He had designed the attack to appear to the British that this was his main assault and had augmented the infantry with a limited amount of armoured forces. Meanwhile, his main motorized and armoured forces were to outflank the enemy positions to the south. On the second morning of his offensive, Rommel sliced through the enemy flank and attacked to the north, spurring a major running tank battle, and resulting in heavy losses to both sides. Whether due to tactics, or superior British strength in equipment, the Germans were unsuccessful in their attempted encirclement of the enemy at Gazala. In the encounter, they lost more than a third of their heavy tanks.

The determined Rommel tried again, on the 28th, to encircle and destroy the enemy armour, but a powerful British counterattack soon forced him onto the defensive. In a renewed effort on the 30th, he attacked to the east, attempting to link up with the Italian X Corps. They had just finished clearing a route through the Allied minefields, enabling an Axis supply line. This move was followed on 2 June when the Italian Trieste Division, together with the 90th Light Division, were able to encircle the Allied strongpoint at Bir Hakeim, which they captured on the 11th. Once again, Rommel seized what he saw as an opportunity and attacked northward, shoving the British back, while counting on the minefields near the Gazala line to protect his own left flank. In what was soon referred to as the "Gazala Gallop," the British forces there began a rapid retreat to escape being cut off by the Germans.

The situation worsened for the British and Commonwealth forces from Gazala. By the 15th, the Axis force arrived at the sea coast, ruling out escape for the other side. With renewed confidence and dedication, Rommel's forces went after the balance of the retreating Allied units who were disorganized and somewhat confused. His intention was to capture Tobruk while the enemy was still in that condition. Tobruk would be his gateway to Egypt. In one of his most significant victories, Rommel launched a savage, well-coordinated attack on the city on 21 June and Tobruk was surrendered with its 33,000 Commonwealth defenders, most of whom were members of the South African 2nd Division. For the achievement, Hitler promoted Rommel to the rank of Field Marshal.

The spectre of Rommel's recent victories brought great concern to the Allies, who saw him as both ready and able to proceed now with his intended conquest of Egypt. Their greatest fear was that, in so doing, Rommel would then roll northeast to take the highly prized oilfields of the Middle East. The effort, though, would need significant reinforcements, which Hitler was then unwilling to provide. Hitler had had doubts about sending Rommel to the North African desert and had only agreed to do it in order to relieve his Italian allies. Now Rommel was driven to keep the British enemy from establishing a new front line; he determined to exploit the weakness of the enemy formations through a main thrust into Egypt. He met considerable criticism over the plan from fellow officers concerned again about his lengthening supply lines in such an undertaking. Luftwaffe Generalfeldmarschall Albert Kesselring objected strenuously to the plan as it required substantial air support which would mean postponing a planned German attack on Malta. But Hitler ultimately approved Rommel's plan, with a view towards achieving total victory in Africa.

Rommel's armoured and infantry forces proceeded eastward as planned on 22 June, running into little resistance. Outrunning their supply lines did pose a problem for the armoured units, but they managed to reach and surround Mersa Matruh on the 26th. The fortification fell to the Germans on the 29th, with all its equipment and supplies, and they took 6,000 prisoners of war.

EL ALAMEIN

There were two principal battles of El Alamein, the first between 1 and 27 July 1942; the second between 23 October and 11 November 1942. Key events in the Western Desert Campaign of the Second World War, the battles of El Alamein were fought near that northern Egyptian railway station, between the German and Italian forces of Panzer Army Africa under the command of Generalfeldmarschall Erwin Rommel, and the British Imperial (Allied) forces of Britain, Australia, South Africa, New Zealand, and British India, commanded by General Claude Auchinleck in the first battle, and by General Sir Harold Alexander and Lieutenant-General Bernard Montgomery in the second. The first battle resulted in a stalemate, but did stop the Axis advance into Egypt. However, that first battle led inevitably to a second which resulted in an Allied victory and the turning point in the North African campaign, ending the German threat to Egypt, the Suez Canal, and the Middle East and Persian oilfields via North Africa. Importantly, it was the first big victory for the Western Allies since the beginning of the European war in 1939.

In the westernmost part of the Qattara Depression in northern Egypt lies the only permanently inhabited settlement in all of the 7,500-square-mile basin, the Qara Oasis, home to about 300 residents. With an average summer daily temperature of around 100 degrees fahrenheit, and a geography dominated by dry lake beds, salt marshes, blowing sand and occasional sticky mud, the Qattara never ranks highly in most people's travel plans. But this 200-mile-long, 70-mile-wide teardrop-shaped stretch of sun-cracked earth played an unforgettable part in modern history.

The Qattara was thought to be impassable by tanks and most military vehicles other than the lightest examples running on relatively narrow tracks. Tanks and other heavy tracked vehicles would simply sink into the fine, powdery sand surface (known as fech fech) of the dry lake beds, and were wholly unsuited to the natural features of the area such as the high cliffs and escarpments. In the establishment of their defensive lines for the battles of El Alamein, both the Allies and Germans developed them in a line from the sea coast of the Mediterranean to the Qattara Depression, utilizing the high cliffs as a boundary to the battlefield. Their wartime role has led to the defensive positions being referred to as the "Devil's Gardens" and, to a large extent, they still exist today, massive, formidable and still threatening minefields.

In the summer of 1942, General Auchinleck, in command of the British Eighth Army, was preparing for battle with the armoured and infantry forces of Generalfeldmarschall Erwin Rommel whose skill and leadership in the desert war had earned him the nickname Wüstenfuchs (The Desert Fox).

Auchinleck was well aware of the Qattara's characteristics and planned to take full advantage of them by establishing a fairly short defensive line directly south of the depression so he could not be outflanked due to the virtual impossibility of operating armour in that strange, hazardous landscape.

In the days leading up to the first battle, Rommel's forces continued to plod eastward, but their pace had slowed dramatically. Interference by Allied forces from Malta, combined with a devastating series of attacks by the R.A.F. on his transports had left him with an unresolved supply problem. The near exhaustion his men were suffering after more than a month of almost constant warfare made the feasibility of a new offensive on El Alamein slim at best. He had only thirteen operational tanks on reaching El Alamein. But the first battle there did begin on 1 July.

From Rommel's perspective, his panzer army had been fighting superior enemy forces for five weeks, four of them in the Tobruk area. The enormous effort had reduced the strength of his forces to a minimal level. He had few reserves of any kind and his resupply situation was practically hopeless with only a tiny fraction of his actual requirement arriving. As he saw it in the days before the first Alamein action, there were several reasons for the failure of the Axis authorities to resupply his forces. The protection of his resupply convoys at sea was the job of the Italian Navy, many of whose officers did not support Hitler's ally, Mussolini and would have preferred an Allied victory in North Africa, and it is belived that some contributed to sabotaging the resupply effort to Rommel, as did some of the higher Italian Fascist authorities who wanted as little as possible to do with the North African war. Rommel questioned the motivation, or lack of motivation, on the part of many of the Italian authorities at the other end of the supply chain, whom he believed failed to understand and appreciate the gravity of the Axis supply situation in North Africa. He felt that many of them did not realize that the North African campaign was nearing an end. He was deeply critical of their lack of inititiative and ingenuity and thought they were hopeless and should have been sacked and replaced long since by men of competence and capability. Unquestionably, it angered him that the minority of good and able supply people in Rome were forced to fight an uphill battle, mired in red-tape and over-organization. Rommel: "When it is remembered that in modern warfare supplies decide the battle, it is easy to see how the clouds of disaster were gathering for my army."

In one the key events leading up to the first battle of El Alamein, General Auchinleck, the Commander-in-Chief of Middle East Command, relieved Lieutenant-General Neil Ritchie as commander of the Eighth Army, assuming that role himself. Feeling somewhat uncomfortable about the position of the British forces at Mersa Matruh because of an exposed left flank to the south, of the sort likely to be exploited by the Germans, Auchinleck chose to delay the coming confrontation by withdrawing his forces about 100 miles further east to what he considered a far more defendable position near the Mediterranean coast by El Alamein. He knew that the high cliffs of the Qattara would eliminate any possibility of Rommel's tanks rolling round the British southern flank, and this new position would also limit the width of the British line of defence. Before the war, the British Eighth Army had been ordered to start construction of a number of what they referred to as "boxes" (facilities with dug-outs and surrounded by minefields and barbed wire). The most extensively developed of these boxes was the facility built near the railway station at El Alamein.

Prior to the start of the battle, the British position in the area was precarious. While Auchinleck believed his forces could halt Rommel's at El Alamein, his confidence was not total, and on the chance that the Desert Fox might outmanoeuvre or outfight him, he had to plan for a possible additional retreat. At the same time, it was vital that he maintain the morale of his troops, and the support of the Egyptians. As the British preparations for the battle proceeded, Auchinleck had additional defensive positions constructed to the west of Alexandria and on the roads leading to Cairo. Meanwhile, in Italy, Benito Mussolini, the Italian fascist leader, was sure that a great Axis victory was nearly at hand and he flew off to Libya to be ready for the celebrations in Cairo.

30 June. Rommel now drove his nearly exhausted warriors forward towards Alamein in the belief that, in spite of their state, the losses he had incurred, and his monumental resupply problems, the momentum he had built up would carry him, his tanks and infantry through the enemy there and on to the Nile. He expected little significant opposition. He organized the remains of his forces, and the 90th Light Infantry Division, the 15th and 21st Panzer Divisions of the *Afrika Korps*, and opened the attack at 3 a.m. 1 July and, of an initial inventory of fifty-five tanks, only thirty-seven remained at the end of the day's fighting. By the afternoon, the 90th had freed itself from the El Alamein box defences and headed east again until having to dig in when it was exposed to a deadly rain of artillery fire from three South African brigades.

Rommel resumed his offensive the next day and with no significant advancement by the 90th, he ordered the *Afrika Korps* up to join with them in an attempt to break through to the coast road by attacking the British to the east near Ruweisat Ridge. By late in the afternoon the British armoured brigades had driven back a series of Axis armoured attacks. On 3 July Rommel again sent the *Afrika Korps* in to attack the enemy force at Ruweisat Ridge. At that point the *Afrika Korps* had only twenty-six operational tanks remaining. By the end of the day, the Italian Ariete Division had just five tanks operational. With his forces further reduced, Rommel was unable to resume his advance to the coast.

From *The Rommel Papers*: 3 July. ". . . I sent the Afrika Korps forward once more against the British line. After an initial success, the attack finally became pinned down in concentric defensive fire. On the same day, signs of disintegration began to show amongst the Italians. An attack by the New Zealanders against the Ariete, which had been detailed to protect the Panzer Army's southern flank, met with complete success. Twenty-eight out of thirty guns were lost to the enemy; 400 men were taken prisoner and the remainder took to their heels in panic.

"This reverse took us completely by surprise, for in the weeks of fighting round Knightsbridge, the Ariete—covered, it is true, by German guns and tanks—had fought well against every onslaught of the British, although their casualties had not been light. But now the Italians were no longer equal to the very great demands being made of them.

"The resulting threat to our southern flank meant that the *Afrika Korps'* intended knock-out attack now had to be carried on by the 21st Panzer Division alone, and the weight of the attack was consquently too small. The 90th Light Division joined up with them later, but was equally unable to force a decision. The attack came to a standstill.

"In these circumstances a continuation of the attack next day would have resulted in nothing more than a useless attrition of our strength. However valuable a breathing space might be to the British command, we had to give the troops a few days' rest and try to carry out an extensive refit. We intended to return to the attack as soon as possible."

By 4 July Erwin Rommel had accepted the fact that his exhausted, under-supplied men could no longer sustain their advance and had to be rested and regrouped. In his report to German High Command he stated that the personnel remaining in his three divisions numbered less than 1,500 each. He also outlined his resupply problems including the near constant harassment his units had been experiencing by aircraft of the Allied Desert Air Force which had been concentrating their attacks on his long and tenuous supply routes. These R.A.F. attacks, together with the greatly reduced resupply shipments from Italy were contributing substantially to his lack of progress. Rommel noted that the enemy's Eighth Army was currently in a rebuilding and reorganizing mode and was being reinforced by the arrival of the Australian 9th Division and the Indian 161st Brigade. He concluded with an expectation that his forces would have to operate defensively for at least the next few weeks.

General Auchinleck directed Lieutenant-General William Ramsden, his new XXX Corps commander, on 8 July to take the ridges at Tel el Eisa and Tel el Makh Khad and then to send raiding units to the airfields of the El Daba area. Ramsden ordered the Australian 9th Division and the 44th Royal Tank Regiment into the Tel el Eisa attack and the tanks of the South African 1st Division to the Tel el Makh Khad effort. At 3.30 a.m. of 10 July, the members of Australian 26th Brigade made their presence known through the heaviest artillery barrage ever launched in Africa when they attacked the Tel el Eisa ridge objective. The attack panicked many of the inexperienced Italian 60th Infantry Division troops occupying defences in the sector. In the action, more than 1,500 Italian prisoners were taken and the German Signals Intercept Company 621 was overrun. The South Africans, meanwhile, had taken their objective position at Tel el Makh Khad. Through the late afternoon and evening, the tanks of the 15th Panzer Division and the Italian Trieste Division were counter-attacking against the Australian positions, but were finally overwhelmed by Allied artillery and the Australian anti-tank guns. From dawn on the 11th, the tanks of the 44th Royal Tank Regiment, together with the Australian 2/24th Battalion, attacked and captured Tel el Eisa ridge, which they managed to hold through the day. More than 1,000 additional Italian prisoners were taken.

Auchinleck had forces dug in on the coastal plain and they would feature in his planned Operation Bacon which began just before midnight of 14 July. The action involved attacking the Italian Brescia and Pavia Divisions at the Ruweisat ridge. The effort was mounted by two New Zealand brigades at dawn on the 15th, but in taking their objectives they had to get through the minefields and pockets of enemy resistance, all of which hampered the provision of reserves, artillery and other support, leaving the New Zealanders trying to hold highly exposed positions on the ridge, supported only by a few anti-tank guns. Importantly, their communications capability with the supporting British armoured brigades broke down, leading to the failure of the British tanks to move up and protect the infantry. In a major reversal for the New Zealanders, elements of the 15th Panzer Division counter-attacked against the New Zealand 4th Brigade, destroying their anti-tank guns and leaving the New Zealanders unprotected, with no option but to surrender. 350 became prisoners of the Germans.

To ease the pressure on the Brescia and Pavia at Ruweisat, Rommel hurriedly brought in reinforcements from the 15th and 21st Panzer Divisions, putting them under the command of Lieutenant-General Walther Nehring. Nehring opened a counter-attack against the 4th New Zealand Brigade, quickly overwhelming them and taking nearly 400 additional prisoners, including Captain Charles Upham. Upham was awarded the Victoria Cross for destroying a German tank, several guns and vehicles, with hand grenades despite suffering a broken arm when shot by machine-gun fire. With nightfall, Nehring ended the action.

In a savage resurgence on 16 July, the Germans beat back an Australian attack on the German position at Point 24. The Australians incurred nearly fifty percent casualties in the action. In the week of combat around Tel el Eisa, the Axis forces lost more than 2,000 men killed with 3,700 taken prisoner. Significantly, the German Signals Intercept Company 621 had been captured by the Australians, robbing Rommel of an important intelligence source for the interception of British radio communications.

In the action on Tel el Eisa, thirty-three-year-old Australian Private Arthur Stanley Gurney's company was being held up by withering machine-gun fire that inflicted heavy casualties. All the officers of his company were killed or wounded in the combat. Gurney risked his life by charging the nearest machine-gun post. He silenced the guns by bayoneting three of the enemy crew. He then went on to another machine-gun post where he bayoneted two more gunners. At that point he was severely wounded by a grenade, but managed to get to a third machine-gun post which he tried to charge. He died of his wounds but his sacrifice made possible the advance of his unit. Gurney was posthumously awarded the Victoria Cross for his actions in the First Battle of El Alamein.

By the third week in July the British in North Africa enjoyed a considerable material advantage over their Axis opponents. General Auchinleck launched a bold operation in which his Indian 161st Brigade infantry mounted an attack on the Ruweisat ridge during the night of 21 July with the objective of capturing Deir el Shein. While that was under way, the 6th New Zealand Brigade attacked the enemy south of the ridge to the El Mreir depression. With daylight, the 2nd and 23rd British Armoured Brigades were to roll through the gap made by the Allied infantry units. The attacks began in the late afternoon of the 21st, but early successes were thwarted by the failure of many vehicles with supporting arms to arrive. In the morning of the 22nd, the British armoured brigades were prevented from advancing and German Lieutenant-General Nehring counter-attacked, overruning the New Zealanders who were again exposed in the open, and inflicting 900 casualties. In the evening, the men of the 24th Australian Brigade, with support of tanks from the 50th Royal Tank Regiment launched an attack on Tel el Makh Khad. The tankers had not been trained in close infantry support methods and lacked proper coordination with the Australian infantry units. This led to the armour and infantry units advancing independently and when they reached the objective, 50th RTR had lost twenty-three tanks due to the lack of infantry support.

The British attack ended disastrously when Lieutenant-General William Gott, commander of XIII Corps, ignored the suggestion of Major-General Alexander Gatehouse, commanding the 1st Armoured Division that the attack be cancelled in the belief that a path through the minefields had not been adequately cleared. Gott gave the go-ahead for the attack, resulting in his forces being caught under heavy enemy fire in the minefields. As they struggled, they were attacked by the 21st Panzer Division and made to withdraw. With the loss of forty tanks, and forty-seven more badly damaged, the British

23rd Armoured Brigade was routed.

Even with far greater strength of numbers, the Eighth Army had thus far failed in its effort to destroy Rommel's forces. As for Rommel, "the situation," as he reported was "critical in the extreme," his men having taken very heavy losses.

The final major attack of the First Battle of El Alamein, the British Eighth Army's third attempt at a breakthrough in the northern sector, was a fiasco—hurriedly and badly planned, and poorly executed. Operation Manhood, as Auchinleck called it, began around midnight of 26/27 July with XXX Corps, reinforced by the 1st Armoured Division, the 4th Light Armoured Brigade, and the 69th Infantry Brigade all operating in concert to break the Axis line south of the Miteirya ridge and push on northwest. The South Africans had been given the job of making and marking a gap through the minefields southeast of Miteirya, to be completed by the midnight opening of the attack. One hour later, the 24th Australian Infantry was to have captured the eastern end of the ridge. The British 69th Infantry Brigade, meanwhile, was to move through the minefield gap made by the South Africans, on to Deir el Dhib, clearing and marking gaps in additional minefields as they went. They would then be followed by the 2nd Armoured Brigade and the 4th Light Armoured Brigade, which were assigned the task of attacking the Axis lines of communication.

The Germans and Italians had anticipated this Allied attack and were ready for it. For the Allies, virtually the entire operation was a catalog of horrors. By 31 July, the 69th Brigade had taken 600 casualties; the Australians 400, for no net gain. Auchinleck's exhausted forces were ordered to stand down from the offensive to beef up their defences against the big counteroffensive he expected.

Rommel, in his retrospective comments on the stalemated First Battle of El Alamein, directed much of the blame on the Italian Supreme Command in Rome: "If success had depended, as in times gone by, on the strength of will of my men and their officers, then we would have overrun Alamein. But our sources of supply had dried up—thanks to the idleness and muddle of the supply authorities on the mainland.

"And then the power of resistance of many of the Italian formations had collapsed. The duties of comradeship, for me particularly as their field Commander-in-Chief, compel me to state unequivocally that the defeats which the Italian formations suffered at El Alamein in early July were not the fault of the Italian soldier. The Italian was willing, unselfish and a good comrade, and, considering the conditions under which he served, had always given far better than the average. There is no doubt that the achievement of every Italian unit, especially of the motorised forces, far surpassed anything that the Italian Army had done for a hundred years. Many Italian generals and officers won our admiration both as men and soldiers.

"The cause of the Italian defeat had its roots in the whole Italian military and state system, in their poor armament and in the general lack of interest in the war shown by many of the leading Italians, both officers and statesmen. This Italian failure frequently prevented the realisation of my plans."

In the battle, the British Eighth Army suffered 13,000 casualties, killed, wounded and captured, and took 7,000 German and Italian prisoners. The Axis suffered 17,000 casualties, killed, wounded and captured. In the aftermath of that First Battle of El Alamein, British Prime Minister Winston Churchill, together with his Chief of the Imperial General Staff, General Alan Brooke, stopped in Cairo on their way to a meeting with Soviet Premier Joseph Stalin in Moscow. While in Egypt, they replaced General Auchinleck with XIII Corps commander Lieutenant-General William Gott. They also appointed General Sir Harold Alexander as Commander-in-Chief, Middle East Command. While on the way to take up his new post, the aircraft that was carrying Gott was shot down by a German fighter. Churchill then appointed Lieutenant-General Bernard Montgomery to replace Gott in command of the Eighth Army.

In July 1942, the German and Italian mechanized and infantry units of *Panzerarmee Afrika* had advanced into Egypt. Generalfeldmarschall Erwin Rommel's forces were threatening Alexandria, Cairo, and the Suez Canal. British General Claude Auchinleck, in command of the Eighth Army, then withdrew his forces to a point fifty miles from Alexandria and where the Qattara Depression came within forty miles of El Alamein on the coast. There, Auchinleck would have the shortest possible front to defend, and his flanks were relatively secure because heavy tanks and other tracked vehicles could not travel on the soft surface of the depression.

After the stalemate of the First Battle of El Alamein, the Eighth Army had launched some unsuccessful counter-offensives in July, followed by Auchinleck ending all offensive action in order to regroup, rest and rebuild the strength of the Eighth. There followed the replacement of Auchinleck by Alexander as Commander-in-Chief, Middle East Command, and of Gott with Montgomery, as commander of the Eighth.

It was during the British rebuilding process in August that Rommel, aware of the massive reinforcements and resupply the Allies were receiving, elected to attack them before their rebuilding effort was complete. Rommel's force was made up of two *Afrika Korps* armoured divisions and reconnaissance units of *Panzerarmee Afrika*. The Germans attacked on 30 August but were stopped at Alam el Halfa ridge and, in anticipation of a British counter-attack, the *Panzerarmee Afrika* force dug in. The British continued their build-up for an additional six weeks in their determination to achieve overwhelming force superiority, effect a major breakthrough, and wipe out the *Panzerarmee Afrika*. Rommel used the time to ready the German defensive positions, laying extensive barbed wire and roughly 500,000 mines. With completion of its build-up, the Eighth Army had a renewed strength of 220,000 men and 1,100 tanks, while Rommel was able to field 115,000 men and 559 tanks.

In Operation Lightfoot, Montgomery's initial plan for the Second Battle of El Alamein, he wanted to open two cleared paths through the enemy mine-fields of the north, one to the southwest towards the middle of Miteirya Ridge; the other to the west, running two miles north of the western end of the ridge. He would use these paths to send his armoured forces through for what he estimated would be a twelve-day battle to defeat the enemy force and would supplement the effort with diversionary attacks on Ruweisat Ridge near the centre of the German line, as well as to the south of it.

The supply lines to the Axis forces were greatly exceeded and, after their failure at Alam el Halfa, they had been subsisting on captured Allied sup-plies which were rapidly depleted. Rommel had insisted on pressing his advance to El Alamein despite strong warnings from both his German and Italian staffs that the supply echelons would not be able to get the vitally needed supplies from the Benghazi and Tripoli ports to the front line. The British, on the other hand, were readily being reinforced and resupplied with troops and materiél from the U.K, Australia, New Zealand, and India, as well as tanks and trucks from the United States. Rommel's supply problems were partially due to complacency in Rome and incessant Allied air attacks, and partly to the massive demands of the German-Soviet campaign on the Eastern Front, severely limiting the Axis ability to meet Rommel's needs in Africa. Rommel became ill around this time and returned to Germany for treatment in early September, which necessitated the transfer of Lieutenant-General Georg Stumme from the Russian Front to temporarily replace Rommel in North Africa. Rommel fully expected the rejuvenated British Army to launch a major new offensive against his forces soon. He clung to the hope that the German battle at Stalingrad would shortly result in a Soviet defeat, enabling the German troops to be moved south through the Trans-Caucasus to threaten Persia and the Middle East. Such a result would then lead to the British having to reinforce their troops in Persia with British and Common-wealth forces from Egypt, postponing for a while at least, the new offensive he was anticipating near El Alamein. Rommel nursed the notion that this delay might allow him to pursuade High Command to arrange a link-up between Panzerarmee Afrika and the German forces that would be moving south from the Soviet Union. So his forces were dug in in Egypt awaiting the expected British attack and the German victory at Stalingrad. While they waited, Rommel used the opportunity to enhance his defences further with many thousands of Teller anti-tank mines and the smaller anti-personnel mines, as well as restrictions on the areas in which the enemy tanks would need to manoeuvre, near the area known as the Devil's Gardens.

It was hugely in Rommel's interest to restrict and narrow the field of battle to the area of his defended zones, and to quickly and efficiently stop any British breakthrough because his greatly reduced numbers and very limited fuel supplies would not allow him to compete with, much less defeat the enemy in the circumstances. He also reorganized his infantry and armoured formations to tighten their ability to prevent any breakthrough attempts.

23 October. The German 15th Panzer Division fell under a brief but very heavy barrage of shell fire by the 24th Australian Brigade. Montgomery's Operation Lightfoot kicked off that night at 9.40 with an unusual opening round of artillery fire from field guns and medium batteries sending shells all across the entire forty-mile width of the front at once. The shelling continued for twenty minutes before switching to precise targets to support the advancing British infantry. The firing went on for more than five hours. The operation had been called Lightfoot because the men of the British infantry would be required to lead the attack across the fields of anti-tank mines which would not be set off by the weight of a soldier.

When four infantry divisions of XXX Corps headed out at 10 p.m. for the strongest of the enemy defences in the desert and reached the minefields, the British mine removers and markers moved up to clear a path for the armoured divisions of X Corps. It was slow going and the first of 500 British tanks moved out and began entering the passage through the minefields. The dust created reduced visibility in the area to near zero and a massive traffic jam soon developed as many of the tanks were bogged down. Now very heavy Axis defensive fire made the continuing clearing of the passage through the minefields even slower and more difficult. By dawn the paths were still not fully cleared.

Early the next morning R.A.F. aerial reconnaissance confirmed no change in the Axis positions. Montgomery then redoubled the efforts of the Eighth Army from the previous day in his determination to break through the enemy minefields with his armour. A counter-attack by German tanks was turned back by the 51st Highland Division. In an odd turn of events on 24 October, when Lieutenant-General Stumme read the reports of the previous days' action and decided to go up on the front line to observe the situation, the unit he was observing suddenly came under enemy fire. Stumme suffered a heart attack and died. His command (Rommel's) was temporarily given over to Major-General Wilhelm Ritter von Thoma, and when Hitler learned of Stumme's death he ordered Rommel back to North Africa. Making a brief stop in Rome to demand more fuel and ammunition for *Panzerarmee Afrika*, he arrived to resume command in the desert the evening of the 25th. In the late afternoon tanks of the 15th Panzer Division and the Italian Littorio Division rolled out to meet their opposite number from the British 1st Armoured Division in the first large tank battle of El Alamein. Rommel: "The tactics which the British were using followed from their apparently inexhaustible stocks of ammunition. Their new tank, the General Sherman, which came into action for the first time during the battle, showed itself to be far superior to any of ours.

"Attacks against our line were preceded by extremely heavy artillery barrages lasting for several hours. The attacking infantry then pushed forward behind a curtain of fire and artificial fog, clearing mines and removing obstacles. Where a difficult patch was struck they frequently switched the direction of their attack under cover of smoke. Once the infantry had cleared lanes in the minefields, the heavy tanks moved forward, closely followed by infantry. Particular skill was shown in carrying out this manoeuvre at night and a great deal of hard training must have been done before the offensive.

"In contact engagements the heavily gunned British tanks approached to a range of between 2,000 and 2,700 yards and then opened concentrated fire on our anti-tank and anti-aircraft guns and tanks, which were unable to penetrate the British armour at that range. The enormous quantities of ammunition which the enemy tanks used—sometimes they fired over thirty rounds at one target—were constantly replenished by armoured ammunition carriers. The British artillery fire was directed by observers who accompanied the attack in tanks."

By nightfall more than 100 tanks were involved in the action and within a few hours, half of them had been destroyed, with no appreciable change to either side's position. Throughout the night the attempts by various British armoured formations to break through the German defences were driven back. In one such effort, by 22nd Armoured Brigade, thirty-one of their tanks were disabled. Progress for the British came on Sunday, 25 October, when they were finally able to advance through the German minefields five miles to take Miteira Ridge in the southeast. Now Montgomery decided to refocus the battle at El Aqqaqir, the "Kidney Feature", and Tel el Eisa until his forces could make a breakthrough in a northern thrust. R.A.F. bombing during the night put more than one hundred tons of bombs on enemy targets in the battle area and thirteen tons on the Stuka dive-bomber base at Sidi Haneish. To complicate matters more for Rommel on his return to the desert, in addition to the many casualties his formations had been suffering, most of his units were under-strength, the men were on half-rations, many were ill, and his fuel supplies for his entire army were down to barely enough for three more days' operation. To make his situation seemingly hopeless, R.A.F. Baufort torpedo bombers located and sank the oil tanker *Proserpina* near Tobruk, virtually ending any possibility of his being resupplied with fuel. But with all Rommel's problems, the British forces seemed somehow incapable of fully exploiting their advantages and the Allied offensive stalled, causing Churchill to grumble: "Is it really impossible to find a general who can win a battle?" Confusion, chaos, miscommunication, lack thereof, and enormous difficulty for the tank and other vehicle crews navigating through the choking dust, shell fire, swirling sand and smoke of the battle areas seemed to constantly hamper the advance efforts of the British.

On the 27th, Rommel began a major attack with his German and Italian tanks, moving against a large force of enemy anti-tank guns and an anti-tank battery. After losing twenty-two German and ten Italian tanks, the Germans were defeated in the action, but oddly, the British withdrew their battle group and failed to replace it that evening. In the action, Lieutenant-Colonel Victor Buller Turner of The Rifle Brigade, was a battalion commander, whose unit had just overcome a German position when his battalion had to fight off an Axis counter-attack by ninety tanks. The British unit destroyed or immobilized at least fifty of the tanks. Colonel Turner joined with a short-handed six-pounder gun crew as a loader. The three men soon managed to destroy five more enemy tanks. In the effort, Turner suffered a significant head wound for which he declined treatment until the three had repulsed the last of their tank targets. For his deed Coloner Turner received the Victoria Cross for gallantry.

The regimental historian for the Royal Sussex Regiment, Brigadier C.E. Lucas-Phillips, described the action at the Axis point of resistance known as 'Snipe' "The desert was quivering with heat. The gun detachments and the platoons squatted in their pits and trenches, the sweat running in rivers down their dust-caked faces. There was a terrible stench. The flies swarmed in black clouds upon the dead bodies and excreta and tormented the wounded. The place was strewn with burning tanks and carriers, wrecked guns and vehicles, and over all drifted the smoke and the dust from bursting high explosives and from the blasts of guns."

The next day brought a powerful effort from the Australian 20th and 26th Infantry Brigades, supported by the 40th and 46th Royal Tank Regiments in a broad attempt to move against the enemy's rear in the coastal salient. Many of the infantry troops were riding on the British Valentine tanks as well as on the carriers. Trouble developed for the Allied units when the infantry and armoured units lost contact with each other during a combat engagement with the Axis forces, bringing the Allied advance to a halt. The Australians suffered considerable casualties and with the coming of darkness, the offensive was called off. Rommel's words on a memorial to the Italian Bersagliere (marksmen), all but twenty of whom were killed or died of their wounds in the days' action: "The German soldier has impressed the world, however, the Italian Bersagliere has impressed the German soldier."

The imbalance of power extended on 29 October. While the British retained about 800 operational tanks, the Axis forces had just 148 German and 187 Italian tanks left. News of the sinking of the Italian oil tanker *Luisiano* by an R.A.F. bomber caused Rommel to tell his commanders, "It will be quite impossible for us to disengage from the enemy. There is no gasoline for such a manoeuvre. We have only one choice and that is to fight to the end at Alamein."

A subtle change seemed to come over Montgomery towards the end of 29 October. It was as though he must have sensed (rather than known), something of the extent of Rommel's troubles and limitations at that stage in the campaign. He was now persuaded that Rommel thought the next coming offensive from the British would be in the coastal sector and that persuasion led Montgomery to shift that next offensive much further south and to set the date for it to begin as the night of 31 October. It would actually have to wait until the following night when the British reorganization of their reserves was completed. During the night of the 31st, the German commander launched no fewer than four separate savage attacks on the position known as Thompson's Post, attacks that involved intense, viscious hand-to-hand combat with no appreciable gains for the Germans. One notable participant in battle was Australian Sergeant William Henry Kibby of the 2/48th Infantry Battalion, South Australia. Kibby had shown great skill in leading his platoon following the death of his commanding officer in the initial Allied attack on Miteira Ridge. On 23 October, Kibby single-handedly charged an enemy machine-gun position, killing three soldiers with his Thompson sub-machinegun, capturing twelve others and taking the position. From that day, until the 31st, Sergeant Kibby motivated, inspired and directed the fire of his men and maintained the communications capability of the unit by making several repairs to the platoon's telephone line while under extreme enemy machine-gun and mortar fire. In the fighting of the 30th-31st, nearly all the men of Kibby's platoon were killed or wounded. In his final act, he was attempting to destroy a remaining enemy machine-gun position with grenades when he was brought down by the machine-gun fire and died of his wounds. For his actions in the Second Battle of El Alamein, the quiet, well-regarded, selfless Sergeant Kibby received the posthumous award of the Victoria Cross.

It seems clear that by 1 November Erwin Rommel must have known that his forces had lost the battle of El Alamein. Nearly all the news he got was bad. On that day Allied aircraft had torpedoed and sunk the two urgently awaited Italian supply transport ships, *Ostia* and *Tripolino*, near Tobruk. All his sources of resupply were disappearing and his losses to date were catastrophic. He now had to count on the help of the head of German Army Command South, Generalfeldmarschall Albert Kesselring, to fly in a supply of vitally needed fuel from Crete—a tenuous possibility in light of the recent intense bombardment of the airfields on that island by the Royal Air Force. Rommel knew now that he had to begin planning a retreat. In a letter to his wife on 1 November, Rommel wrote: "It's a week since I left home. A week of very, very hard fighting. It was often doubtful whether we'd be able to hold out.

Yet we did manage it each time, although with sad losses. I'm on the move a lot in order to step in wherever we're in trouble. Things were very bad in the north yesterday morning, although it was all more or less cleaned up by evening. The struggle makes very heavy demands on one's nervous energy, though physically I'm quite well. Some supplies are supposed to be on their way. But it's a tragedy that this sort of support only arrives when things are almost hopeless."

Bernard Montgomery's agenda for 2 November called for a new operation to force Rommel's forces out to fight in the open, to attack and occupy his supply routes and reduce or eliminate his petrol supply, to destroy his remaining infantry and armoured forces. It would call for an entirely new and much more destructive intensity than had yet been unleashed in the campaign, and would be aimed at Tel el Aqqaqir, Rommel's defensive base. Montgomery code-named the offensive Operation Supercharge and it began at 1 a.m. It was to be carried out by four infantry brigades, an infantry battalion, and an armoured brigade, all of them under the command of New Zealand Lieutenant-General Bernard Freyberg.

A devastating seven-hour aerial barrage on Tel al Aqqaqir and Sidi Abd el Rahman, followed by a four-and-a-half hour 360-gun barrage launched the operation. Then came successful moves by two assault brigades on their initial objectives. A new salient was formed with the relatively easy capture of the left and right flank positions, enabling a team of New Zealand engineers to enter the minefields and efficiently clear five passages through which other Allied elements were able to move into the open area and attack Axis communications facilities.

When the 130 tanks of the British 9th Armoured Brigade moved out from El Alamein railway station at 8 p.m. on 1 November it was against the best judgement of General Freyberg, who had tried without success to convince Montgomery of what he saw as excessive risk to his men in the effort. He had said that brigade would be attacking on too wide a front without reserves and would most probably incur upwards of fifty percent losses in the attempt. Freyberg: "We all realise that for armour to attack a wall of guns sounds like another Balaclava; it is properly an infantry job. But there are no more infantry available, so our armour must do it." Montgomery: " . . . was aware of the risk and accepted the possibility of losing 100 percent casualties in the 9th Armoured Brigade to make the break, but in view of the promise of immediate following through of 1st Armoured Division, the risk was not considered as great as all that."

In the attack, only twenty-four of the original Allied force of 130 tanks survived in operational condition. Many of the others were repairable, however. Of the more than 400 tank crewmen, 230 were killed, wounded or captured. The objective of opening up the enemy gun line and creating a new passage for the 1st Armoured Division tanks to roll through was not initially achieved, though heavy damage had been done to the Axis force there. The German-led Axis armoured 15th, 21st panzers and the Littorio Armoured Division launched a counter-attack at 11 a.m. of 2 November against the 1st Armoured Division and what was left of the 9th Armoured Brigade, but were overwhelmed by the anti-tank guns, artillery, and heavy air support of the Allies. The Axis lost at least 100 tanks that day. Actually, the tank losses on both sides were roughly equal for the day, but for Rommel the losses were far worse, representing as they did a much higher proportionate loss to his remaining armoured resources than did the British losses. The British would later refer to the action as the "hammering of the Panzers."

As Montgomery planned his activity for the next day, Rommel listened to a report from General der Panzertruppe Thoma, that he would have a maximum of only thirty-five tanks ready to fight the next day; and just a third of his anti-tank and artillery weaponry remained useable. The information focused Rommel on what he now saw as his highest priority, saving the remains of his entire army by withdrawing it to a pre-planned position at Fuka in the Egyptian Delta. He immediately ordered his XX Corps, the *Afrika Korps*, the 90th Light Division, and the 19th Flak Division to make a fighting withdrawal, and his other formations to withdraw with their limited available transport.

When Rommel notified Hitler on the 2nd that ". . . the army's strength was so exhausted after its ten days of battle that it was not now capable of offering any effective opposition to the enemy's next break-through attempt . . . With our great shortage of vehicles an orderly withdrawal of the non-motorized forces appeared impossible . . . In these circumstances we had to reckon, at the least, with the gradual destruction of the army." Hitler's reply arrived the following day: "To Field Marshal Rommel. It is with trusting confidence in your leadership and the courage of the German-Italian troops under your command that the German people and I are following the heroic struggle in Egypt. In the situation which you find yourself there can be no other thought but to stand fast, yield not a yard of ground and throw every gun and every man into the battle. Considerable air force reinforcements are being sent to C-in-C South. The Duce and the Comando Supremo are also making the utmost efforts to send you the means to continue the fight. Your enemy, despite his superiority, must also be at the end of his strength. It would not be the first time in history that a strong will has triumphed over the bigger battalions. As to your troops, you can show them no other road than that to victory or death. Adolf Hitler". Rommel: "We were completely stunned, and for the first time in the African campaign I did not know what to do. A kind of apathy took hold of us as we issued orders for all existing positions to be held on instructions from the highest authority." Rommel considered the situation and chose compromise. He ordered X and XXI

Corps, and the 90th Light Division to stand and hold their positions. He had the *Afrika Korps* withdraw in the evening of 3 November to a point six miles west and had the XX Italian Corps and the Ariete Division fill in the positions that had been occupied by the *Afrika Korps*. He then informed Hitler that he was determined to hold the positions on the battlefield.

Though operating with flawed intelligence information about the status of the enemy positions, Montgomery's forces attacked and captured a few of their objectives that day and by the 4th, the Allied chase was on in pursuit of the retreating Axis forces. Various factors, including the dispersion of some Allied formations from the earlier fighting, and heavy traffic congestions on the paths through the minefields greatly hampered Montgomery's progress. But on the occasions when his armoured forces did encounter enemy resistance, it did not go well for the Germans and Italians. When the 7th Armoured Division moved against the Ariete Armoured Division, the latter put up a strong fight but was finally annihilated. The same fate met the Littorio Division and the Trieste Motorized Division that day. Of the actions, Berlin Radio stated: "The British were made to pay for their penetration with enormous losses in men and material. The Italians fought to the last man." When Colonel Dall'Olio, commanding the Bologna Division, finally surrendered his force to the Allies, he reportedly said, "We have ceased firing not because we haven't the desire but because we have spent every round."

The true depth of Rommel's situation by mid-day of the 4th had absorbed him: "The picture in the early afternoon of the 4th was as follows: powerful enemy armoured forces . . . had burst a twelve-mile hole in our front, through which strong bodies of tanks were moving to the west. As a result of this, our forces in the north were threatened with encirclement by enemy formations twenty times their number in tanks . . . there were no reserves, as every available man and gun had been put into the line. So now it had come, the thing we had done everything in our power to avoid—our front broken and the fully motorized enemy streaming into our rear. Superior orders could no longer count. We had to save what there was to be saved." Rommel wired Hitler for his permission to retreat to Fuka. Then General Thoma was captured. Rommel waited until 5.30 p.m. for a reply from Hitler and, failing that, ordered the retreat. His earlier compromise to Hitler sealed the fate of his remaining unmotorized Italian forces, now too far forward to be part of an organized withdrawal.

On 5 November Montgomery was convinced it would require deeper and more powerful tank attacks to defeat and / or destroy the Axis forces and so ordered the 1st and 7th Armoured Divisions, but relatively little was achieved that day. By noon of the 6th, heavy rain came and much of his armoured equipment became bogged down. That day, American heavy bombers raided the port at Tobruk, sinking the Italian supply vessel Ethiopia. The planes later attacked Benghazi, setting fire to the Italian tanker *Portofino*, thwarting yet another potential fuel lifeline to Rommel, with much of his forces in the Mersa Matruh area. His last rearguard troops left Matruh during the night of 7/8 November, as Rommel planned to fight a delaying action at Sidi Barrani, some eighty miles west of Matruh, to buy time for the bulk of his forces to escape through the Halfya and Sollum passes at the escarpment. In the morning of 11 November, the 5th New Zealand Infantry Brigade reached and stormed the Halfya pass, capturing more than 600 Italian prisoners. At the end of the day the border area had been cleared of German and Italian forces. Now Montgomery was sharing Rommels supply problem, having outrun his own resupply transport. The end of the El Alamein campaign had finally come for Rommel, the *Afrika Korps*, and the *Panzerarmee Afrika*.

In his prolonged retreat effort, Rommel was determined to keep the British Eighth Army at arm's length in order to give his men the best chance of escape. He had them destroying all facilities and equipment, while laying mines and booby traps extensively, and he established a defensive line by Wadi Zemzem near Buerat, 230 miles east of Tripoli. He requested permission to withdraw his remaining forces all the way to Tunisia where he felt they would be in better position to stage a last-ditch defensive action and perhaps join his forces with the Axis forces then forming to deal with the Allied Operation Torch landings. On 19 December that permission was denied by Hitler and Rommel was instructed to hold position at Buerat and fight to the last man.

Rommel continued to withdraw his forces towards Tunisia and was forced to make a fighting retreat as they went. The Allied forces took Tripoli on 23 January. Now the Germans and Italians were faced with the two-pronged threat of the Eighth Army coming at them from the east and the Americans, French and other British forces approaching them from the west. But Rommel wasn't quite finished in the desert war yet. In February he launched a punishing assault on the American II Corps in the Battle of the Kasserine Pass, the first major engagement between American and German forces in the Second World War. While the Germans inflicted considerable damage on the U.S. II Corps forces at Kasserine in the initial contacts, causing heavy American casualties and driving the Americans back some fifty miles from their positions west of Faid Pass, that situation would change over the course of the Kasserine action. The inexperiened and poorly-led Americans there were soon reorganized and given reinforcement with British reserves and were, ultimately, able to defeat the Axis force there. On 23 February 1943, Rommel met with Kesselring, and his Chief of Staff, Siegfried Westphal, both of whom tried unsuccessfully to persuade Rommel to continue trying to exploit any remaining combat possibilities in the Kasserine campaign. Rommel, however, was adament at that point about calling off the offensive.

On 9 March Rommel flew to Rome for what turned out to be a fruitless meeting with Mussolini and, on the following afternoon Rommel arrived at

Hitler's headquarters in Russia where he had tea at the Fuehrer's headquarters. Hitler was visibly upset about the disaster at Stalingrad and was wholly unreceptive to Rommel's arguments and proposals about re-equipping and revitalizing his troops in Africa. Hitler ordered Rommel to take sick leave and put himself right to be ready for further command.

El Alamein had been the first major campaign against the Germans where the Western Allies achieved a decisive victory. German and Italian casualties had totalled over 37,000—more than thirty percent of their entire force. In contrast, Allied casualties amounted to only 13,500—a far smaller percentage of their total forces.

One important factor that Erwin Rommel either never knew about, or never acknowledged, was the Allied code-breakers' of Bletchley Park reading the encrypted Enigma/Ultra messages, many of which included the daily reports from the German forces in North Africa. These vital messages provided the Allies with current information about the Axis supply shipments on the Mediterranean, making it possible for the limited Allied naval and air forces there to locate and sink many of those ships.

Winston Churchill had two memorable comments on the campaign: "This is not the end, it is not even the beginning of the end. But it is, perhaps, the end of the beginning", and "Before Alamein we never had a victory. After Alamein we never had a defeat."

KURSK

Believing that the historic Soviet victory at Stalingrad may have been some sort of aberration, the German armies struggled in a mighty effort to regroup, reorganize, and recover from the most hellish experience any modern army had faced. From that effort emerged the plan for a new offensive the Germans hoped to launch in May 1943. The offensive was called Operation Zitadelle (Citadel) and its objective was to surround and destroy the five Soviet armies positioned in the area of the Kursk salient, between Orel and Belgorod. It has often been called the greatest tank battle in history.

As the summer of 1943 began, two-thirds of the entire German Army was based in Russia. The brutal impact of armoured warfare had been amply and repeatedly demonstrated since 1939 in the German campaigns for Poland, the low countries, France, North Africa and the Soviet Union. A number of spectacular German successes resulted from the powerful and truly shocking blitzkrieg attacks of the panzers—until the staggering defeat of the German Army at Stalingrad in February 1943. In that clash, the Germans lost 1,500 tanks; the Soviets lost 4,341 tanks . . . but they won the battle.

Since their loss at Stalingrad, the Germans had been retreating on the Eastern Front. Hitler and the German High Command were desperate to halt that retreat as soon as possible, to dispell any belief among Germany's enemies that she had lost her military power with the defeat at Stalingrad. They worried about the morale of their retreating army who also faced the threat of attack from Russian partisans in the withdrawal.

The German High Command thought it essential to organize and launch a huge and ambitious offensive against the Russians to prove that the armed forces of Germany were still a force to be feared and taken very seriously. The Germans appreciated, too, that if they could win a major victory over the Russians in a time when the Russians were rapidly losing patience with America and Britain for an apparent unwillingness to open a second front in the west, the possibility of a resulting split in the relationship between Russia and the western Allies would certainly be to Germany's advantage.

In spite their many problems in the Soviet Union, the Germans were managing to be extremely productive in armaments under the supervision of Albert Speer, despite the increasingly intense Allied bombing of Germany and German-occupied Europe. In mid-1943 Germany was producing roughly twice as many heavy and medium tanks as she had the previous year; twice as many military aircraft, and three times as much ammunition.

Before the start of Operation Citadel, the Germans had assembled 2,700 tanks, 2,000 planes, 10,000 artillery guns, and 900,000 troops in the battle zone—equivalent to one-third of Germany's entire military strength. The

Germans were evidently persuaded that the Allies would not be launching a second front during 1943, and at least partly on that basis felt safe in sending an enormous number of personnel to the Eastern Front.

The renewed German strength saw the wide-scale introduction of the formidable Focke-Wulf Fw-190A fighter plane, and the limited production of the threatening new Henschel Hs 129 ground attack aircraft. Nicknamed the *Panzerknacker* (tank cracker), the Hs 129 was developed to meet a need identified by the Condor Legion during the Spanish Civil War. But the plane never actually performed to its specified requirement. Being grossly underpowered, it handled poorly and was not produced in sufficient numbers to make a significant contribution to the German war effort. Strangely, Henschel had been ordered to equip the 129 with low-horsepower, low-priority engines that were not in demand for other production aircraft, thus greatly limiting its performance and sealing its fate. For a time, though, its very existence posed a powerful psychological threat. Much more important was the introduction on the Eastern Front of the new and genuinely threatening Tiger, King Tiger, and Panther German tanks, together with the new Ferdinand self-propelled gun.

The Russians, on the other hand, had not been static, but had made substantial advances against the enemy. In the aftermath of the German defeat at Stalingrad, a salient or bulge was created in the lines near the city of Kursk, south of Orel and north of Kharkov, roughly 280 miles south of Moscow. The Germans wanted to shorten their lines through the elimination of the Kursk salient and hoped to break through the northern and southern flanks, to encircle and trap the forces of the Red Army there. Intelligence reports, provided in part by the British, informed the Russians about the intended German offensive at Kursk. That knowledge, together with a delay in the start of the offensive while the Germans awaited adequate numbers of their new weapons, especially the Tiger tank, allowed the Red Army sufficient time to build new defences and assemble sizeable reserves in preparation for a major counterattack.

Armed with the knowledge of Citadel, the impending German offensive, the Russians planned their own effort, to redirect, slow, exhaust, and gradually wear down the panzers. The plan called for making the German tanks run their attack through the minefields, artillery kill zones, and hidden anti-tank strong points established through eight spaced defence lines 250 km deep. It was easily the most extensive defensive facility ever built. Between November 1942 and February 1943, Russian forces advancing west threatened to isolate the German Army Group A in the Caucasus, adding additional pressure on the Germans to launch the Citadel offensive. In the meantime, innovative methods were needed to disrupt the Russian advances, form up new divisions whose members would include non-combatant personnel, and equip new armoured units with every available tank including those being serviced and repaired in rear area workshops. In this period, a variety of armoured and motorized formations were arriving in German assembly areas. These included the 6th, 11th, and 17th Panzer Divisions, and the SS Panzer Corps which had recently been in France.

In his order of 15 April 1943, Hitler expressed his support and intention for Citadel: "This offensive is of decisive importance. It must end in swift and decisive success Every commander, every private soldier, must be indoctrinated with awareness of the decisive importance of this offensive. Victory at Kursk will be a beacon for the whole world."

The German Field Marshal Erich von Manstein was keen to open Citadel with the German Army on the strategic defensive and stressed the delivery of powerful counter-attacks by their panzer divisions. In a two-pronged approach, he wanted to maintain a strong force on the left flank while retreating on the right at the Dnieper River and delivering a heavy counter-attack against the flank of the Red Army. Hitler was not impressed with Manstein's idea and would not even consider giving up such territory as a part of the plan. The Manstein plan also met profound disfavour at the High Command level where Colonel General Kurt Zeitzler and other officers preferred to focus on the Kursk salient where the Red Army was maintaining the Voronezh and Central Fronts within and near the salient. Those positions provided the Germans with an opportunity to entrap between fifteen and twenty percent of the Red Army's entire forces. Such an action would straighten and reduce the front line and lead to the Germans recapturing the strategically important railway city of Kursk, which was sitting on the main north-south rail line between Moscow and Rostov. Plans for the attack were set by March. The German 9th Army under Generalfeldmarschall Walter Model was charged with attacking to the south from Orel, as Generaloberst Hermann Hoth's 4th Panzer Army together with Manstein's Army Group Kempf would swing in from the north near Belgorod. The two forces were to link up at Kursk and, if events there favoured the Germans, they were authorized to roll on to establish a new line at the Don River well to the east. In their favour, these German commanders knew they were in command of powerful attack forces, that the German Army boasted a proud record of having smashed Russian front line defences pretty much at will, and that the travel distance to Kursk was not that great.

Initially, the attacks were set to open on 4 May, but were immediately deferred pending the arrival in the war zone of the new, eagerly anticipated weaponry for the German forces, including the highly touted Tiger and Panther tanks. The attack date was reset for 12 June, which was soon changed to 20 June by Hitler under the threat of a potential Allied landing in Italy, coupled with continuing delays in the delivery of the new tanks. He would again postpone the start date to 3 July and later to 5 July.

A crucial flaw in the German plan for the coming blitzkrieg assault on the

Kursk salient was that it would lack the essential element of surprise. The scope and nature of the German build-up in personnel and armoured equipment was so vast as to make their intentions quite plain. Even the key aspect of German success in such past efforts, attacking unanticipated locations, would not be part of this operation. And the highly regarded tank expert and blitzkrieg specialist, Generaloberst Heinz Guderian, powerfully expressed his concern, and that of many fellow German commanders, when he confronted Hitler about the Kursk offensive: "Is it really necessary to attack Kursk, and indeed in the east this year at all? Do you think anyone even knows where Kursk is? The entire world doesn't care if we capture Kursk or not. What is the reason that is forcing us to attack this year on Kursk, or even more, on the Eastern Front?" To which Hitler responded: "I know. The thought of it turns my stomach."

The Russian command structure placed two generals with the responsibility for the defense of Kursk, Marshal of the Soviet Union Konstantin Rokossovsky, and General Nikolai Vatutin. The man put in charge of the massive Soviet reserve force to be employed in a counter-offensive was General Ivan Konev, and overseeing all of these commanders was Marshal of the Soviet Union Georgy Zhukov.

Their many highly credible intelligence sources had provided the Russians with virtually all they needed to know about the offensive operation coming from the Germans. They knew how and where it would be launched, they had a reasonably accurate estimate of the enemy numbers in equipment and personnel involved, and they knew, within days, when it would begin. Initially, Stalin failed to accept Zhukov's conclusion about Kursk as the German objective, but on consultation with other Soviet commanders, he concurred. In devising their own strategy for the offensive, the Russians determined to follow one that would essentially allow the Germans to wear themselves down to the point where they could no longer fight.

Armed with substantial intelligence information about the coming German offensive, Stalin and some of his military advisors favoured a first strike approach to beat the Germans to the punch. But Zhukov and the majority of the commanders favoured a more cautious posture which he outlined in a letter to Stalin at the time: "I consider it inadvisable for our forces to go over to the offensive in the very first days of the campaign in order to forestall the enemy. It would be better to make the enemy exhaust himself against our defences, and knock out his tanks and then, bringing up fresh reserves, to go over to the general offensive which would finally finish off his main force."

With some fifty divisions assembled for the offensive, including seventeen panzer and panzergrenadier divisions, upwards of 780,000 men, nearly 3,000 tanks, 10,000 guns and mortars, and 2,100 aircraft, the German forces prepared for the opening encounters of what was expected to be the most massive and extraordinary tank and infantry battle in history. For their part, the Russians had prepared 1.3 million men, 3,600 tanks, 20,000 guns and mortars, and 2,800 aircraft. With the intelligence provided him by the Swiss Lucy spy organization, together with decoded cipher informtion from Bletchley Park, Marshal Zhukov was able to pinpoint the location of the impending attack by 8 April. His defensive strategy recommendation to the Red Army General Staff: "According to the situation of the Soviet-German front, the enemy will attempt to cut off the Kursk salient, encircle and destroy the Soviet forces of Central Front and Voronezh Front deployed here. At the moment, both fronts have only fifteen tank divisions, meanwhile the German forces at Belgorod-Kharkov direction have already gathered seventeen tank divisions, most of them include the new types of tanks such as Tiger I, improvised Panther, Jagdpanzer IV and some kinds of tank destroyers such as Marder II, Marder III."

Based on intelligence reports, the Russians were able to predict where the German armoured divisions would want to employ their tanks in depth, and were able to position a large number of anti-tank guns there, as well as preparing many trenches and anti-tank traps. Their defences included the laying of 504,000 anti-tank and 440,000 anti-personnel mines, and, with the progressive delays and deferments of the German attack, the Russians were able to employ about 300,000 civilians to help in the construction of defences along the Kursk salient, as well as repairing vital access roads and digging literally thousands of miles of trenches.

The primary role of the Red Army when the German offensive started would be to exhaust and grind down the panzer formations, using artillery, anti-tank guns and anti-tank obstacles to slow, obstruct, and halt them, preparatory to the launching of a Soviet counter-offensive. Soviet machine-gun posts, mortar and howitzer crews were charged with destroying German infantry attempting to approach the Soviet anti-tank guns. Additionally, the Russians would utilize the support of a great many tanks that were to be dug in in hull-down positions to be used as static gun platforms.

Much earlier in the German offensive on the Soviet Eastern Front, the Red Air Force had performed poorly and erratically, encumbered as it was with an inventory of largely obsolete, inadequate aircraft and insufficiently trained airmen. By the time of the Kursk offensive in mid-1943, however, the air force had improved dramatically. Training and training standards had been lifted, and new, highly capable aircraft like the Yak-9 fighter and the Ilyushin IL-2 Sturmovik ground attack plane were in wide-spread operation and were extemely impressive performers.

Along with all the actual weaponry, defences, and personnel assembled and positioned for the fight by the Soviets, an elaborate assortment of deceptions and dummy positions and facilities were created. Fake airfields were populated with mock aircraft; effective use was made of camouflage, and a campaign of radio and communications misdirection was launched. So good was much of the battlefield camouflage that the first indication to the Germans of Russian guns in the area was the sight and sound of their own vehicles exploding.

Throughout the period of delays and postponements of the Kursk / Citadel operation, the Germans were adding to their arsenal of weaponry to be used in that offensive. The new additions included seventy-nine formidable Henschel Hs 129 ground attack aircraft, 270 new Tiger tanks, a number of new, late-model Mark IV Panzer tanks, as well as several captured Soviet T-34 tanks. To help counter the effectiveness of the Soviet Sturmovik ground attack plane, the Germans would bring Junkers Ju87G Stuka dive-bombers with cannon mounted in gun pods.

The final, actual date and order for beginning the Kursk offensive was issued on 1 July for the attack to start on 5 July. By the 2nd, that information was given to the Russian front line commanders, thanks to Soviet intelligence sources. Prior to the outbreak of the action, some German prisoners who had been captured by Russian shock troops before the start of the battle, informed their Russian captors that the attack would begin on the 5th, confirming the intelligence reports already in the hands of the Red Army commanders. That knowledge led to the Russians launching a huge artillery bombardment against the German forces beginning at 2 a.m. on 5 July, a bombardment by Russian artillery on the Voronezh Front ordered by General Vatutin. The psychological effect of the shelling took a heavy toll on the morale of the German troops on the receiving end as they realized that the German attack plans had been compromised.

It began in the afternoon of the 4th. It began with Stuka dive-bombers raiding the front lines to the north and then withdrawing to allow German artillery to start pounding the line. Early, probing attacks by the 3rd Panzer Corps against Soviet positions near Zavidovka; the 11th Panzer Division at the area around Butova, and west of there, the *Grossdeutschland* Division and the 3rd Panzer Division, and then the 2nd SS Panzer Corps went up against heavy enemy resistance until it was assisted by special assault troops wielding flamethrowers to eliminate the threat from outposts and bunkers. A substantive reply from the Soviets arrived at 2.30 a.m. of the 5th in a breath-taking shelling by upwards of 3,000 guns and mortars firing approximately half of the artillery ammunition used by them in the entire offensive, silencing roughly half of the German artillery batteries on the Central Front, delaying, slowing and disorganizing the enemy advance.

The main thrust of the German tank and infantry attack began at 5.30 a.m. following an artillery barrage. Luftwaffe air support arrived and the force of some 500 tanks, with heavys in the lead, mediums coming next, and then the infantry behind the armour. The Russians knew precisely where the German 9th Army would be attacking on the Soviet Central Front and were ready for them. Quite soon the Germans were trapped in the massive minefield defences and had to call up engineering units to clear lanes through the fields, working all the while under intense artillery fire which slowed their efforts and wrought heavy German casualties. Of the forty-nine Ferdinand heavy tank destroyers (later renamed *Elefant*) sent in against the Red Army that day, thirty-seven were lost or made inoperative in the minefields by 5.00 p.m. In that first day of the offensive, the Germans managed to advance six miles into the Soviet lines, for a loss of 1,287 men killed and missing, and 5,921 wounded. They also discovered the vulnerability of the Ferdinand, and some of their other armoured vehicles, for their lack of secondary armament. In the days immediately after the 5th, savage attacks by the German forces were greeted with equally savage responses from the Soviets. After 10 July, the German 11th Panzer Division had lost two-thirds of its tanks. The Germans were finding, too, that their vaunted Tiger tank was indeed vulnerable to the anti-tank guns of the Russians as the Russian tank commanders soon realized that the armour of the Tiger was thinner on its sides.

Two days later, what many historians have called the "greatest tank battle of World War Two" began about fifty miles southeast of Kursk at a place called Prokhorovka. The encounter, according to some, involved upwards of 1,500 tanks, although later research indicates that number to be closer to 600, still an enormous cast. In the run-up to the Battle of Kursk, German forces managed to recapture the city of Kharkov on 14 March 1943 after four days of house-to-house fighting. They pushed the Red Army back across the northern Don River and, in so doing, created the bulge in the Soviet lines which became known as the Kursk salient. In the effort, the Germans captured 9,000 Soviet troops and killed 23,000.

The Kursk offensive took on a new dimension on 12 July 1943 when German formations, mainly the 4th Panzer Army, engaged the tanks of the Red Army's 5th Guards Tank Army near the town of Prokhorovka. To that point in the Battle of Kursk, the German forces had been largely stopped in the northern Orel sector, but to the south of the Kursk salient, the Germans had made a greater penetration and were approaching Prokhorovka. Their advance had forced the Red Army to involve much of it operational reserves earlier than it had intended, leading to one of the biggest tank battles in history. In it, the intention of the German tank forces was the encirclement and elimination operationally of much of the Soviet armoured capability. The station was their primary objective at Prokhorovka and taking it would, the Germans believed, allow their 4th Panzer Army to break through in the sector and the Wehrmacht to reach the rear of the Soviet forces and encircle them in and around Kursk.

The panzers did succeed in getting to the station and were threatening to encircle the Soviet 1st Tank Army, but on 11 July Marshal Zhukov ordered a counter-offensive involving five Soviet armies to begin on the 12th. Of the participating Soviet forces, the 5th Guards Tank Army lacked proper artillery preparation for the coming battle and its tank commanders were ordered to operate at high speed as a means of overcoming their own shortcomings in tanks and weaponry. They were also required to make their main attack in a sector containing an anti-tank ditch that had been dug by the Soviets and would now work in favour of the enemy forces. A further negative factor for the Russians was that the bulk of available Red Air Force aircraft were then tied up in operations in the north, essentially sacrificing control of the air over the Prokhorovka area to the German Air Force for the present.

The 2nd SS Panzer Corps opened their attack at 6.50 in the morning of 12 July. Both sides needed strong air support to sustain the efforts of the ground formations, but despite nearly 900 sorties being flown by the Soviets and 654 by the Germans, that support was unable to give a significant edge to either side that day. The panzers had to launch their attacks on the 5th Guards Tank Army without the diversionary support they required. The 2nd was spearheading the German attack for Generaloberst Hermann Hoth's 4th Panzer Army which had been greatly reinforced with additional tanks and personnel. In the rolling hills and farmlands to the west of Prokhorovka, the panzers clashed with the Guards tanks in an eight-hour battle fought in choking dust and broiling heat. Some accounts claim that the Germans brought an operational force of nearly 500 tanks and self-propelled guns to the scene, and still found themselves considerably outnumbered by their Russian enemy. The spearheading 2nd SS Panzer Corps somehow held its formation against the massive power of the Guards tanks, but in the action it lost half its own tanks. Meanwhile, the tanks of the 3rd SS Division were fighting the Soviet 31st Guards Tank Corps and the 33rd Guards Rifle Corps to a virtual draw, with the Russians having the edge through their close-in firing at the relatively vulnerable side armour of the Tiger tanks.

The Soviets had launched their own attack at 9.15 a.m. The air situation then changed dramatically in the Germans' favour. The Soviet General Rotmistrov fielded more than 400 tanks and assault guns in a first wave, backed up by a second wave of seventy more tanks. This time the German Air Force arrived in strength and in time to catch the Russians out in the open. The Luftwaffe came in with large formations of bomb-carrying Fw-190s, Ju 87 dive-bombers, and Hs 129 tank-killer ground attack planes. David M. Glantz and Jonathan M. House in *The Battle of Kursk*: ". . . four squadrons of Henschel Hs 129 aircraft, specially equipped with 30mm automatic cannon for anti-tank missions, broke up the Soviet attack, perforating the thin overhead armour of the tanks and leaving a hideous, burning wasteland. This unprecedented action, in which a tank attack was halted by air power alone, set a dangerous precedent. Indeed, throughout this entire savage battle, Soviet troop movements had to be conducted at night to minimize such losses. This in turn delayed the arrival of reserves to block the German penetration."

The German tanks were also effectively supported by their artillery units. In the thick, heavy smoke created by the many exploding and burning Russian tanks, visibility became minimal for both sides. In the attack that morning, the Russians lost 400 of the 800 tanks they had fielded. The heavy Russian tank losses were attributed, in part at least, to the lack of efficient Soviet air-to-ground communications and co-ordination. Their aircraft were either not available due to other commitments or were unable to react quickly enough when required. The Soviet 31st Tank Corps commander stated that their air support was absent until 1 p.m. Another tanker, of the 5th Tank Army reported that the German aircraft were constantly over the Soviet tank formations throughout the battle, while their own Red Air Force fighters were not up to the task.

By nightfall, most of the German formations in the day's battle had been bested by the Soviet armoured forces and guns. The German tanks had suffered heavily too in strikes by Sturmovik ground attack aircraft, as well as from waves of Stukas and the new Henschel Hs 129 tank destroyer planes. Soviet tank losses were extremely high as well, halting their own advance. The principal fighting formations of both sides failed to achieve their objectives that day.

The prepondrance of Soviet reserve strength and the ability of the Red Army armoured units and infantry to halt the German advances, combined with the need to abort the assault of the German 9th Army on the northern portion of the Kursk salient, to cause Hitler to call off the attack. Kursk was the last major offensive launched by the Germans in Russia. While not a clear tactical victory for the Soviets, Prokhorovka and the wider Kursk battle, after the German defeat at Stalingrad, left the Red Army with the strategic initiative for the balance of the war.

ARDENNES

Hitler had ordered his commander in Paris, General Dietrich von Choltitz, to destroy the city rather than simply surrender it to the Allies when they arrived to liberate it in summer of 1944. But Choltitz negotiated an agreement to refrain from destroying the city and to surrender it in return for the safe withdrawal of his occupying garrison there. The arrangement was an expensive one for the Allies, in fuel, resources, and personnel commitments, and especially time—substantially delaying their progress towards the Rhine and Germany. Out of Paris, Hitler's armies were feeling the heat of the approaching Russians from the east, Yugoslav partisans in the Balkans, and the American forces moving through Belgium.

In one of several pronounced differences of opinion between General Dwight Eisenhower, Supreme Commander of the Allied Forces in Europe, and Field Marshal Bernard Montgomery, Allied ground forces commander, Montgomery was a proponent of a narrow frontal assault on Germany to be followed by a concentrated attack on Berlin. Ike, on the other hand, opted for an approach to Germany along an extended front, to let his supply chain catch up and keep pace with his rapidly advancing armies, and to consolidate their positions along the Rhine River. By September, a massive Allied airborne assault on the Dutch towns of Arnhem, Nijmegen, and Eindhoven ended in a chaotic, disastrous mess in which the British First Airborne Division suffered nearly seventy-five percent casualties. In October, the American forces captured Aachen, once a part of Charlemagne's empire. Advancing through the Hürtgen Forest, they experienced heavy losses as they trudged and rolled over the snow-covered German minefields.

The Allied armoured forces had achieved much success in the Normandy campaign, but were unable to effectively support a three-pronged attack into the follow-up action, which might have enabled them to end the European war in 1944. The Allies got to the Siegfried Line in September, but by then they had been considerably weakened. At that point it was no longer possible to keep them supplied with the food, fuel, ammunition, spare parts, and the maintenance required for their continued advance. And, approaching from the east, the Russians were experiencing similar problems and were also stalled. It was to the great advantage of the Germans, who fully capitalized on it to assemble a large and powerful armoured force with which to push the Allied forces back into the English Channel. It was to be the last great opportunity of the war for the Germans.

Now the Germans faced a monumental challenge in putting together the armoured force they needed. They had to significantly increase German mobilization, contain the Russian advances in Poland, displace many thou-

sands of workers from their falling industrial base to use as replacements for
the huge losses they were taking in combat, and perhaps most difficult, they
had to somehow find, equip, train and field at least nine complete new panzer divisions and twenty infantry divisions.

With Germany's basic infrastructure in near total ruin from the massive,
continuing Allied combined bombing offensive towards the end of 1944, the
Germans were helpless to slow the flow of vital oil from their war reserves.
Armaments Minister Albert Speer had worked minor miracles resurrecting
the German armoured capability, but Germany's oil reserves had been reduced
by nearly two-thirds by the spring, and the incessant Allied bombing campaign had all but ruined German synthetic oil production. By August, the Red
Army had eliminated the important Ploesti oilfields as a precious Romanian
source, making it necessary for the German army to transport their tanks by
train, putting a further drain on their limited coal supply, rather than on their
vitally important oil reserves. Further complicating the situation for the
Germans was the ever increasing level of attacks by Allied bombers, as well
as by fighters in the ground-attack role, on the German railways. This intensified air activity required the Germans to restrict much of their high-priority rail transport of hardware such as tanks to nighttime.

In what for the Allies was a rather new wrinkle following the D-Day landings at Normandy, the Nazis attempted to retake the initiative and, hopefully, shift the outcome of the war in their favour. They dropped a new form of
terror weapon into the mix—the V-1 flying bomb. With it, Hitler hoped to
recapture the initiative and possibly alter the entire course of the European
war. The British and the Americans called the V-1s "Buzz Bombs" or
"Doodlebugs". The weapons were relatively small, pulse-jet-powered early
cruise missiles. They were not very sophisticated devices, incapable of
reaching and hitting a specific target with much reliability or accuracy. But
by late summer 1944, lifting from their launch sites on the Channel coast
of France, the V-1s managed to destroy about 75,000 buildings and kill
more than 6,000 people in southern England. They were quickly followed
by a far more frightening flying bomb in the form of the massive V-2 rocket.
Beginning in September, the supersonic V-2 rockets began falling, silently
and without any warning, on London and the south of England, destroying
far greater areas than the V-1s and spreading a new kind of terror among
the British people. Thankfully, for their sake, these terrible new weapons
became operational too late for the Germans to change to course of the war
with them.

Hitler's belief in the value and capability of those V-weapons, and the need
for the launch sites in northern France for their attacks on Britain, coupled
with his need to retake the port facilities of Antwerp, and his then-shrinking
resources, powerfully influenced the decision to address his final major

attack on the Western Allies, instead of on the steadily advancing Soviets. Interestingly, he decided to launch the action through the Ardennes forest in Belgium, taking advantage of the limited American force presence there, and of the often difficult and rather unpredictable weather conditions in that region, which virtually assured a minimum of Allied aerial reconnaissance and air opposition there. In such an attack, Hitler expected to sever the Allied supply lines, shatter their alliance and sufficiently ruin their morale, to alter the course of the war and then force a negotiated settlement. Much of his expectation was based on his low opinion of the American soldier, whom he believed would be utterly terrorized by such a blitzkrieg attack and left incapable of further opposition. On 11 and 12 December he held a final planning conference for the Ardennes offensive: "Gentlemen, before opening the conference I must ask you to read this document carefully and then sign it with your full names." General Hasso von Manteuffel, General Officer Commanding, 5 Panzer Army: "The date was 3 November 1944, and I had assumed that the conference would be merely a routine meeting of the three army commanders who held the northern sector of the Western Front under Field Marshal Model's Army Group B. Each officer present had to pledge himself to preserve complete silence concerning the information which Jodl intended to divulge to us: should any officer break the pledge, he must realize that his offence would be punishable by death. I had frequently attended top secret conferences presided over by Hitler at Berchtesgaden or at the 'Wolf's Lair' both before and after 20 July 1944, but this was the first time that I had seen a document such as the one I now signed. It was clear that something most unusual was afoot.

"The German commanders knew the terrain in the Ardennes well. We had advanced across it in 1940 and retreated through it only a few months before. We knew its narrow, twisting roads and the difficulties, not to say dangers, they could cause an attacking force, particularly in winter and in the bad weather conditions which were an essential prerequisite to the opening of our operation. The main roads contained many hairpin bends, and were frequently built into steep hillsides. To get the guns of the artillery and flak units, as well as the pontoons and beams of the bridging engineers around these sharp corners was a lengthy and difficult business. The guns and trailers had to be disconnected and then dragged around the corner by a capstan mechanism, naturally one at a time. Vehicles could not pass one another on these roads."

General Sepp Dietrich, General Officer Commanding, 6 Panzer Army: "All I had to do was to cross the river, capture Brussels and then go on and take the port of Antwerp. And all this in December, January and February, the worst months of the year; through the Ardennes where snow was waist-deep and there wasn't room to deploy four tanks abreast, let alone six armoured divisions; when it didn't get light until eight in the morning and was dark again at four in the afternoon and my tanks can't fight at night; with divisions that had just been reformed and were composed chiefly of raw untrained recruits; and at Christmas time."

The operation began in the early morning of 16 December under a heavy fog cover, as eight panzer divisions rolled through the minimal defences of the Allies on the eighty-five-mile front. Initially, the German forces were able to roll up substantial advances through the forest to the complete shock of the Americans there. The large dent the Germans created in the Allied line there led to the operation becoming known as the Battle of the Bulge. American Brigadier-General Anthony McAuliffe, in command of the 101st Airborne Division, arranged for the panzers to receive a hot reception as they rolled on towards the American-occupied town of Bastogne, a strong defence of the town, costing the armoured and infantry forces of the German commander, General Heinrich Freiherr von Lüttwitz, and causing him to issue the following:

"To the U.S.A. commander of the encircled town of Bastogne:
The fortune of war is changing. This time the U.S.A. forces in and near Bastogne have been encircled by strong German armoured units. More German armoured units have crossed the river Our near Ortheuville, have taken Marche and reached St. Hubert by passing through Hompre-Sibret-Tillet. Libramont is in German hands.

"There is only one possibility to save the encircled U.S.A. troops from total annihilation: that is the honorable surrender of the encircled town. In order to think it over, a term of two hours will be granted beginning with the presentation of this note.

"If this proposal should be rejected one German Artillery Corps and six heavy A.A. Battalions are ready to annihilate the U.S.A. troops in and near Bastogne. The order for firing will be given immediately after this two hours term.

"All the serious civilian losses caused by this artillery fire would not correspond with the well-known American humanity. —The German Commander

And General McAuliffe's reply:

"To the German Commander:
NUTS!
The American Commander
(the reply was explained to the German negotiators as the equivalent of 'Go to hell!')

This exchange was followed by an order from General Eisenhower to General George Patton to assist the Americans at Bastogne. Patton sent the 37th Tank Battalion under the command of Lieutenant Colonel Creighton Abrams,

Jr. to spearhead an armoured column to break the German encirclement of Bastogne. In his illustrious military career, Abrams went on to become a four-star general in command of all U.S. forces in the Vietnam War. Today's American main battle tank is named in his honour.

Another famous American general, Matthew B. Ridgeway: "I remember once standing beside a road leading through a pine wood, down a slope to the road junction of Manhay, where a hot fight was going on. That whole Ardennes fight was a battle for road junctions, because in that wooded country, in the deep snows, armies could not move off the roads. This particular crossroads was one of many that the Germans had to take if they were to keep up the momentum of their offensive, and we were fighting desperately to hold it. I had gone up to this point, which lay not far forward of my command post, to be of what help I could in this critical spot. As I was standing there, a lieutenant, with perhaps a dozen men, came out of the woods from the fighting, headed towards the rear. I stopped him and asked him where he was going and what his mission was. He told me that he and his men had been sent out to develop the strength of the German units that had reached Manhay, and that they had run into some machine-gun fire that was too hot for them, so they had come back.

"I relieved him of his command there on the spot. I told him that he was a disgrace to his country and his uniform and that I was ashamed of him, and I knew the members of his patrol were equally ashamed. Then I asked if any other member of the patrol was willing to lead it back into the fight. A sergeant stepped up and said he would lead it and see to it that it carried out its mission.

"Another incident occurred which I remember with regret. In the fierce fighting, the town [Manhay] changed hands several times. The Germans had brought up some flat trajectory guns, and they started shelling our little group. Fragments whizzed everywhere. One struck an artillery observer, who was standing by me, in the leg, and another punctured the [fuel] tank of his jeep. As this shell exploded an infantry sergeant standing nearby became hysterical. He threw himself into the ditch by the side of the road, crying and raving. I walked over and tried to talk to him, trying to help him get hold of himself. But it had no effect. He was just crouched there in the ditch, cringing in utter terror. So I called my jeep driver, Sergeant Farmer, and told him to take his carbine and march this man back to the nearest M.P., and if he started to escape to shoot him without hesitation. He was an object of abject cowardice, and the sight of him would have a terrible effect on any American soldier who might see him. That's the sort of thing you see sometimes. It is an appalling thing to witness—to see a man break completely like that—in battle. It is worse than watching a death—for you are seeing something more important than the body die. You are witnessing the death of a man's spirit, of his pride, of all that gives meaning and purpose to life."

Many more important combat actions were to follow, and by 26 December, momentum and the initiative had changed over to the Americans. The lengthy period of fog and poor weather conditions had finally lifted on Christmas eve, allowing Allied aircraft, including tank-destroying Hawker Typhoons of the R.A.F., to hit and quickly wreck many German tanks and other armoured vehicles. The Germans mounted another major armoured assault on Bastogne, but without success. It was then clear to General Manteuffel that the great German counter-offensive the Americans referred to as the Battle of the Bulge, had failed and a full-scale German retreat followed with the Americans in hot pursuit.

American losses in the Battle of the Bulge were 10,276 killed, 47,493 wounded, and 23,218 missing. British losses in the action included 200 killed of a total of 1,400 casualties. On the German side, the casualties amounted to approximately 100,000 killed, wounded, or missing. The fighting in the Ardennes in late 1944 and early 1945 was among the most savage and intense of the entire war. The aggression of the German forces had been whipped up to great intensity early in the offensive when a rumour began circulating among them that the British and American armies were about to turn over their German prisoners to the Russians. The Germans fighting in the Ardennes attacked their Allied opposition thereafter with a new level of ferocity. Some of the actions led to several of the German commanders being tried for war crimes committed during the Ardennes offensive.

In the Allied pursuit of the German forces retreating from the Ardennes, American armoured and infantry units were advancing on them from the south while the British forces came after them from the north. In a panicky move to try holding off the rapidly advancing Russians towards Poland, the Germans sent much of their remaining tank forces there, leaving few armoured reserves to cope with the Allies pursuing the large force out of Belgium towards Germany. The last of the German troops from the Ardennes were across the Rhine into Germany by 22 March.

As the Russians were closing in on Berlin in the spring of 1945, Fritz-Rudolf Averdieck was a radio operator / sergeant in Armoured Grenadier Regiment 90 of the German Army. He was a crew member of a *Schützenpanzerwagen* or SPW, a light armoured vehicle with half-tracks. It was also used as a troop carrier, was open at the top and mounted a machine-gun. It was used during operations as a command centre by his commander. It was a command-communications and fighting vehicle. The wireless operator sat beside the driver, with the commander behind him on the carrier. Averdieck:"In early 1945, the last barrier before Berlin was the Seelow Heights near the Oder River. After incurring heavy casualties in our numerous attacks which failed to throw the Soviet bridgehead back over the Oder, the great Soviet offensive began on 16 April. The superior strength of the enemy overwhelmed our battle-weary troops, and reached the Seelow Heights. Our weakened regiment counter-attacked, but was unable to regain the old front lines. Nevertheless, we strengthened and held a position on the Heights the night of 19 April. But the continuous Soviet heavy artillery and mortar fire took a heavy toll, tearing large rents in our lines. One thing was clear from the sound of the ongoing battles. The enemy had already passed us to the north and south on its march to Berlin."

BEST OF THE BEST

To be fair, there are several contenders for the title—best of the best tanks in the world, and reaching an objective concensus with any number of experts may well be impossible. What follows then is simply a brief exposure to the main battle tanks that are currently thought—by most people who should know—to be the best in the world. Which is the best of the best? The jury is still out. Here, in no particular order, are the nominees.

The German Leopard 2 was developed in the 1970s for the West German Army by Krauss-Maffei Wegmann Maschinenbau of Kiel, as the successor to the Leopard 1. The Leopard 2 has proven quite popular with various customer countries including Austria, Canada, Norway, Sweden, Portugal, Spain, Poland, Denmark, Finland, the Netherlands, Greece, Switzerland, Chile, and Turkey. More than 3,480 Leopard 2 tanks have been produced. Germany has purchased 2,125 of the tanks for its modern army.

The Leopard 2 first entered combat with the German contingent of the Kosovo Force, and the Dutch contingent in Bosnia-Herzegovina during the 1990s, and they were employed by Canada in Afghanistan in August 2007. Denmark also fielded some Leopard 2s in Afghanistan that autumn and the crew of one of them suffered the first fatality in the combat operations of the type when it was hit by an improvised explosive device. Three members of the four-man crew were wounded and managed to escape from the vehicle, but the badly wounded driver did not and, despite on-site treatment by Danish medics, he did not survive the attack.

For its armoured protection, the Leopard 2 has spaced multi-layered composite material overall with additional armour added on the turret front, hull and side skirts. The A4M and A6M variants have an additional mine protection plate on the belly to protect the crew against mines and IEDs. Leopard variants after the 2A6 are built with spall liners for crew protection. A definition of spall is: flakes of material that are broken off a larger solid body and can be produced as a result of projectile impact, corrosion, weathering, cavitation, or excessive rolling pressure. Spalling is defined as a process of surface failure in which spall is shed. One Leopard 2 variant is made with additional slat armour to increase the tank's protection against rocket-propelled grenades.

Smoke to mask the tank's movement can be generated by smoke mortars mounted on either side of the turret and can be fired electrically as single rounds or as salvos of four.

Four Halon fire extinguisher bottles are installed to the right, behind the driver's station and are automatically activated by the tank fire detection system when the temperature rises above 82 degrees centigrade in the fighting compartment, or manually by a control panel near the driver. An extra Halon extinguisher is stored on the floor near the main gun. There is crew protection against nuclear, biological, and chemical threats through an NBC overpressurization system.

The Leopard 2 is armed with the Rheinmetall 120mm smoothbore gun, the current variant of which has twenty-seven rounds of ammunition stored in the forward part of the hull left of the driver's station and an additional fifteen rounds in the left side of the turret bustle. Should the ammunition storage area be hit, a blow-off panel in the roof of the turret is designed to direct an explosion upwards away from the crew compartment. The fully-stabilized gun can fire a variety of round types, including the German DM33 anti-tank round which is reputed to be capable of penetrating twenty-two inches of steel armour at a range of 2,200 yards. A newer version of the round, a multi-purpose anti-tank round, is said to be able to penetrate thirty-two+ inches of the armour. A newer version of the Rheinmetall gun system is designed to fire the LAHAT anti-tank guided missile through the main gun to engage a target at a range of up to 6,600 yards. The thermal sleeve and bore evacuator on the barrel of the main gun are made of glass-reinforced plastic and are designed to regulate the barrel temperature. The tank commander has a stabilized panoramic periscope for day-night observation and target identification. The periscope can traverse 360 degrees and projects a thermal image on a monitor in the fighting compartment. The rotation time for the turret itself is ten seconds. The fire control suite can provide up to three range values in four seconds. The fire control system enables the tank to engage moving targets at ranges up to 5,500 yards while moving over rough terrain.

Secondary armament on the Leopard 2 (German model) includes two MG3 7.62mm machine-guns with 4,750 rounds of ammunition carried on board.

The Leopard 2 is powered by an MTU liquid-cooled V-12 twin-turbo diesel engine of 1,479 hp. The tank has a maximum road range of about 310 miles. The entire engine power pack can be changed in the field in thirty-five minutes.

There are several engineering variant models of the Leopard 2. The *Bergepanzer* armoured recovery vehicle comes in a "bulldozer" mode and a version with a crane and integral winch for rescuing damaged vehicles enabling it to tow them to safety even over rough, battlefield terrain. There is a *Panzerschnellbrücke* that can carry a folding mobile bridge to be used in fording a river. The bridge is strong enough to support a Leopard tank. When the mission is completed, the tank-bridge is then retrieved and re-stowed. The *Pionierpanzer Kodiak* is a bulldozer-excavator with dual capstan winches and is used for clearing obstacles and minefields. The *Fahrschulpanzer* is a driver training tank for Leopard 2 crews. A weighted, fixed observation cab replaces the standard turret and has forward and side-facing windows as well as a dummy gun. Positions are provided for an instructor and two additional students.

The maximum combat weight of the Leopard 2 is about sixty tons and the top speed is forty-two mph, placing it among fastest tanks in the world, if not *the* fastest.

The unit cost in 2007 was $5.74 million.

The British entry in the main battle tank stakes is the Challenger 2, developed by Vickers Defence Systems, which is now known as BAE Systems Land and Armaments. The Challenger 2 is a substantially redesigned version of the Challenger 1, having very few parts that are interchangeable with the 1. Challenger 2 has served in Kosovo, Bosnia, and Iraq and was initially developed in 1986 by Vickers as a private venture. A formal deal for a demonstrator vehicle resulted when the company submitted its design to the Ministry of Defence and, following a competition with the tanks of other manufacturers, including the American M1A2 Abrams MBT and the German Leopard 2, the MoD ordered 127 Challenger 2s and thirteen driver training versions in June 1991. That order was followed in 1994 by another for an additional 259 tanks and nine driver training vehicles. The first of the new tanks were delivered in 1994 from the production facilities at Barnbow, Leeds, and Elswick, Tyne and Wear.

The new tank was then subjected to an extensive range of performance reliability and in-service reliability testing, simulating an operational experience of 285 days. The performance aspect included seventeen miles of on-road travel; twenty-one miles of off-road travel; thirty-four main armament rounds fired; 1,000 7.62mm machine-gun rounds fired; sixteen hours of weapon system operation; ten hours of main engine idling; and three and a half hours of main engine running. In the in-service reliability demonstration, twelve fully-crewed Challenger 2s were tested at both the Bovington test tracks and the Lulworth Bindon ranges. They passed, exceeding all staff requirements.

Operationally, Challenger 2 went into British Army service in 1998 with the Royal Scots Dragoon Guards stationed in Germany. The tanks are planned to stay in service until 2035, serving with the Royal Scots Dragoon Guards, the Royal Dragoon Guards, the Queen's Royal Hussars, and the 2nd Royal Tank Regiment. In addition to the tanks ordered for the British Army use, the Sultanate of Oman ordered thirty-eight Challenger 2s, with delivery completed in 2001. Additional versions of the Challenger 2, the Trojan minefield breaching vehicle, and the Titan bridge-laying vehicle, were developed in and displayed in 2006. Sixty-six of these specialized vehicles are on order for the Royal Engineers. The Trojan is a combat engineering vehicle intended to replace the Chieftain AVRE. It carries an articulated excavator arm, a bulldozer blade, and attachment rails for fascines, or stick bundles used in construction. The Titan Armoured Vehicle Launched Bridge carries a single twenty-six-metre bridge, or two twelve-metre bridges, and can also be fitted with a bulldozer blade.

The Challenger 2 is armed with a 120mm gun fitted with a thermal sleeve and a muzzle reference system and fume extractor. The gun system is controlled through an all-electric control and stabilization system. The 360 degree rotation of the turret is completed in nine seconds. It is believed that this main gun in the Challenger 2 is the only MBT main gun whose barrel is rifled. The British Army continues to require the use of high-explosive squash head (HESH) rounds, in addition to armour-piercing rounds. The HESH rounds have a longer range—up to five miles—and are more effective against thin-skinned vehicles and buildings. Ammunition storage for forty-nine rounds is provided in the turret and hull. Additional armament includes a 7.62mm chain gun, to the left of the main gun, and a 7.62mm machine-gun mounted on a pintle on the loader's hatch ring. 4,200 rounds of 7.62mm ammunition are carried on board. A risk analysis for the possible incorporation of an automatic loader for the main gun of the tank indicated the probability of reduced battlefield survivability under such a system, so the Army elected to retain a four-man crew that includes a loader, for the Challenger 2. The results of the analysis pointed to the possibility of mechanical failure and the time needed for such a repair as the primary concerns leading to the Army's decision.

The tank commander has a panoramic gyro-stabilized sight with a laser rangefinder. His station is equipped with eight periscopes for 360 degree vision. Night vision is provided through a thermal observation and gunnery sight, the image being displayed on both the commander's and gunner's sights and monitors. The gunner has a primary sight whose laser rangefinder has a range of 218 yards to six+ miles. The driver's position is equipped with an image-intensifying passive driving periscope for night driving.

Among the most heavily armoured and best protected tanks in the world today, the turret and hull of the Challenger 2 are protected with second generation Chobham armour, a British invention whose details are classified, but the British Army claims the armour is twice as strong as steel. Kits of explosive reactive armour (ERA) are also fitted as required. A nuclear, biological, chemical (NBC) protection system is fitted in the turret bustle, and the turret is equipped with five smoke grenade dischargers on each side. The tank is also able to create smoke by injecting diesel fuel into the exhaust manifolds.

As in all British tanks since the Centurion, Challenger 2 is equipped with a boiling vessel (BV), sometimes referred to as a kettle. This system can be used for brewing tea and other hot beverages, and for heating the boil-in-the-bag meals provided in ration packs. This feature is unique to the British armed forces.

The first use of the Challenger 2 in combat occurred in March 2003 during the invasion of Iraq when 120 of the tanks belonging to the 7th Armoured Brigade of the 1st Armoured Division went into action during the siege of Basra. The tanks gave fire support to the British forces there and were praised for their availability. Earlier problems relating to sand filters had long since been resolved. In one incident, an urban encounter, a Challenger 2 was attacked by irregular forces using rocket-propelled grenades and machine-guns. In the attack, the driver's gunsight was damaged and, as he was trying to back away under the commander's direction, damage occurred to the other sights and then the tank threw its tracks when it entered a ditch. An easy target at that point, the tank was soon hit at close range by fourteen RPGs and a MILAN anti-tank missile. The only significant damage was to the sighting system. All of the crew were safe and unhurt, remaining in the tank until it was recovered for repairs. The tank was operational again within six hours. In another incident, a Challenger 2 was struck in August 2006 by a Soviet RPG which penetrated the hull through the explosive reactive armour in the driver's cabin area. The driver suffered the partial loss of a foot and two more of the crew were injured, but the driver was able to reverse the tank some one and a half miles to an aid station. Later the MoD commented: "We never claimed that the Challenger 2 is impenetrable."

On 25 March 2003, Challenger 2s were involved in a "friendly fire" incident in Basra when a tank of the 2nd Royal Tank Regiment mistakenly engaged another Challenger 2 (of the Queen's Royal Lancers) when the first tank crew detected what they believed to be an enemy flanking manouevre, on their thermal equipment. The attacking tank fired two HESH rounds, the second round hitting the open hatch of the commander and showering hot fragments into the turret, causing an explosion of the stowed ammunition, which destroyed the tank and killed two crew members. It was the only Challenger 2 ever to be completely destroyed on operations. In another incident, on 6 April 2007, also in Basra, an IED shaped-charge penetrated the underside of a Challenger 2 and in the explosion the driver suffered the loss of three of his toes and one other crewman suffered minor injuries. To guard against such incidents in future, Challenger 2s have been upgraded with a new passive armour package using add-on armour from Rafael Advanced Defense Systems of Israel.

Other upgrades have been added to the Challenger 2 line, including the Challenger Lethality Improvement Programme (CLIP) to replace the L30A1 rifled main gun with the 120mm Rheinmetall L55 smoothbore gun, the same as that used on the Leopard 2, enabling the Challenger 2 to use the standard NATO ammunition, including the tungsten-based kinetic energy penetrator rounds that do not attract the environmental and political objections levelled against depleted uranium rounds. The 2006 cost estimate for fitting the Rheinmetall gun to all British Army Challengers was £386 million.

A further version of the Challenger 2 is the Challenger Armoured Repair and Recovery Vehicle for recovering damaged tanks on the battlefield. With seating for a mixed-trade crew of up to five, instead of armament this vehicle is fitted with a main winch and a smaller pilot winch, an Atlas crane which can lift more than seven tons over a distance of 4.9 m., a bulldozer blade, and a large set of heavy repair and recovery tools including gear for air-compressed tools and arc-welding.

The 2002 unit cost of the Challenger 2 was £4,217,000. The tank's Perkins diesel engine delivers 1,200 hp and maximum road and cross-country speeds of 37mph and 25mph respectively. Challenger 2 has a range of 280 miles (road) and 156 miles (cross-country).

From Chrysler Defense, which is now General Dynamics Land Systems, comes the M1A2 Abrams MBT. It is named after General Creighton Abrams, the former U.S. Army Chief of Staff and Commander of U.S. military forces in Vietnam from 1968 to 1972. Abrams is believed to be the original source for "They've got us surrounded, the poor bastards," uttered during the Battle of the Bulge. The Abrams M1A2 was developed during the Cold War era and was the first tank to adopt the British Chobham armour. Prior to the Gulf War Operations Desert Storm and Desert Shield, the Abrams was fitted with better firepower and improved nuclear, biological and chemical protection. The tank was considerably better than the Iraqi tanks it faced and very few Abrams tanks were hit in their encounters. Experience gained in Iraq led to improvements in the sighting and fire control systems, and to some extent, the tank's vulnerability to RPGs and mines was reduced through the introduction of the Tank Urban Survival Kit (TUSK). The TUSK field-installable kit enables the Abrams tank to be upgraded without the need for a recall to a maintenance depot.

Heavily armoured and well armed, the Abrams is powered by a Honeywell multi-fuel 1,500 hp gas turbine engine that is normally run on JP8 jet fuel. The tank is protected with a sophisticated composite armour. For the safety of the crew, the ammunition storage is in a separate blow-out compartment. The Abrams is among the heaviest of main battle tanks in service today, at nearly sixty-eight tons. The unit cost in fiscal year 1999 was $6.21 million (estimated inflation-adjusted 2012 at $8.58 million).

The M1A1 Abrams entered service with the U.S. Army in 1980, replacing the M60 Patton main battle tank. The Abrams remains the main battle tank of the United States Army and Marine Corps, and of the armies of Australia, Egypt, Kuwait, Saudi Arabia, and Iraq. It has been built by the Lima Army Tank Plant since 1980 and was also built by the Detroit Arsenal Tank Plant from 1982 to 1996. The tank is operated by four crew members: commander, gunner, loader, and driver. General Dynamics Land Systems Division purchased the Chrysler Defense company in 1982, after Chrysler had built 1,000 of the Abrams tanks. Between 1979 and 1985, 3,273 of the tanks were produced. The total production of the Abrams M1 and M1A1 amounted to 9,000 tanks at an approximate unit cost of $4.3 million. A 1990 a U.S. government report criticized the cost and fuel efficiency of the M1 when compared with other MBTs of similar power and performance, such as the German Leopard 2.

It was not until 1991 in Operation Desert Storm of the Gulf War, that the M1A1 Abrams was tried in combat. In that initial engagement, 1,848 Abrams tanks had been sent to Saudi Arabia to take part in the liberation of Kuwait. The Soviet T-55, T-62, and T-72 tanks of the Iraqi Army under Saddam Hussein were clearly outmatched by the Abrams. Of all the tanks fielded by the Americans, only nine were destroyed in the action, seven of them by friendly fire. Two were deliberately destroyed when they were disabled, to prevent their being captured. Others received minor battle damage but remained fully operational. In fact, relatively few of the Abrams tanks were even hit by enemy fire. There was just one American fatality among the tank crews and very few wounded.

In that desert conflict, the Abrams had an effective killing range of more than 2,700 yards, a vital advantage over the Soviet tanks of the opposition whose maximum effective range was 2,200 yards. In survivability, the M1A1 was able to sustain and survive direct hits to the front armour and fore side turret armour by armour-piercing rounds in friendly fire incidents. They could not sustain similar hits to the side armour of the hull or the rear armour of the turret, with both areas being penetrated on at least two occasions by depleted uranium ammunition.

American forces invaded Iraq in 2003 to find and depose the Iraqi leader, Saddam Hussein, in Operation Iraqi Freedom. By March of 2005, eighty Abrams tanks were put out of action in enemy attacks. A new emphasis on "urban warfare" for armoured units emerged from that Iraq experience, resulting in many Abrams tank crews being issued shoulder-fired anti-tank weapons based on the likely need to engage heavy tanks in tightly restricted urban areas in which the Abrams' main gun could not be readily used.

In the Iraq campaign, a number of M1s that were immobilized in combat had to be destroyed—often by other Abrams crews—to prevent capture by the enemy forces. Some M1s were ambushed by Iraqi infantry units using short-range anti-tank rockets fired at the tracks, the rear, and the tops of the tanks, but the majority of the M1s damaged after the invasion were hit by improvised explosive devices. The Iraqi experience added to the urban warfare requirement and the development and deployment of the Tank Urban Survival Kit, giving extra side and rear protection.

For concealment purposes, the turret of the Abrams is mounted with two six-barreled smoke grenade launchers capable of creating smoke thick enough to block thermal imaging as well as vision. Like the British Challenger 2, the Abrams is also able to create smoke by spraying fuel into the hot turbine exhaust, but with a slightly higher degree of fire risk to the engine compartment than in the case of the Challenger. For that reason, the system has been disabled on most Abrams tanks.

Another protective system in the Abrams is a Missile Countermeasure Device (MCD) that is designed to impede the guidance system function of many semi-active control line-of-sight wire and radio guided anti-tank missiles and thermally, and infrared guided missiles. The device emits a huge, condensed infrared signal that confuses the seeker of an anti-tank guided missile.

The armour protection of the Abrams is based on the British-designed Chobham armour, a composite armour that is formed through the spacing of multiple layers of various steel alloys, plastic composites, ceramics, and kevlar. The tank can also be fitted with reactive armour over the track skirts if needed, as in urban warfare situations, and with slat armour on the rear of the hull and the rear fuel cells to protect against anti-tank guided missile hits. The interior is lined with kevlar to protect against spalling. M1A1 tanks began being fitted with improved armour packages in 1987 which contained depleted uranium mesh to protect the front of the turret and the front of the hull. This armour reinforcement substantially improves the tank's resistance to most anti-tank weaponry. The penalty, though, is added weight on the tank, with depleted uranium being 1.7 times denser than lead. This upgrade was implemented on an emergeny basis for the tanks being deployed in Operation Desert Storm and has since been added to all M1A1 Abrams tanks on active service. It comes as standard equipment on the M1A2.

Like the German Leopard 2, the Abrams is equipped with a Halon fire suppression system that detects and automatically engages and extinguishes a fire in seconds. A second fire suppression system is installed in the engine compartment, and a number of small, hand-held fire extinguishers are stowed in the crew compartment. The fuel and ammunition storage is in armoured compartments equipped with blow-out panels for the protection of the crew should the tank be damaged.

Originally, the M1 tank was equipped with a 105mm rifled main gun which fired a variety of high-explosive, white phosphorus, high-explosive anti-tank, and anti-personnel rounds. The continuing arms race competition, and tank science, have moved on, however, and now the main gun armament of the M1A1 and the M1A2 is the Rheinmetall 120mm smoothbore, similar to that used on the Leopard 2. Motivated by the Russian introduction of Relikt, a new and formidable type of explosive reactive armour that is replacing Kontakt-5, the ERA used on the Russian main battle tanks through the T-90, the Abrams main gun can fire a new round designed to be effective against the latest Russian ERA. The Abrams Rheinmetall gun can also shoot the HEAT shaped-charge rounds claimed to be effective against armoured vehicles, low-flying aircraft, and personnel. Another deadly capability of the gun is the M1028 120mm anti-personnel canister cartridge introduced in the aftermath of the invasion of Iraq. The cartridge canister contains nearly 1,100 9.5mm tungsten balls which, on firing, spread from the gun muzzle in a shotgun effect that is lethal to a distance of 660 yards. The typical uses for such a terrifying weapon are against infantry attacks, to break up ambushes in urban areas, breaching walls, and in support of infantry assaults by providing covering fire. Conventionally, the Abrams gun uses manual loading.

The secondary weaponry of the Abrams tank includes a .50 calibre machine-gun at the front of the commander's hatch and can be fired through a magnifying sight with all the tank's hatches buttoned up to protect the crew. There is a 7.62mm machine-gun in front of the loader's hatch, with a night-vision scope; and another 7.62mm machine-gun in a coaxial mount on the right side of the main gun. The TUSK upgrade kit includes a 12.7mm machine-gun that can be mounted above the main gun in a remote weapons platform.

The Abrams fire-control system computer uses data supplied from a variety of sources to reach a ballistic solution that ensures a hit percentage greater than ninety-five percent at nominal ranges.

The Honeywell powertrain of the Abrams, a 1,500 hp Lycoming-designed, multi-fuel gas turbine engine with a six-speed (four forward and two reverse) transmission, gives the tank a top road speed of forty-five mph and a cross-country speed of thirty mph. The engine can be run on diesel, kerosene, any grade of motor gasoline, or jet fuel, generally JP8 universal jet fuel for U.S. military vehicles and aircraft. Fuel economy is a continuing issue with the tank as the engine burns in excess of 1.67 U.S. gallons per mile in cross-country travel. The turbine, however, is quieter than a diesel tank engine and is less audible from a distance.

For carrying troops, the soldiers of a battle-equipped infantry squad can ride on the rear of the tank, behind the turret, using ropes and equipment straps to provide handholds and snap-links to secure themselves.

The Abrams is a heavy main battle tank and when time in a threat situation allows, it is transported to where it is needed by ship, as was the case in the first Persian Gulf War. But when the strategic requirement is urgent, two combat-ready M1A2s can be air-lifted in a C-5 Galaxy transport aircraft or one in a C-17. When the U.S Marines take their Abrams tanks to a combat zone, they are normally transported as a platoon of four to five tanks attached to the deployed Marine Expeditionary Unit aboard a Wasp-class LHD vessel. On land, the Abrams is transportable by truck on a heavy equipment transporter (HET) which also accomodates the four tank crew members.

A new version of the Abrams tank, the M1A3, is under development. Prototypes are expected to be available in 2014 and the new tank is anticipated to be operational in 2017. The M1A3 is intended to have a lighter

120mm main gun, new road wheels with improved suspension, more durable tracks, improved lighter armour, long-range precision armaments, an infrared camera and laser detectors. A weight saving of approximately two tons is expected to result from the addition of a new internal computer system with fiber-optic cabling replacing the current cabling.

The Russian third-generation main battle tank is the T-90, an extensive modernization of the long-serving T-72. The T-90 serves with the Russian Ground Forces and the Russian Naval Infantry, and has been designed and manufactured by Uralvagonzavod of Nizhny Tagil, Russia. It is also used by Algeria, Azerbaijan, India, and Turkmenistan. The 2011 estimated unit cost of the T-90 is approximately $4.25 million. It is believed that at least 1,667 T-90s have been built.

The Russian source, Moscow Defense Brief: the T-90 entered combat in the 1999 Chechen invasion of Degestan, where one of the tanks was hit by seven anti-tank rocket-propelled grenades, remained operational and continued in action. MDB refers to the T-90 as the best protected Russian tank.

It is believed that Russia has a new tank weapon system under development called the T-99 Universal Combat Platform, nicknamed Armata, which is expected to be introduced in 2015 and to enter service in 2020. The T-99 is anticipated to have a more powerful engine than the 830 hp engine, or the uprated 1,000 hp and 1,250 hp engines, that power various examples of the T-90, as well as improved armour, an improved main gun, an autoloader, and storage for ammunition that is separated from the crew compartment.

The main gun of the T-90 is the 2A46M 125mm smoothbore tank gun, the same gun as used on the T-80 series tanks. The gun is capable of firing armour-piercing, fin-stabilized discarding sabot rounds, high-explosive anti-tank, high-explosive fragmentation ammunition, and Refleks anti-tank guided missiles which have semi-automatic laser beam-riding guidance and a tandem hollow-charge high-explosive anti-tank warhead. The missile has an effective range of from 110 yards to 6,500 yards, takes up to 17.5 seconds to reach maximum range, can penetrate thirty-seven inches of steel armour, and can engage low-flying aircraft. The gun is fed by an automatic loader, reducing the crew to three, a commander, a gunner, and a driver. The T-90 fire-control system includes a day-night sighting system mounted at the commander's station. Later models of the tank use an upgraded thermal imaging sight for accurate firing to a range of 8,750 yards. The gunner also has the use of a day-sighting system with a laser rangefinder and a missile guidance channel.

The current diesel engine for the T-90 is made by Uralvagonzavod and delivered by the Chelyabinsk Tractor Plant. It powers the tank to thirty-seven mph on roads and twenty-seven mph cross-country.

The T-90 is protected by a composite armour shell containing alternating layers of aluminium and plastics with a controlled deformation capability. A second level of protection is provided by third generation Kontakt-5 explosive reactive armour to degrade the kinetic energy of armour-piercing fin-stabilized discarding sabot ammunition. The Kontakt-5 blocks protect the turret and the turret roof from top-attack weapons. The turret also has a forward armour package of steel plating with a sandwiched filler of Russian composite armour between layers of steel plates, for less weight and greater protection than steel-only armour. In addition to the aforementioned protective systems, the T-90 is equipped with the *Shtora* (curtain) countermeasures suite which includes two electro-optical red-eye "dazzlers" mounted on the front of the turret, four laser warning receivers, two aerosol grenade discharging systems, and a computerized control system. Shtora warns the crew when the tank has been 'painted' by a weapon guidance laser, enabling them to slew the turret to face the threat. The tank is also equipped with nuclear, biological and chemical (NBC) protection equipment. The T-90 can be fitted with an electro-magnetic counter-mine system which emits a pulse to disable magnetic mines and disrupt electronics ahead of the tank's progress.

Nexter (GIAT) of France builds the French AMX-56 Leclerc main battle tank, which is named to honour General Philippe Leclerc de Hauteclocque, the commander who led the Free French 2nd Armoured Division on the drive towards Paris in the Second World War. The tank has been operated by the French Army and the army of the United Arab Emirates since 1991. With production completed, the French Army has taken delivery of 406 Leclercs and the UAE Army has received 388. The unit cost as of 2008 was approximately $22.5 million.

The Leclerc was initially developed by GIAT Industries in 1978. Prototypes were introduced in 1989 and production began in 1991. It is considered by many in the defence world to be the best main battle tank in current operation, though probably as many 'experts' would disagree with that assessment.

The project leading to the Leclerc began in 1975 when a working committee was established to identify the necessary and desired specifications for the vehicle. In 1980 a memorandum of understanding was signed with the Federal Republic of Germany for the joint French-German development of a main battle tank to be called Napoléon 1 in France and Kampfpanzer III in Germany. Some fundamental disagreements ended the joint project in December 1982, and the French decided to create a purely French MBT. One of the stated goals for the design was to achieve at least twice the level of protection against kinetic-energy penetrator weapons that was then common to main battle tanks of the fifty-ton weight class. In their effort to limit the unit cost of the new tank, the French were interested in attracting a foreign partner to share the burden. The United Arab Emirates became that partner. The French employ the Leclerc in four armoured regiments of sixty tanks each and maintain 100 of the tanks in combat-ready reserve status. As of 2011, 254 Leclercs were maintained in fully operational status.

The main gun armament of the Leclerc is the GIAT 120mm smoothbore cannon capable of firing the standard NATO 120mm rounds, as are the American Abrams and German Leopard tanks. The French gun also uses French-made ammunition. It has a thermal sleeve insulation and automatic compressed air fume extraction. The tank is equipped with an autoloader system specially designed for it. The system eliminates the need for a loader (4th) crew member. The Leclerc autoloader can fire at a rate of twelve shots a minute and carries twenty rounds of ready ammunition. It can utilize up to five different types of ammunition. The tank can shoot the main gun while traveling at thirty-one mph at a target 4,400 yards distant. Secondarily, the tank is equipped with a 12.7mm coaxial machine-gun and a remote-controlled 7.62mm machine-gun. In a system capability similar to that of the Abrams M1A2, the Leclerc battlefield management system automatically reports to the command post the tank's location, fuel state and quantity of ammunition remaining.

The hull and turret of Leclerc are made of welded steel which is also fitted with modular armour allowing for easy repair, replacement and upgrading. French Army officials considered and rejected Chobham armour for Leclerc in the late 1970s in the belief that Chobham was 'overly specialized' in optimization to defeat hollow-charge weapons. They elected instead to develop a steel perforated armour system similar to that of the early German Leopard 2. As standards of tank armour protection increased in the 1990s, however, the French decided to apply a titanium-tungsten non-explosive reactive armour system to the tanks produced from 2001.

The digital fire-control system of Leclerc can track six targets concurrently, similar to the system equipping the British Challenger 2. The Leclerc is powered by a 1,500 hp Hyperbar diesel engine and an automatic transmission of five forward and two reverse gears. The top speed of the tank on roads is forty-four mph and thirty-four mph cross-country. The range is 340 miles, extendable to 400 with the use of removable external fuel tanks. Leclerc is among the lightest main battle tanks at just fifty-six tons and has one of the best power-to-weight ratios (twenty-seven hp per tonne). Provided the crew is safely strapped in and secured by their harnesses, the tank's hydrokinetic retarder system can slow it down very impressively i.e. to avoid being hit in a combat situation.

While having been deployed in Kosovo and in Lebanon in 'low-intensity' conflict situations, Leclercs have not yet been subjected to high-intensity war zone situations.

Chariot is the English translation of the Hebrew word Merkava, the main battle tank of the Israeli Defense Forces, developed in the early 1970s and introduced into operational service in 1978. Pronounced 'mur-kuh-vuh', this tank first saw combat in the 1982 Lebanon War.

Mantak/IDF builds the Merkava and the estimated unit cost is approximately $6 million. The requirements for the design of this tank included exceptional crew safety and survivability, rapid repair of battle damage, cost-effectiveness, and good off-road performance. In addressing the crew safety aspect, an early design decision positioned the turret assembly nearer the rear of the hull than on most main battle tanks, and the engine in the front for added protection against frontal attack. This layout provides for greater than normal storage capacity, and a rear entrance to the crew compartment for easy access when the tank is under enemy fire. Thus, in addition to its fighting role, the Merkava can be readily utilized as a forward command-and-control station, an armoured personnel carrier, and as a platform for medical disembarkation.

Merkava's origins go back to 1964 when Major-General Israel Tal took command of the Israel Armoured Corps, then an organization of about 1,000 tanks, a combination of American Shermans and Pattons, French AMX-13s, and British Centurions. At that point, the quality of Israeli tank gunnery and tank maintenance was, at best, uneven. With the arrival of the Pattons and Centurions, such a casual approach was no longer tolerable. These vehicles were far more sophisticated and demanding than the IAC's old Shermans. Suddenly, a great deal more was required of the crews and personnel. When Major-General Tal took over, he soon implemented reforms that completely revitalized the corps. Bringing discipline and inspiring new confidence, he standardized and tightened training, and helped the crews to master their tanks and their capabilities.

In the '70s Major-General Tal and the Israeli tank planners considered the basic traditional compromise required in the development of a new and better tank: fire power, mobility, and crew protection. Israel had suffered such heavy losses of its tank crews in the October 1973 War that they determined to make crew protection the highest priority in planning the Merkava.

The Israelis have been involved in enough conflicts involving armoured warfare to have learned a lot about what happens to tanks and tank crews in combat. They set out to learn as much as possible about ballistics in relation to tanks and, after exhaustive studies, concluded that it was as important to protect the tank itself as it was the crew. The greater the protection of the tank, the greater the opportunity would be to get in closer to the enemy.

They decided to position the entire crew at the centre of the tank, to surround them by both the armour of the vehicle, and all the other elements and materials, for extra layers of shielding from incoming fire. And, while most modern main battle tanks have the engine positioned at the rear of the hull, they chose to put the engine and the transmission towards the front of the tank to add another barrier between the crewmen and their enemy. The guiding precept they followed through the design phase was that every operating part of the vehicle had to both function optimally and add to protection of the crew. Even the fuel tanks are designed into the walls of the hull, which are comprised of an outer layer of cast armour and a welded inside layer, with the fuel contained between the two layers. The fuel tanks have been designed to generate a hydrostatic pressure on impact from an incoming projectile. That pressure turns the fuel itself into a more resistant medium which actually pushes back at the projectile, turning the projectile's own energy against it. Additional protection is afforded through the installation of chain netting at the rear of the turret, to disperse and destroy rocket-propelled grenades and anti-tank rockets before impacting the primary armour.

The designers went on to devise a system of panels of high explosive that is sandwiched between metal plates which explode outward when struck by an incoming projectile. This explosive reactive armour was used on the earlier Merkavas, but has since been superseded by a newer, passive system of modular panels that are quickly and easily replaceable. The crew compartment layout positions the driver forward and to the left, with the engine to his right.

The Merkava is powered by a 1,500 hp turbocharged diesel engine that can drive the tank at forty mph on roads and 34 mph cross-country. The tops of the tracks are shielded by steel covers backed with plates of a special armour to protect the tracks and the suspension from damage by high-explosive anti-tank weapons. The design of the turret is well-sloped at the front and has a small cross-section, presenting a minimal target to enemy gunners. The turret too is protected by the special armour. The commander and the gunner sit to the right in the turret, the loader to the left. The current mark of the Merkava is armed with a 120mm smoothbore gun equipped with a tracking device that can lock it onto a target, keeping it accurately aimed even when the tank is moving at speed. The tank is also armed with two 7.62mm machine-guns, and a 60mm mortar that can be loaded and fired internally.

In 1995, the BAZ system was introduced on the Mark III Merkava. It incorporates an upgraded fire-control system, laser designators, upgraded ammunition storage containers to minimize ammunition 'cook-off', the Kasag modular armour system providing rapid replacement and repair on the battlefield, and other unspecified armour upgrades. Upgrades and improvements introduced with the 2003 Merkava Mark IV include new, removable modular armour, a V-shaped belly armour pack, a wider ammunition capability for the main gun including HEAT and sabot rounds, and 12.7mm machine-gun. There is also a new fire-control system making the Merkava capable of shooting down helicopters, and a new digital battlefield management system.

In its combat history, the Merkava performed well in the 1982 Lebanon War against the T-62 Syrian tanks and proved basically immune to the anti-tank weapons of the time. The Israelis incurred substantial casualties in the 2006 Lebanon War, many of them Merkava tank crewmen. Nearly half of the Israeli tanks involved were hit by anti-tank missiles and many experienced some degree of armour penetration. Fifteen tank crewmen were killed in the action. In one instance, a Merkava IV with the additional V-shaped belly pack installed ran over an improvised explosive device. One of the crewmen was killed, the only fatality among the seven soldiers on board (four crewmen and three infantrymen). In this conflict, five Merkavas were destroyed by Hezbollah. In general, however, the Israelis were well satisfied with the tank's overall performance. Author, analyst and a founding member of the Israeli Armoured Corps, Col. David Eshel: ". . . summing up the performance of the Merkava tanks, especially the latest version Merkava IV, most tank crews agree that, in spite of the losses sustained and some major flaws in tactical conduct, the tank proved its mettle in its first high-saturation combat."

TANK MAN

The story of 'Tank' has appeared many times on internet websites, unattributed. It may or may not be true. I would be pleased to give due credit for it to the author, if only I knew his or her identity.

"They told me the big black Lab's name was Reggie as I looked at him lying in his pen. The shelter was clean, and the people really friendly. I'd only been in the area for six months, but everywhere I went in the small college town, people were welcoming and open. Everyone waved when you passed them on the street.

"But something was still missing as I attempted to settle in to my new life here, and I thought a dog couldn't hurt. Give me someone to talk to. And I had just seen Reggie's advertisement on the local news. The shelter said they had received numerous calls right after, but they said the people who had come down to see him just didn't look like 'Lab people,' whatever that meant. They must've thought I did.

"But at first, I thought the shelter had misjudged me in giving me Reggie and his things, which consisted of a dog pad, a bag of toys almost all of which were brand new tennis balls, his dishes, and a sealed letter from his previous owner. See, Reggie and I didn't really hit it off when we got home. We struggled for two weeks (which is how long the shelter told me to give him to adjust to his new home). Maybe it was the fact that I was trying to adjust, too. Maybe we were too much alike.

"For some reason, his stuff (except for the tennis balls—he wouldn't go anywhere without two stuffed in his mouth) got tossed in with all of my other unpacked boxes. I guess I didn't really think he'd need all his old stuff, that I'd get him new things once he settled in, but it became pretty clear soon that he wasn't going to.

"I tried the normal command the shelter told me he knew, ones like 'sit' and 'stay' and 'come' and 'heel,' and he'd follow them—when he felt like it. He never really seemed to listen when I called his name—sure, he'd look in my direction after the fourth or fifth time I said it, but then he'd just go back to doing whatever. When I'd ask again, you could almost see him sigh and then grudgingly obey.

"This just wasn't going to work. He chewed a couple shoes and some unpacked boxes. I was a little too stern with him and he resented it, I could tell. The friction got so bad that I couldn't wait for the two weeks to be up, and when it was, I was in full-on search mode for my cell phone amid all of my unpacked stuff. I remembered leaving it on the stack of boxes for the guest room, but I also mumbled, rather cynically, that the 'damn dog probably hid it on me.'

"Finally I found it, but before I could punch up the shelter's number, I also found his pad and other toys from the shelter. I tossed the pad in Reggie's direction and he sniffed it and wagged, some of the most enthusiasm I'd seen since bringing him home. But then I called, 'Hey, Reggie, you like that? Come here and I'll give you a treat.' Instead, he sort of glanced in my direction—maybe 'glared' is more accurate—and then gave a discontented sigh and flopped down, with his back to me.

"Well, that's not going to do it either, I thought. And I punched the shelter phone number.

"But I hung up when I saw the sealed envelope. I had completely forgotten about that, too. 'Okay, Reggie,' I said out loud, 'let's see if your previous owner has any advice.'

" 'To Whoever Gets My Dog: Well, I can't say that I'm happy you're reading this, a letter I told the shelter could only be opened by Reggie's new owner. I'm not even happy writing it. If you're reading this, it means I just got back from my last car ride with my Lab after dropping him off at the shelter. He knew something was different. I have packed up his pad and toys before and set them by the back door before a trip, but this time . . . it's like he knew something was wrong. And something is wrong . . . which is why I have to try and make it right. So let me tell you about my Lab in the hopes that it will help you bond with him and he with you.

" 'First, he loves tennis balls, the more the merrier. Sometimes I think he's part squirrel, the way he hordes them. He usually has two in his mouth, and he tries to get a third in there. Hasn't done it yet. Doesn't matter where you throw them, he'll bound after it, so be careful—really don't do it by any roads. I made that mistake once, and it almost cost him dearly.

" 'Next, commands. Maybe the shelter staff already told you, but I'll go over them again: Reggie knows the obvious ones—'sit', 'stay', 'come', 'heel', and 'over' if you put your hand out right or left. 'Shake' for shaking water off, and 'paw' for a high-five. He does 'down' when he feels like lying down—I bet you could work on that with him some more. He knows 'ball' and 'food' and 'bone' and 'treat' like nobody's business.

" 'I trained Reggie with small food treats. Nothing opens his ears like little pieces of hot dog. Feeding schedule: twice a day, once about seven in the morning, and again at six in the evening. Regular store-bought stuff; the shelter has the brand.

" 'He's up on his shots. Call the clinic on 9th Street and update his info with yours' they'll make sure to send you reminders for when he's due. Be forewarned: Reggie hates the vet. Good luck getting him in the car—I don't know how he knows when it's time to go to the vet, but he knows.

" 'Finally, give him some time. I've never been married, so it's only been Reggie and me for his whole life. He's gone everywhere with me, so please include him on your daily car rides if you can. He sits well in the back seat, and he doesn't bark or complain. He just loves to be around people, and me most especially.

" 'Which means that this transition is going to be hard, with him going to live with someone new. And that's why I need to share one more bit of info with you . . . His name is not Reggie. I don't know what made me do it, but when I dropped him off at the shelter, I told them his name was Reggie. He's a smart dog, he'll get used to it and will respond to it, of that I have no doubt, but I just couldn't bear to give them his real name. For me to do that, it seemed so final, that handing him over to the shelter was as good as me admitting that I'd never see him again. And if I end up coming back, getting him, and tearing up this letter, it means everything is fine. But if someone else is reading it, well, it means that his new owner should know his real name. It'll help you bond with him. Who knows, maybe you'll even notice a change in his demeanor if he's been giving you problems.

" 'His real name is Tank. Because that is what I drive.

" 'Again, if you're reading this and you're from the area, maybe my name has been on the news. I told the shelter that they couldn't make 'Reggie' available for adoption until they received word from my company commander. See, my parents are gone. I have no siblings, no one I could have left Tank with . . . and it was my only real request of the Army upon my deployment to Iraq, that they make one phone call to the shelter . . . 'in the event' . . . to tell them that Tank could be put up for adoption. Luckily, my colonel is a dog guy too, and he knew where my platoon was headed. He said he'd do it personally. And if you are reading this, then he made good on his word.

" 'Well, this letter is getting too downright depressing, even though, frankly, I'm just writing it for my dog. I couldn't imagine if I was writing it for a wife and kids and family. But still, Tank has been my family for the last six years, almost as long as the Army has been my family. And now I hope and pray that you make him part of your family and that he will adjust and come to love you the same way he loved me.

" 'That unconditional love from a dog is what I took with me to Iraq as an inspiration to do something selfless, to protect innocent people from those who would do terrible things . . . and to keep those terrible people from coming over here. If I had to give up Tank in order to do it, I am glad to have done so. He was my example of service and of love. I hope I honored him by my service to my country and comrades.

" 'All right, that's enough. I deploy this evening and have to drop this letter off at the shelter. I don't think I'll say another good-bye to Tank, though. I cried too much the first time. Maybe I'll peek in on him and see if he finally got that third tennis ball in his mouth.

" 'Good luck with Tank. Give him a good home, and give him an extra kiss goodnight—every night—from me. Thank you, Paul Mallory.'

"I folded the letter and slipped it back in the envelope. Sure, I had heard of Paul Mallory, everyone in town knew him, even new people like me. Local kid, killed in Iraq a few months ago and posthumously earning the Silver Star when he gave his life to save three buddies. Flags had been at half-mast all summer.

"I leaned forward in my chair and rested my elbows on my knees, staring at the dog. 'Hey, Tank,' I said quietly. The dog's head whipped up, his ears cocked and his eyes bright. 'C'mere boy.'

"He was instantly on his feet, his nails clicking on the hardwood floor. He sat in front of me, his head tilted, searching for the name he hadn't heard in months. 'Tank', I whispered. His tail swished.

"I kept whispering his name, over and over, and each time, his ears lowered, his eyes softened, and his posture relaxed as a wave of contentment just seemed to flood him. I stroked his ears, rubbed his shoulders, buried my face into his scruff and hugged him.

" 'It's me now, Tank, just you and me. Your old pal gave you to me.'

"Tank reached up and licked my cheek. 'So what do you say we play some ball?' His ears perked again 'Yeah? Ball? You like that? Ball?' Tank tore from my hands and disappeared into the next room. And when he came back, he had three tennis balls in his mouth."

The tank is more than a killing machine, more than a battlefield menace. In many parts of the world since the Second World War, tanks on the streets have often been the first sign of violent political change, a military coup or the imposition of a repressive regime.

Politicians have long recognized the value of the tank in the initimidation and repression of civilian populations. Its awesome appearance can be traumatizing, especially in an ordinary urban contect. Patrick Wright, author of *Tank*, a superb cultural history of the weapon, comments: "People talk about the tank as a rational instrument of warfare—you get lots of them, then you mass them together and you advance—but it's always had a symbolic dimension as well. It is a monstrous object that crawls towards you and you don't know what it can do to you, but it scares you almost to death. It would be quite wrong to ignore this. The symbolic force of this weapon makes it very well attuned to modern peacekeeping-type operations. It may take two months to get it there, but if you put a tank on a bridge things tend to settle down."

In the last half of the twentieth century, ordinary citizens of several nations faced invading tanks and, for a while at least, stood their ground in defiance of clearly overwhelming force and fear.

On 4 November 1956, Hungarian Prime Minister Imre Nagy spoke to his people in a dramatic radio broadcast as Soviet armour assaulted Budapest. "Soviet troops attacked our capital with the obvious purpose to overthrow the legitimate Hungarian government. Our troops are fighting. The government is in its place."

Shortly after the death of Premier Joseph Stalin in 1953, the Soviet leadership became aware of a growing disenchantment with the oppressive communist system in the satellite nations, Hungary being a prime example. The Soviets ordered the hardline Hungarian Communist Party boss, Matyás Rakosi, to Moscow for consultation. He was directed to relax the pressures then being applied by his regime on Hungary's industry and collective farms, to soften his "reign of terror" approach, and to work towards a higher living standard for his people. Finally, he was required to ordain fellow communist Imre Nagy as the new Hungarian Prime Minister. Nagy was a moderate with considerable popular support. He was known for opposing the communist policies of terror and forced industrialization and collectivization. He was a reformer who wanted to liberalize communism in his country, but without any major shift towards capitalism. He began his programme in July with what he called "the new stage in building socialism."

In little more than a year after the death of Stalin, the Soviet flirtation with a more relaxed form of communism appeared to be ending as hardline policies came back into vogue. In Hungary, Rakosi saw the opportunity to regain his former stature and embarked on a programme to de-stabilize Nagy's government. In March 1955, emboldened by the Russian winds of change, he sacked Nagy and reimposed terror on the Hungarians. But with the coming of a new Soviet Communist Party chief, Nikita Krushchev, and his February 1956 denunciation of Stalin, Rakosi's little empire in Hungary began to unravel and by the summer he had been dismissed.

Unrest in Hungary, Poland, and elsewhere in the Soviet satellite states was growing rapidly. On 22 October the people of Budapest learned of a change of leaders in the Polish communist party. Wladislaw Gumulka, like Nagy, a relative moderate, was the new party boss, ousting the former Stalinist regime in Warsaw. His rise to power triggered a prompt Soviet reaction. Krushchev flew to the Polish capital as Soviet military forces mobilized to move on the rebellious satellite state. A clash was averted, however, as the clever Gomulka carefully maintained his stance within the federal system of the Warsaw Pact. On hearing of the party changes in Poland, students of the Budapest Technical University created a 16-point list of demands. They then called for a peaceful gathering on 23 October to demonstrate their solidarity with the people of Poland and declare their demands. Walls all over the city were plastered with posters calling for freedom. The demonstrators were demanding a complete withdrawal of the troops, the abolition of censorship, establishment of a multi-party political system with free elections, economic independence and the re-establishment of traditional national symbols and holidays. They were supported by much of the citizenry. A broad spectrum of politics was represented as leftists, communist reformers, social democrats, religious leaders, conservatives, and even some right-wing elements joined the movement. Ordinary citizens defied the government and got their news by listening to the banned Radio Free Europe. The Hungarian Revolution was under way.

The initial violence occurred when Hungarian secret police opened fire on activists who were attempting to occupy the headquarters of Radio Budapest on the 23rd. Elsewhere in the country revolutionary groups were quickly being formed and a general political strike was organized. Student and general demonstrations erupted in the many town squares where the protestors frequently focused their attentions on dismantling and destroying the hated symbols of repression. Down came Soviet war memorials, red stars and, in perhaps the most defiant of vandalisms, the activists set about the massive statue of Stalin in central Budapest, attacking it with hammers, toppling and decapitating it. In the wake of all this action, Imre Nagy was once again brought in as Prime Minister.

By the 25th the Hungarian situation had worsened significantly. In an ugly scene at the parliament building, unarmed demonstrators were fired on by soldiers in an effort to suppress the uprising. There, and in other parts of the country, hundreds of protesters were killed. Gradually, however, many Hungarian soldiers began changing sides and joining the ranks of revolutionaries.

Two days after the shootings, Imre Nagy told the nation that he had formed a new government which incorporated non-communists and intended to negotiate the withdrawal of Soviet forces from Hungary. Under new management, Hungarian Radio followed the Nagy announcement with one in which it supported the protestors. But while the Soviet troops had withdrawn from Budapest, they remained poised in the countryside, ready to move forcefully against the activists. On 1 November, with the troops refusing to withdraw further, Nagy acted by withdrawing Hungary from the Warsaw Pact alliance and declaring the nation's neutrality. In doing that Nagy renounced the policies of his own party and the international communist movement. The Kremlin reacted immediately.

On 3 November, Soviet Army generals were in discussions with officers of the Hungarian army about troop withdrawal. The talks were a sham and the Hungarian delegation was then arrested by Soviet security forces. On 4 November, the Soviet military moved in a savage attack on Hungary and in a few days put an end to the rebellion. Imre Nagy and his top officials, who had sought refuge at the Yugoslav embassy in Budapest, were given assurances of safe conduct out of the country. When they tried to leave, they were quickly taken into custody by the Soviets who then installed their own puppet government headed by János Kádár, who had won Soviet support by opposing the rebellion.

Now Soviet tanks and armoured vehicles clattered down the main streets and boulevards of Budapest, firing indiscriminately as they rolled. Young armed activists fought back, shooting, shouting, and hurling Molotov cock-tails (bottles filled with gasoline) at the tanks. Many homes and buildings were destroyed as the Soviets forcibly put down the revolt. Token resistance continued until early in 1957, but the revolution had failed. A new reign of terror had begun. Some 25,000 Hungarians were arrested and incarcerated in the two years following the revolt; 230 were executed. Almost 200,000 refugees fled the country to freedom in Britain, the United States and else-where.

In 1949 Mao Zedung stood in Beijing's Tiananmen Square and proclaimed a "People's Republic" on behalf of the people of China. The square, near the Gate of Heavenly Peace leading into the Forbidden City, had been the scene of student demonstrations as early as 1919 and has, since 1949, been the venue where the Chinese leadership reviews the troops of the People's Liberation Army.

Forty years after Mao's proclamation student and worker members of China's pro-democracy movement gathered to take back Tiananmen Square for a seven-week period in the spring of 1989. They were joined by educa-tors, doctors, soldiers and others and eventually numbered more than one million, many of whom had seen operating democracies while on visits to the United States and Britain.

The demonstration had started on 15 April after the death of Hu Yao Bang, the former Secretary General of the Communist Party of China, who had been demoted and disgraced when he was accused of being in sympathy with stu-dent pro-democracy demonstrators in 1987. Thousands of students went to Tiananmen Square to honour Hu Yao Bang and were soon joined by workers and intellectuals. The action of the demonstrators was quickly condemned by the government in a letter to the *People's Daily*, describing the students' behaviour as "an act of treason". Police freely used their truncheons to con-trol the demonstrators. This caused many more thousands of students and their supporters to come to the square to denounce the violence and express their anti-government views.

The dissidents produced a daily newspaper which protested against gov-ernment corruption and demanded political democracy in their country. They broadcast their message, and the speeches of their heroes, from a radio tent in the square and they created a 30-foot statue which they named the Goddess of Democracy. It was erected to face the massive poster of Mao there. At the southwest corner of the square was a Kentucky Fried Chicken shop which the demonstrators used as their headquarters and meeting place. Their struggle for human rights had been non-violent and a remarkable expression of will and determination.

On 14 May more than 2,000 of the protestors were engaged in a hunger strike as more than 100,000 occupied the square. In the following days their

numbers grew rapidly to nearly one million. They began shouting for government reforms and the resignation of the Chinese leader, Deng Xiaoping.
Their calls were a supreme embarrassment to the government which, at that
moment, was hosting Mikhail Gorbachev, the first Soviet head of state to visit
China in thirty years. In a conciliatory gesture, Deng Xiaoping called on the
hunger strikers in hospital and then agreed to meet with the student protest
leaders. In the meeting Deng did not accede to their demands. He warned
the Chinese people of the repercussions that awaited those who became involved
in the protest movement. On 20 May the hardline Premier Li Peng branded
the protest action a "riot". He declared martial law in Beijing and called in
troops from the countryside. By the following day the People's Liberation
Army had taken over all newspapers, television and radio stations in Beijing.
On the 22nd the government shut down the satellite feed to North America
and Europe.

Key members of the government were divided over what measures they
should take to quell the protest. Deng advocated suppression by the use of
any force necessary, but others around him wanted no part of that. Unarmed
soldiers had no effect on the demonstrators who surrounded their vehicles.
By 29 May the government had declared the students and the other demonstrators "hooligans" and "bad elements"; counter-revolutionaries who were
liable to be arrested and shot. On 2 June more than 200,000 soldiers had
moved into Beijing. Deng's patience was exhausted. He ordered the army to
retake Tiananmen Square at all costs. By noon on the 3rd, PLA soldiers had
entered the square and were hitting people with truncheons as well as toss-
ing tear gas cannisters to disperse the crowds. In a broadcast the government
then warned that it had the right to deal forcefully with the "rioters". The
people of Beijing were instructed to stay indoors. At 2 a.m. on 4 June, units
of the PLA 27th Field Army surrounded the square and, by 4 a.m. it's soldiers had opened fire on the protestors. The army brought in tanks from all
directions towards the square and hundreds of the unarmed demonstrators,
including many children, were killed. The Chinese Red Cross estimated that
up to 2,600 students and civilians died in the tragic action, which quickly
attracted worldwide condemnation of the Chinese government.

The next day the shocked and outraged activists steadfastly refused to
leave Tiananmen. Elements of the People's Liberation Army occupied the
square and were endeavouring to secure their supply lines, as a column of
eighteen Norinco Type 69/59 main battle tanks advanced down Chang'an
Boulevard, the Avenue of Eternal Peace. The BBC's Kate Adie described
what happened next: "Just after midday the tanks rolled out of the square. A
lone young man stood in front of the first one. The tank faltered; came to a
stop . . . It was an extraordinarily purposeful but mundane way of doing
things . . . It seemed impromptu. There he was with his little plastic bag—
such a human touch, as if he had been shopping."

Wang Weilin. It may or may not be the real name of the unknown rebel who defied the Chinese Communist regime that day in one of the most courageous acts of all time. He was a slight figure in white shirt and dark slacks. In his left hand he held a shopping bag. He moved towards the approaching tank column and positioned himself directly in front of the lead tank, which stopped and then attempted to swerve to the right around the man, who moved left to block it. It then tried to swerve to the left and he moved right. The man then climbed up onto the tank to speak to the driver. The writer Pico Iyer reported the rebel's words to the driver as: "Why are you here? My city is in chaos because of you."

Little is known about the young man who defied the might and power of his government that June day. Time magazine has cited the unknown protestor as one of the "top twenty leaders and revolutionaries of the 20th century." It is widely believed that he was a nineteen-year-old universitystudent. His actual identity is still a mystery, as is his fate, and, according to the Information Center for the Human Rights and Democracy Movement in China, the Communist Party authorities have never found Wang. They quote Jiang Zemin, the Party General Secretary in 1990, as saying: "We can't find him. We got his name from journalists. We have checked through computers but can't find him among the dead nor among those in prison." When asked about the fate of the young rebel, by the American television interviewer Barbara Walters in a 1992 conversation, Jiang responded: "I think never killed."

The powerful image of The Tank Man, Wang Weilin, or whatever his name may be, posed resolute in front of that Chinese tank, is a familiar one to hundreds of millions of people around the globe. It has become an icon of defiance and one of the most famous and recognized photographs of all time. of The Tank Man, Patrick Wright has written: "The image has been subject to much interpretation in the West." Eminent military historian John Keegan declared it a "merely poetic image, a story of impersonal armed might of the army lined up against the unvanquished human spirit." One report confirmed Wang's status as a student by putting books in his bag, and there were diverse variations on the words he is said to have shouted at the tanks, from the simple "Go away" of the *Sunday Express*, to "Go back, run around, stop killing my people" elaborated by *Today* a week or so later.

On 4 June 1998, the ninth anniversary of the Tiananmen Square tragedy, United States Senator Paul Wellstone addressed the Senate: "Like everyone who witnessed that brutal massacre, I cannot forget the image of that lone, courageous figure, Wang Weilin, standing firm and holding his ground against the oncoming PLA tanks. China's leaders have tried to convince the world that freedom and democracy are Western ideals, contrary to Asian values. Their rhetoric would have us believe that maintaining repressive policies is essential to the preservation of their cultural and national identity.

The image of Wang Weilin tells a different story; a story of the human spirit's incredible determination and sacrifice for liberty and freedom."

Since the events of June 1989, the Chinese government has sought to mollify the people with the prospect of greater individual material wealth to be achieved through an increase in the pace of economic development, this in lieu of greater political rights. Some personal freedoms have also come to pass, including the right to choose one's job and to relocate. Such gains have functioned as a limited diversion from the political activism of the recent past, but the memory of Tiananmen Square, of The Tank Man and the spirit of the demonstrators there, survives and continues to inspire the peoples of China and the world.

Matilda II tank driver-operator/W-T operator T.G. Needham recalled: "I joined the Royal Tank Corps on my eighteenth birthday, 4 January 1938, and remained a tankie until my demob 1946. After depot training at Bovington I was posted to the 7th Battalion at Catterick. On the outbreak of war and army re-organization, the unit was renamed 7th Royal Tank Regiment. There I became a loader-operator on *Grimsby*, the third tank in 5 Troop, A Squadron. After Dunkirk, as part of the BEF, we had lost all our tanks in the counter-attack at Arras and were hurriedly re-equipped with a mixture of Matilda Is and Valentines.

"In September 1940, we were sent with other units to the Middle East to reinforce the peacetime garrison of the 1st and 6th RTR and ancillary units. This was an inspired decision by Churchill as Britain's back was to the wall awaiting an invasion. We had our tanks entrained on railway flats in sidings for whenever the invasion took place. We used nice, perishable parcel trucks as barracks.

"Our move was top secret and entailed a five-week voyage round Ireland, out into the Atlantic, round the Cape, up through the Suez Canal to Port Said where the drivers had the frightening job of unloading onto a pier of lighters. Then by land to a base at Alexandria where the tanks were adapted for desert work with racks fitted for water cans, and large air filters fitted to the engines as protection against the fine clouds of dust and fine sand that covered all transport in the western desert. The garrison engineers had constructed a single-line railway up to the Egyptian border and beyond. The end of the line, or railhead, had reached a desolate spot called Sidi Haneiph, a few miles east of Mersa Matruh.

"Before we left Alexandria we had taken six casualties among the tank crews. As we were on a war footing, every tank was always ready for instant action, fully loaded with guns and ammunition. Part of the readiness procedure was to try every two-pounder round in the gun breech to ensure there were no bulged or damaged cases to jam when in action. The shell and case were then ejected and stacked in the storage racks in the hull. The first tank in trouble had a bulged or oversize case stuck with 1/8 inch to go fully home to allow the breech block to spring up and close the breech. The round was then ejected by the breech mechanism lever. The round, now checked, had a safety clip covering the firing cap in position, and the shell and case stacked in a rack in the hull or turret. The proper drill to remove a jammed round was to use a case-removal tool, a steel implement with a split screwdriver at one end and a blank screw at the other. A wooden handle was then fitted cross-wise which allowed the loader to use full strength of both legs, arms and back to pull the case out. This was time-consuming and, without great care, a dangerous process. The loader decided to give the stuck case a sharp tap with a hammer to force it fully home. The shell exploded in the open breech and the full force of the explosion came back on the three men working in the turret, killing or badly wounding them all.

"The enquiry team established the cause of the explosion and all the men were warned of the dangers of using a hammer on live ammunition. The warning finished with the observation that, if in some dire emergency, you had to force a stuck round home, for goodness sake, use a wooden block. Then there was another explosion. The second enquiry found that the second loader had indeed used a piece of wood, to wit, the hammer handle, but the nip of hard wood left in the handle after turning it on the lathe, made it a very effective firing pin. I got myself out of this quandary by equipping myself with a thick, short stubby screwdriver. When the blade was held behind the rim of the jammed round, the handle could be levered back onto the top of the breech block and then given a sharp blow with the heel of the hand; it acted like another extractor lever and could remove quite a hard jam.

"We loaded our tanks on flat cars again at Alexandria and, as Egypt was a hotbed of spies and intrigue, we officially went up the desert to train. We unloaded at Sidi Haneiph. The force rolled ponderously over the Libyan border and formed a defensive arc of fortified positions inside Egypt with many tanks, guns and lorries, all covered by a large air arm. Wavell's troops had discovered a big gap in the Italian defensive arc and a preemptive strike was planned to catch the Italians off balance. 7 RTR were to spearhead the strike. Now the good reconnaissance work of the Long Range Desert Group slipped up and caused 7 RTR much hard work and heartburn. They reported that the Fort Nibweiwa position was defended by a large ditch and wall about eight feet high and twelve feet wide. This, in effect, did not exist, but we had to be prepared to cross it as it was our main objective. In WWI, tanks had crossed the German Hindenburg line by using fascines, tightly bound bundles of brushwood, to allow the tanks which dropped them into the trench to step down and then step out, so crossing the trench system.

"The miracle workers at Base Workshops had produced modern-type fascines, long octagonal frames made of heavy four-inch square wood timbers bolted on a central beam with strengthening struts like the spokes of a wheel. They were slung round the Matilda's turret by a cable. The tank ran alongside the trench; the tank commander reached out and pulled a release toggle and the fascine rolled down into the trench. A second tank crew did the same and the fascines laid formed a step down into and a step out of the trench. Fixing these arrangements was hard and heavy work, but, as *Grimsby* was the third tank of 5 Troop, we didn't have to carry one.

"The approach through the gap was done at night, guided by hurricane lamps placed in empty four-gallon petrol cans with nail holes knocked in the sides. These pinpricks of light were enough to let us cross right through the gap in pitch darkness, right to the other side of the Italian positions, where we ate the proverbial bully, biscuits and tea and settled down for a few hours' sleep.

"There was strict wireless silence in force so the troop leaders ordered 'Start engines' with hand signals. Radios were switched on and we waited, eager and raring to go. Then the radio crackled into life and Major Rew, the squadron leader, oredered 'All stations, Lee Hay (our call sign), ADVANCE!' and we were off.

"The day broke all Mussolini's attempts at conquest, as our thickly-armoured tanks smashed everything the Italians had. Although the desert looked flat, there was a rise of eight or nine feet between us and Nibweiwa and the Italians hadn't a clue that we were there until fifty tanks burst in upon them. This successful action was cleverly enlarged upon until it took the entire Italian North African territory. Truly our first victory of the war."

BIBLIOGRAPHY

Adams, Simon, *World War I*, Dorling Kindersley, 2001

Ambrose, Stephen, *Band of Brothers*, Simon & Schuster, 1992

Arnold, James, *The Battle of the Bulge*, Osprey, 1990

Barker, A.J., *Afrika Korps*, Bison Books, 1978

Beevor, Antony, *Stalingrad*, Viking, 1998

Bethell, Nicholas, *Russia Besieged*, Time-Life Books, 1980

Boscowan, Leo, *Armoured Guardsmen*, LeoCooper, 2001

Canby, Courtland, *A History of Weaponry*, Hawthorn Books, 1963

Carruthers, Bob, *German Tanks at War*, Cassell, 2000

Clancy, Tom, *Armored Cav*, Berkley Books, 1994

Clark, Alan, *Barbarossa*, Quill, 1965

Cooper, Belton, *Death Traps*, Presidio Press, 2000

Cooper, Matthew and Lucas, James, *Panzer*, Purnell Book Services, 1976

Coppard, George, *With a Machine Gun To Cambrai*, Cassell, 1999

Crow, Duncan, *Modern Battle Tanks*, Profile Publications, 1978

Davies, J.B., *Great Campaigns of World War II*, Macdonald & Co., 1980

Delaforce, Patrick, *Taming The Panzers*, Sutton Publishing, 2000

Delaney, John, *The Blitzkrieg Campaigns*, Caxton Editions, 2000

Deighton, Len, *Blitzkrieg*, Jonathan Cape, 1979

Diaz, Octavio, *Tanks and Armoured Vehicles*, Lema Publications, 2000

Doubler, Michael, *Closing With The Enemy*, Univ. Press of Kansas, 1994

Dunstan, Simon, *Challenger Squadron*, Crowood Press, 1999

Eshel, David, *Chariots of the Desert*, Brasseys', 1989

Fletcher, David, *Tanks and Trenches*, Sutton Publishing, 1994

Fletcher, David, *The British Tanks 1915-19*, Crowood Press, 2001

Folkestad, William, *The View from the Turret*, Burd Street Press, 2000

Forbes, Colin, *Tramp in Armour*, Collins, 1969

Ford, Roger, *The World's Great Tanks*, Grange Books, 1999

Forty, George, *Afrika Korps at War*, Ian Allan, 1978

Forty, George, *Royal Tank Regiment*, Guild Publishing, 1989

Forty, George, *Tank Action*, The History Press, 1995

Gervasi, Tom, *Arsenal of Democracy II*, Evergreen, 1981

Glantz, David & House, Jonathan, The Battle of Kursk, Univsity Press of Kansas, 1990

Green, Michael, *M1 Abrams Main Battle Tank*, Motorbooks, 1992

Guderian, Heinz, *Achtung Panzer*, Arms & Armour, 1992

Guderian, Heinz, *Panzer Leader*, Penguin Books, 2000

Halberstadt, Hans, *Inside The Great Tanks*, Crowood Press, 1998

Healy, Mark, *The Tiger Tank Story*, The History Press, 2010

Hogg, Ian, *Tank Killing*, Brown Packaging Books, 1996

Houston, Donald, *Hell on Wheels*, Presidio Press, 1997

Jensen, Melvin, *Strike Swiftly!*, Presidio Press, 1997

Jones, Kevin, *The Desert Rats*, Caxton Editions, 2001

Jorgensen, Christer and Mann, Chris, *Tank Warfare*, Spellmount Ltd, 2001

Keegan, John, *The First World War*, Hutchinson, 2001

Kershaw, Robert, *Tank Men*, Hodder, 2008

Kurowski, Franz, *Panzer Aces*, J.J. Fedorowicz Publishing Inc., 1992

Lande, D.A., *Rommel in North Africa*, MBI Publishing, 1999

Lucas, James, *Panzer Army Africa*, Purnell Book Services, 1977

Macksey, Kenneth, *Tank Facts & Feats*, Sterling Publishing, 1980

Macksey, Kenneth, *Tank versus Tank*, Grub Street, 1999

Mason, David, *Verdun*, The Windrush Press, 2000

Mauldin, Bill, *Up Front*, Henry Holt & Co., 1945

McGuirk, Dal, *Rommel's Army in Africa*, Motorbooks, 1993

Messenger, Charles, *The Art of Blitzkrieg*, Ian Allan, 1976

Orgill, Douglas, *T34 Russian Armor*, Ballantine, 1971

Parker, Danny, *Battle of the Bulge*, Greenhill Books, 1991

Perrett, Bryan, *Desert Warfare*, Patrick Stephens Limited, 1978

Perrett, Bryan, *Iron Fist*, Arms & Armour, 1995

Reynolds, Michael, *Steel Inferno*, Spellmount Ltd, 1997

Rommel, Erwin, *The Rommel Papers*, Harcourt, Brace and Co., 1953

Smithers, A.J., *A New Excalibur*, Leo Cooper, 1986

Tout, Ken, *A Fine Night for Tanks*, Sutton Publishing, 1998

Trewhitt, Philip, *Armoured Fighting Vehicles*, Dempsey Parr, 1999

Wernick, Robert, *Blitzkrieg*, Time-Life Books, 1976

Wright, Patrick, *Tank*, Faber & Faber, 2000

INDEX